The Fiore

and the *Detto d'Amore*

THE WILLIAM AND KATHERINE DEVERS SERIES IN DANTE STUDIES

Theodore J. Cachey, Jr., and Christian Moevs, editors

VOLUME 3
The Design in the Wax: The Structure of the Divine Comedy and Its Meaning, Marc Cogan

VOLUME 2
The Fiore in Context: Dante, France, Tuscany, ed. Zygmunt G. Barański and Patrick Boyde

VOLUME 1
Dante Now: Current Trends in Dante Studies, ed. Theodore J. Cachey, Jr.

The Fiore

and the *Detto d'Amore*

A LATE 13TH-CENTURY ITALIAN TRANSLATION OF THE *ROMAN DE LA ROSE*

Attributable to Dante 

A translation with introduction and notes by

SANTA CASCIANI

and

CHRISTOPHER KLEINHENZ

UNIVERSITY OF NOTRE DAME PRESS
Notre Dame, Indiana

http://www.undpress.nd.edu

Manufactured in the United States of America

Library of Congress Cataloging-in-Publication Data
Fiore. English & Italian.
The Fiore ; and, the Detto d'amore : a late 13th-century Italian translation of the Roman de la Rose, attributable to Dante / a translation with introduction and notes by Santa Casciani and Christopher Kleinhenz.
p. cm. — (William and Katherine Devers series in Dante studies ; v. 4)
Includes bibliographical references and index.
Italian and English on facing pages.
ISBN 0-268-00893-0 (pbk. : alk. paper)
I. Title: Fiore ; and, the Detto d'amore. II. Dante Alighieri, 1265–1321.
III. Casciani, Santa. IV. Kleinhenz, Christopher. V. Detto d'amore.
English & Italian. VI. Title. VII. Series.
PQ4471.F397 E5 2000
851'.1—dc21

00-039220

∞ *The paper used in this publication meets the minimum requirements of the American National Standard for Information Sciences—Permanence of Paper for Printed Library Materials, ANSI Z39.48-1984.*

Contents

Preface

The William and Katherine Devers Program in Dante Studies at the University of Notre Dame supports rare book acquisitions in the university's John A. Zahm Dante collection, funds an annual visiting professorship in Dante studies, and supports electronic and print publication of scholarly research in the field. In collaboration with the Medieval Institute at the university, the Devers program has initiated a series dedicated to the publication of the most significant current scholarship in the field of Dante studies.

In keeping with the spirit that inspired the creation of the Devers program, the series takes Dante as a focal point that draws together the many disciplines and forms of inquiry that constitute a cultural tradition without fixed boundaries. Accordingly, the series hopes to illuminate Dante's position at the center of contemporary critical debates in the humanities by reflecting both the highest quality of scholarly achievement and the greatest diversity of critical perspectives.

The series publishes works on Dante from a wide variety of disciplinary viewpoints and in diverse scholarly genres, including critical studies, commentaries, editions, translations, and conference proceedings of exceptional importance. The series is supervised by an international advisory board composed of distinguished Dante scholars and is published regularly by the University of Notre Dame Press.

The Dolphin and Anchor device that appears on publications of the Devers series was used by the great humanist, grammarian, editor, and typographer, Aldus Manutius (1449–1515), in whose 1502 edition of Dante (second issue) and all subsequent editions it appeared. The device illustrates the ancient proverb *Festina lente,* "Hurry up slowly."

THEODORE J. CACHEY, JR.,
AND CHRISTIAN MOEVS
EDITORS

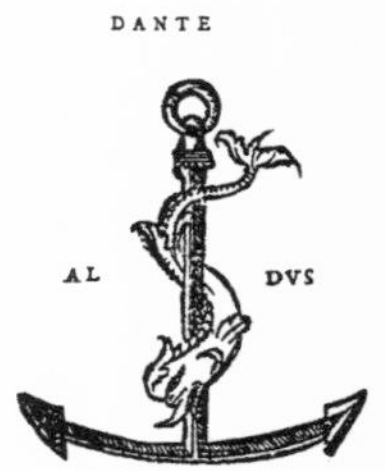
DANTE
AL
DVS

Acknowledgments

We would like to express our thanks to the many individuals who have taken interest in this project, many of them since its inception some years ago. First of all, we are greatly indebted to Theodore J. Cachey, Jr., who first encouraged us in this project and who has been a constant and reliable source of knowledge and inspiration. We owe much to Zygmunt Barański (University of Reading) whose reading—and rereadings—of both the introductory materials and the translation have saved us from a variety of pitfalls on numerous occasions. We thank Patrick Boyde (Cambridge University): his fine literary and linguistic sensitivity to the Italian text and attention to our early attempts to put it into proper English taught us much about the art of translation; what infelicities remain are obviously ours and ours alone. Giuseppe Mazzotta (Yale University) read the introduction and made valuable suggestions for its improvement. Robert R. Edwards (Pennsylvania State University) also read the introduction and provided valuable comments on Ovid and the *Romance of the Rose*. Heather Hayton (Pennsylvania State University) offered useful suggestions for our version of the *Detto d'Amore*. Douglas Kelly (University of Wisconsin-Madison) was an invaluable resource for our questions on the *Romance of the Rose*. We thank Ilaria Marchesi (Rutgers University) whose contributions went far beyond mere editorial expertise. The warm support that Kevin Brownlee (University of Pennsylvania) has given to the project was greatly appreciated. As it is evident from our work, we have profited from the extensive commentary on the *Fiore* and the *Detto d'Amore* by earlier editors: Ernesto Giacomo Parodi, Gianfranco Contini, Claudio Marchiori, and Luca Carlo Rossi. Finally, we are grateful to Theodore J. Cachey, Jr., and Christian Moevs for hosting this volume in the William and Katherine Devers Series in Dante Studies.

Santa Casciani and Christopher Kleinhenz
(October 1999)

The Fiore

Introduction

Background: The *Romance of the Rose*

The *Roman de la Rose* (*Romance of the Rose*)[1] is an allegorical work that was written in the thirteenth century by two Old French poets, Guillaume de Lorris and Jean de Meun. For almost three hundred years after its composition, this poem was one of the most widely read and influential works of medieval French literature.[2] Although its popularity declined during the sixteenth and seventeenth centuries as the reading public increasingly viewed allegory as an archaic vehicle for poorly disguised moralizing, the *Rose* has since regained its preeminence. In this century it was perhaps the work of C. S. Lewis, principally his *Allegory of Love*,[3] that encouraged a renewed interest in medieval allegory, and therefore interest in the *Romance of the Rose*.[4]

The *Romance of the Rose* is not an easy text to read or understand. First of all, the poem is not a unified whole; indeed, its two sections are radically different in tone and purpose. The author of the first part, Guillaume de Lorris, wrote his 4,028 verses in the second quarter of the thirteenth century (1237) and left the work incomplete. Forty years later, another French poet, Jean de Meun, completed Guillaume's unfinished allegorical dream vision, employing a much different style and tone. In the second part of the *Rose* Jean counters Guillaume's courtly idealism with his own extensive

1. All passages from the *Roman de la Rose* in English come from Charles Dahlberg's translation: Guillaume de Lorris and Jean de Meun, *The Romance of the Rose* (Princeton: Princeton University Press, 1995). The French citations come from Guillaume de Lorris and Jean de Meun, *Le Roman de la Rose*, ed. Félix Lecoy, 3 vols. (Paris: Champion, 1965–70).

2. For a study of the medieval reception and manuscript tradition of the *Rose*, see Sylvia Huot, *The "Romance of the Rose" and Its Medieval Readers: Interpretation, Reception, Manuscript Transmission* (Cambridge: Cambridge University Press, 1993).

3. C. S. Lewis, *The Allegory of Love* (Oxford: Clarendon Press, 1936). On the *Romance of the Rose*, see John V. Fleming, *The "Roman de la Rose": A Study in Allegory and Iconography* (Princeton: Princeton University Press, 1969).

4. For an annotated bibliography of the *Rose*, see Heather Arden, *The "Roman de la Rose": An Annotated Bibliography* (New York: Garland, 1993).

philosophical digressions and social commentary. Guillaume framed his poem within the context of "courtly" love and drew his material from Ovid,[5] from the earlier lyric traditions of the troubadours and trouvères and from the treatise by Andreas Capellanus, *De amore*.[6] Guillaume set his poem in springtime, the traditional season for love. On a May morning Guillaume's narrator/protagonist dreams that he enters the Garden of *Deduit*, planted by *Courtoisie*, and sees a beautiful Rosebud. Wounded by Cupid's arrow, he falls in love with the Rose and swears his fealty to the God of Love. Lover's difficult quest to win the Rose is portrayed through the interaction of allegorical personages, who represent different aspects of the complex psychological and social drama. Some of these present obstacles to love: e.g., *Dangier* (Resistance), *Jalousie* (Jealousy) and *Male Bouche* (Bad Mouth), while other characters assist Lover in his quest: e.g., *Ami* (Friend), *Pitié* (Pity) and *Esperance* (Hope). To help Lover overcome these obstacles, Cupid reappears and provides him with a set of rules, the Rules of Love, and the code of courtship behavior first outlined in Ovid's *Ars Amatoria*. Cupid encourages Lover to cultivate the virtues of a courtly knight as a means to conquer the Rose. Thus, Lover embarks on a strategic quest to overcome the various obstacles and to conquer the Rose.

While Guillaume's portion of the *Rose* invokes the fusion of *Amour* and *Courtoisie*, the courtly behavior which comprised a large part of medieval French romance, Jean de Meun, in his continuation of the work, adopts a moralizing tone and encyclopedic scope. He includes a comprehensive disquisition on love and courtship, introducing moral and scientific themes[7] stemming not only from European texts but also from classical authors.[8] In contrast to Guillaume's lyrical and psychological overtones, Jean de Meun's tone is polemical. He often satirizes women, parodies the mendicant orders, and raises questions about the relationship between the sexes and about social and class differences, issues which were of great interest to the rising bourgeoisie.

5. Ovid, *The Art of Love and Other Poems*, ed. and trans. J. H. Mozley 2nd ed. (Cambridge, Mass.: Harvard University Press; London: Heinemann, 1985).

6. Andreas Capellanus, *De amore libri tres*, ed. E. Trojel (Copenhagen: Gadiana, 1892).

7. For the scientific and philosophical modes of treatment, see Douglas Kelly, *Internal Difference and Meanings in the "Roman de la Rose"* (Madison: University of Wisconsin Press, 1995), 52–91.

8. On the subject of classical *auctores*, see John V. Fleming, "Jean de Meun and the Ancient Poets," in *Rethinking the "Romance of the Rose": Text, Image, Reception*, ed. Kevin Brownlee and Sylvia Huot (Philadelphia: University of Pennsylvania Press, 1992), 81–100.

The *Rose* in Italy and the Appearance of the *Fiore*

The presence of a large body of thirteenth- and fourteenth-century manuscripts of the *Romance of the Rose* in Italian libraries attests to the significance of this poem for Italian readers and writers of the period.[9] An even better indication of its influence south of the Alps is the existence of the *Fiore*, a retelling of the *Rose* in 232 sonnets.[10] Many contemporary scholars attribute this series of sonnets to Dante, and this attribution has occasioned much controversy over the years.[11] The 3,245 verses in the Italian sonnets reconstruct and recompose the 21,750 verses of the Old French text.[12] As in the *Rose*, Lover's journey in the Italian text culminates in the thinly veiled erotic description of the "plucking" of the flower. Unlike the French text, however, the *Fiore* does not distinguish between the first part of the *Rose*, written in the refined courtly verse of Guillaume de Lorris, and the second part, composed in the didactic style of Jean de Meun. In the Italian version the author removes the story from its original courtly and didactic cornices,[13] and grounds it in the style of the so-called *giocosi* poets, which is based neither on the lyrical style used by Guillaume nor on the encyclopedic and digressive formulations of Jean de Meun.[14] As some critics have argued, the choice of the sonnet form would indicate the author's intent both to dissociate his work from the French text and to place it within a distinctively Italian poetic tradition.[15] While the sonnet was often used for courtly texts in the high style,[16] it was the preferred poetic form of poets writing in the "low"

9. Luigi Vanossi mentions more than 300 manuscripts (*Dante e il "Roman de la Rose": saggio sul "Fiore"* [Florence: Olschki, 1979], 160–171). On the medieval reception and the manuscript tradition of the *Rose*, see also Huot, *The "Romance of the Rose" and Its Medieval Readers*.

10. All passages from the *Fiore* come from Dante Alighieri, *Il Fiore e il Detto d'Amore attribuibili a Dante Alighieri*, ed. Gianfranco Contini (Milan and Naples: Ricciardi, 1984).

11. See below for a discussion of authorship.

12. Three sonnets (121, 132, 144) are missing one line each.

13. On this point, see Leonardo Sebastio, *Strutture narrative e dinamiche culturali in Dante e nel "Fiore"* (Florence: Olschki, 1990), 99–294; and John Took, "Towards an Interpretation of the *Fiore*," *Speculum* 54 (1979), 500–527.

14. For studies on the *poeti giocosi*, see, among others, Mario Marti, *Cultura e stile nei poeti giocosi del tempo di Dante* (Milan: Rizzoli, 1956); Antonio Enzo Quaglio, *La poesia realistica e la prosa del Duecento* (Bari: Laterza, 1971); and Franco Suitner, "Dante e la poesia satirica del suo tempo," *Letture classensi* 12 (1983), 61–79.

15. Zygmunt G. Barański, "Lettura dei sonetti I–XXX," in *Letture classensi* 22: *Lettura del "Fiore,"* ed. Zygmunt G. Barański, Patrick Boyde, and Lino Pertile (Ravenna: Longo, 1993), 13–35. For studies on the art and the invention of the sonnet in Italy, see Christopher Kleinhenz, *The Early Italian Sonnet: The First Century (1220–1321)* (Lecce: Milella, 1986); Aldo Menichetti, "Implicazioni retoriche nell'invenzione del sonetto," *Strumenti critici* 9 (1979), 1–30; Marco Santagata, *Dal sonetto al Canzoniere* (Padua: Liviana, 1979).

16. See, for example, many of the sonnets by Guido Cavalcanti and Dante.

style, such as Cecco Angiolieri, Rustico Filippi and others.[17] Poems written in this stylistic register co-existed with the more conventional courtly lyrics, a literary situation already present in the Sicilian School.[18] Therefore, the use of the sonnet form as the meter of the *Fiore* may be viewed as a conscious literary choice that enabled its author to represent the pivotal points of the *Rose* in a sort of synthesis and, at the same time, to launch a counterattack against thirteenth- and fourteenth-century French cultural hegemony in Italy.[19] By eliminating Jean's digressions, the author of the *Fiore* concentrates on the art of love as highlighted in the first part of the *Rose* and redirects the discourse of the poem to this end. In fact, the Italian author would appear to re-establish Guillaume's intent in the text; for it is Guillaume who states that "it is the *Romance of the Rose*, in which the whole art of love is contained" ("ce est li *Romanz de la Rose*, / ou l'art d'Amors est tote enclose," vv. 37–38). However, the Italian author is also able to accomplish Jean's principal objective, that of defining the *Romance of the Rose* as a "Mirror for Lovers"—an encyclopedia for lovers ("Le Mirouer aus Amoureus," v. 10,651).[20]

The *Fiore:* Manuscript and Composition

The only existing copy of the poem, published for the first time in 1881 by Ferdinand Castets,[21] is in Codex H. 438 of the Bibliothèque Universitaire of Montpellier. In the same codex with the *Fiore* is bound a copy of *The Romance of the Rose* in a different hand. The handwriting is in a style used in Tuscany.[22] Until 1849 both the *Fiore* and the *Detto d'Amore* were bound together as

17. See Marti, *Cultura e stile.* In *De vulgari eloquentia* (II.iii.5–6), Dante relegates the sonnet (and the *ballata*) to the inferior ranks of poetry.

18. For studies pertaining to the history of Tuscan poetry, see Ignazio Baldelli, "La letteratura volgare in Toscana dalle origini ai primi decenni del secolo XIII," in *Letteratura italiana: Storia e geografia, l'età medievale* (Turin: Einaudi, 1987), 65–77. For the Sicilian School, see, among others, Gianfranco Folena, "Cultura e poesia dei Siciliani," in *Storia della letteratura italiana,* vol. 1: *Le origini e il Duecento,* ed. Emilio Cecchi and Natalino Sapegno (Milan: Garzanti, 1965), 273–347; Kleinhenz, *The Early Italian Sonnet* (especially chapter 2); and Antonio Enzo Quaglio, "I poeti della 'Magna Curia' siciliana," in Emilio Pasquini and Antonio Enzo Quaglio, *Le origini e la scuola siciliana* (Bari: Laterza, 1971), 171–240.

19. See Barański, "Lettura dei sonetti I–XXX," 27–28. For major studies on the relationship between France and Italy and the fortune of the *Romance of the Rose* in Italy, see Gianfranco Contini, "Un nodo della cultura medievale: la serie *Roman de la Rose - Fiore - Divina Commedia," Lettere italiane* 25 (1973), 162–189; Carlo Dionisotti, *Geografia e storia della letteratura italiana* (Turin: Einaudi, 1967); Cesare Segre, *Lingua, stile e società: Studi sulla storia della prosa italiana* (Milan: Feltrinelli, 1976 [1963]); John Took, "Dante and the *Roman de la Rose,*" *Italian Studies* 37 (1982), 1–25.

20. Barański, "Lettura dei sonetti I–XXX," 28–29.

21. *Il Fiore, poème italien du XIIIe siècle, en CCXXXII sonnets, imité du Roman de la Rose par Durante,* ed. Ferdinand Castets (Paris: Maisonneuve, 1881).

22. For the latest study on the handwriting of the codex, see Teresa De Robertis Boniforti, "Nota sul codice e la sua scrittura," in *The Fiore in Context: Dante, France, Tuscany,* ed. Zygmunt G.

one manuscript in the same hand.[23] However, in 1849 Guglielmo Libri stole the folios where the *Detto* appears, and these are now the property of the Laurentian Library in Florence with the shelf number Ashburnham 1234.[24] The dating of the composition of the *Fiore* is not without problems. The references to historical events within the text of the *Fiore* place the writing within the period 1280–1293, based on the following internal evidence: the murder of the philosopher Siger of Brabant around 1280–1284 in Orvieto (sonnet 92); the persecution of the paterines in Tuscany between 1283–1287 (sonnet 126); and the revolt of the bourgeoisie against the nobility between 1282–1293 (sonnet 118). Guido Mazzoni argues for its composition in the period around 1295,[25] while Contini dates it to the years 1286–1290, which are closer to Petrocchi's proposed dates of 1286–1287. Based on her detailed study of the handwriting of the manuscript, Teresa De Robertis Boniforti tentatively proposes a date of composition sometime in the first two decades of the fourteenth century, while recognizing the problems with squaring those dates with Dante's possible authorship of the *Fiore* and / or *Detto*.[26] On the other hand, Barański, basing his position on the Italian polemics against French literary hegemony, believes that it does not make sense to attribute the composition of the *Fiore* to the first two decades of the Trecento because the necessity of establishing an Italian literary tradition was no longer pressing in this period.[27] Contini's and Petrocchi's dates are much more appropriate, because they agree with internal references in the *Fiore* to historical events relating to the period 1282–1293.

The Authorship of the *Fiore*

The most controversial point of the *Fiore* and the *Detto* concerns the question of their authorship. The possible attribution of these two texts to Dante began with Castets,[28] who associated the author's stated name

Barański and Patrick Boyde (Notre Dame: University of Notre Dame Press, 1997), 49–81. In the debate that follows her study (pp. 82–86), De Robertis Boniforti clarifies that, in paleografic terms, Tuscan comprises not only Tuscany but also the geographic area of Umbria and Bologna (82).

23. The titles of the works—*Fiore* and *Detto d'Amore*—do not appear in the manuscript and are modern designations.

24. De Robertis Boniforti, "Nota sul codice," 49–50.

25. Guido Mazzoni, "Se possa *Il Fiore* essere di Dante Alighieri," in *Raccolta di studii critici dedicata ad Alessandro D'Ancona festeggiandosi il XL anniversario del suo insegnamento* (Florence: G. Barbèra, 1901), 681.

26. De Robertis Boniforti, "Nota sul codice," 64.

27. Zygmunt G. Barański, "Il *Fiore* e la tradizione delle *translationes*," *Rassegna europea di letteratura italiana* 5 / 6 (1995), 31–41, 38.

28. Castets, *Il Fiore*, xv.

Durante, found in sonnets 82 and 202,[29] with Dante. While some early scholars such as Rajna[30] and Mazzoni[31] also believed in the possibility of Dante's authorship, Contini[32] and Vanossi[33] are convinced that Dante is the author of the *Fiore*.[34] Among the features that point to Dante as author are the work's narrative qualities, the rhyme scheme of the tercets, the similarities of words and phrases with other works of the Florentine poet,[35] and the moral stance and literary sophistication that the text shares with the *Divine Comedy*.[36]

Prominent among scholars of an earlier era who contested Dante's authorship are Zingarelli,[37] Borgognoni[38] and Parodi.[39] More recent critics who dispute his paternity are Wunderli,[40] Armour,[41] Fasani,[42] Pertile,[43] Cursietti,[44] Fratta,[45] and Buzzetti Gallarati.[46] Some of the arguments against Dante's authorship are the incompatible linguistic and metrical preferences and the absence of many of the *Rose*'s themes in the *Fiore*.[47] Patrick Boyde has provided

29. "For I must help Durante. . ." (82.9); "thus it happened to the good Ser Durante" (202.14).

30. Pio Rajna, "La questione del *Fiore*," *Il Marzocco* 26, no. 3 (16 gennaio 1921).

31. Mazzoni, "Se possa *Il Fiore* essere di Dante Alighieri."

32. Contini, "Un nodo della cultura medievale."

33. Vanossi, *Dante e il "Roman de la Rose."*

34. For others who credit the *Fiore* to Dante, see Aldo Vallone, "Il *Fiore* come opera di Dante," *Studi danteschi* 56 (1984), 141–167; and Gianfranco Contini, "La questione del *Fiore*," *Cultura e scuola* 13/14 (1965), 768–773.

35. For a study of words and phraseology in Dante and other poets of his time, see Letterio Cassata, "Sul testo del *Fiore*," *Studi danteschi* 58 (1986), 187–237.

36. For the latest summary and a bibliography of the debate, see Patrick Boyde, "*Summus Minimusve Poeta?* Arguments for and against Attributing the *Fiore* to Dante," in *The Fiore in Context*, 13–45.

37. Nicola Zingarelli, "La falsa attribuzione del *Fiore* a Dante Alighieri," *Rassegna critica della letteratura italiana* 27 (1922), 236–254.

38. Adolfo Borgognoni, "Il *Fiore*," *La rassegna settimanale di politica, scienza, lettere ed arti* 8, no. 198 (16 ottobre 1881), 247–249.

39. Ernesto Giacomo Parodi, "Prefazione," in his edition, *Il Fiore e il Detto d'Amore*, appendix to *Le opere di Dante* (Florence: Bemporad, 1922), v–xx.

40. Peter Wunderli, "*Mortuus redivivus:* Die Fiore-Frage," *Deutsches Dante-Jahrbuch* 61 (1986), 35–50.

41. Peter Armour, "Lettura dei sonetti LXI–XC," in *Letture classensi* 22, 67–68.

42. Remo Fasani, "L'attribuzione del *Fiore*," *Studi e problemi di critica testuale* 39 (1989), 5–40.

43. Lino Pertile, "Lettura dei sonetti CLXXXI–CCX," in *Letture classensi* 22, 131–153.

44. Marco Cursietti, "Ancora per il *Fiore:* indizi cavalcantiani," *La Parola del testo* 1 (1997), 197–218.

45. Aniello Fratta, "La lingua del *Fiore* (e del *Detto d'Amore*) e le opere di Francesco da Barberino," *Misure Critiche* 14 (1984), 45–62.

46. Silvia Buzzetti Gallarati, "La memoria di Rustico nel *Fiore*," in *Studi di filologia medievale offerti a D'Arco Silvio Avalle* (Milan-Naples: Ricciardi, 1996).

47. For a statistical analysis of the *Fiore* and the view that it is not by Dante, see the studies by Joseph A. Barber, "Prospettive per un'analisi statistica del *Fiore*," *Revue des études italiennes* 31 (1985), 5–24, and "A Statistical Analysis of the *Fiore*," *Lectura Dantis* 6 (1990), 100–122. For another dissenting voice, see Arnaldo Moroldo, "Emprunts et réseaux lexicaux dans le *Fiore*," *Revue des langues romanes* 92 (1988), 127–151.

a fine overview of the debate over the contested authorship of the *Fiore*.[48] In rejecting Dante's authorship, Pertile cites sonnet 82 as providing one possible bit of internal evidence for his position. In this sonnet Love finds it necessary to help Durante because he was "so wise and tenacious and constant / that Reason's speech had no effect at all." Pertile believes that the name *Durante* is used as an epithet, not to name the author, but to synthesize in one word Lover's sexual role throughout the entire text.[49] The practice of *interpretatio nominis* should be viewed in the more general context of Duecento and Trecento literature where it serves both serious and comic ends.[50]

The Content of the *Fiore*

In sonnet 1, Lover (*Amante*), while gazing at a flower in the Garden of Pleasure is wounded by the God of Love. After pledging fealty to the God of Love, Lover tries to pick the Flower but is opposed by Resistance (*Schifo*) (sonnets 2–8). In sonnets 9–10 Reason (*Ragione*) tries to intervene, but Lover does not listen. Sonnets 11–12 contain the first dialogue with Friend (*Amico*), who urges Lover to the quest. Then Mercy (*Pietà*) and Sincerity (*Franchezza*) convince Resistance to allow Lover into the garden. Once there, he finally kisses the Flower, but because of this offence he is banished from the garden (13–21). Chastity (*Castità*) asks Jealousy (*Gelosia*) to take strong precautions; then a fortified castle is built where Chastity and Jealousy imprison Fair Welcome (*Bellacoglienza*) under the surveillance of the Old Woman (*La Vecchia*). Resistance, Modesty (*Vergogna*), Fear (*Paura*) and Bad Mouth (*Mala-Bocca*) guard the doors of the castle (22–32). In sonnets 33–34 we see Lover's suffering, then Reason tries in vain to dissuade Lover from pursuing his amorous quest (35–46). Friend returns to the scene and advises Lover on the trickery of love: in order to conquer the Flower he must either use hypocrisy with Bad Mouth or follow the road of Extravagance (*Troppo-Donare*) controlled by Wealth (*Ricchezza*) (47–72). However, Wealth refuses Lover (73–76). The God of Love wants to reward Lover for his one-year resistance to all of his obstacles and summons the Barons of Love, Forced Abstinence (*Costretta-Astinenza*) and False Seeming (*Falsembiante*) (77–81). Together they plan their

48. See note 36 above.

49. Pertile disagrees with Vanossi's suggestion that the name *Durante* should be interpreted seriously according to the principle of *nomina sunt consequentia rerum* following Dante's practice in the *Vita Nuova* (24.4) and in *Paradiso* (12.79–81); see the note in Vanossi, *Dante e il "Roman de la Rose,"* 139.

50. In this regard Pertile notes the juxtaposition of Beatrice to Becchina ("Lettura dei sonetti CLXXXI–CCX," 152).

strategy to conquer the castle (82–87). At this point False Seeming appears dressed as a Dominican friar; he introduces himself and, in a demonstration of ecclesiastical hypocrisy, assures faithfulness to the God of Love (88–127). False Seeming and Forced Abstinence betray and kill Bad Mouth (128–136). Once inside the castle, Lover strikes a deal with the Old Woman to convince Fair Welcome to yield (137–143). Then the Old Woman delivers a long monologue evoking her youthful errors, urging women to use deceit to betray and profit from men as well as to have several lovers simultaneously (144–197). Fair Welcome receives Lover, but the opposition mounted once again by Resistance requires a new strategy (194–205). The army of the God of Love attacks the castle, and amid battles and combats there is large-scale slaughter, which continues until the God of Love calls a truce (206–214). Venus intervenes, setting fire to the castle and routing the enemy (215–225). Lady Courtesy persuades Fair Welcome to receive Lover (226–227), and Lover deflowers the Flower (228–230). Lover thanks his benefactors and rejoices at the successful accomplishment of his mission in the face of many obstacles (231–232).

The *Fiore* and the *Rose:* Questions of Influence and *Translatio*

As readers of the *Fiore*, we may wonder whether the Italian author, in rebelling against French literary conventions, is devising—and putting into practice—a new art of translation that will help the nascent Italian literary tradition assume its own identity, one different from that of the French. Kevin Brownlee places the *Fiore* with the *Tesoretto* and the *Divine Comedy* as specific texts that do not exemplify the usual historical progression with regard to the Italian reception of French culture.[51] In fact, he suggests that the author of the *Fiore*, in a paradoxical twist, transforms the Old French of the *Rose* into the Tuscan vernacular with a view toward claiming literary primacy and linguistic authority. However, in this transformation the author of the *Fiore* also utilizes a number of gallicisms, such that the French text is simultaneously evoked and denied. The same is true, Brownlee argues, for the *Fiore*'s treatment of French literature. One of the points he uses to explain this concept is the sophisticated transition that the Italian author uses between the first and second part of the *Rose* where the two French authors come into question. Specifically, Brownlee cites verses 9–14 of sonnet 21 in the *Fiore:*

51. Kevin Brownlee, "The Practice of Cultural Authority: Italian Responses to French Cultural Dominance in *Il Tesoretto, Il Fiore,* and the *Commedia,*" *Forum for Modern Language Studies* 33 (1997), 258–269.

And now I will tell you of the fortress
where Fair Welcome was imprisoned,
the one that Love destroyed with his strength.
I will also tell how Resistance became hostile towards me
and kept me in distress for a very long time,
and how Reason returned to me.

They correspond to the following verses in the *Rose*:

> From now on it is right for me to tell you how I struggled with Shame, who gave me a lot of trouble afterward, and how the walls were raised and how there rose the rich and powerful castle that Love seized later through his efforts. I want to pursue the whole history, and I shall never be idle in writing it down as long as I believe that it may please the beautiful lady—may God be her cure—who better than any other shall, when she wishes, give me the reward. (3499–3510)[52]

Brownlee suggests that the Italian author is specifically responding to this crucial point in the *Rose* where Guillaume's text remains narratively incomplete, because, while it predicts closure, this does not occur.[53] Thus, in sonnet 21, the author of the *Fiore* would appear to erase the distinction between the two French authors, as well as those problems associated with the poetics of the *Rose* which link issues of incompletion/closure with those of continuation/*translatio*. Brownlee states that in French literature, *translatio*

> involves the rewriting/continuation of a canonical *auctor* and serves to authorise both a specific vernacular literary enterprise and the vernacular as literary language. At the same time, of course, the model text—usually Latin—is itself valorised.[54]

However, by implicitly ignoring the distinction between the two French texts, the Italian author proposes to rewrite the *Rose* in such a way as to sup-

52. The verse numbers following the translation refer to Dahlberg's English translation. Here is the passage in the original: Des or est droiz que je vos conte/coment je fui melez a Honte, /par qui je fui puis mout grevez, /et coment li murs fu levez/et le chastiaus riches et forz, /qu'Amors prist puis par ses esforz. /Tote l'estoire veil parsuivre, /ja ne m'est parece d'escrivre, /por quoi je cuit qu'il abelise/a la bele, que Dex guerisse, /qui le guerredon m'en rendra/mieux que nule, quant el voudra. (vv. 3481–3492)

53. Brownlee supports Douglas Kelly, "'Li chastiaus. . . Qu'Amors prist puis par ses esforz': The Conclusion of Guillaume de Lorris' *Rose*," in *A Medieval French Miscellany*, ed. Norris J. Lacy (Lawrence: University of Kansas Publications, 1972), 61–78. See also Sylvia Huot, "The *Fiore* and the Early Reception of the *Roman de la Rose*," in *The Fiore in Context*, 153–165.

54. Brownlee, "The Practice of Cultural Authority," 258.

press *translatio* and literary genealogy and to place his work within a precise historical period in Italian literary culture.

Scholars have been debating the sophistication of the *Fiore* for years, and the complex question of its literary/historical intent remains unresolved. Some critics have rightfully emphasized that the goal of the *Fiore* was to amuse and entertain. Lino Pertile, for example, states that

> the *Fiore* is an undoubtedly brilliant work, but one programmatically lacking in complexity. It was rewritten as a comic exercise and as a vehicle designed to make the audience laugh by a skilled author, . . . a highly refined and intelligent poet, but one without discipline and patience, who was well-versed in philosophy and literature, probably being steeped in these up to his neck.[55]

However, it is also legitimate to ask whether the work represents a sophisticated self-awareness of its role in the Italian cultural environment of the time. Brownlee and Barański, while aware of the problems associated with their views, have come to the tentative conclusion that the *Fiore* is critically self aware (as problematic as this may be).

Barański sees the complexity of the *Fiore* as residing in the different ways the Italian author reworks the practice and theory of translation.[56] In a recent study he convincingly shows how, in sonnet 103, *Falsembiante* describes and synthesizes the art of translation:

> Moreover, it seems to me no work at all
> to go around the regions of the world
> seeking out every religious order;
> but in matters of religion I unfailingly
> leave the fruit behind and take the straw,
> for I only want my habit to be like theirs
> and to be able to preach sweet sermons:
> with these two devices the world is blinded.
> And thus I go about changing both tone and verse
> and saying humble and simple words,
> but my actions are quite different from my words;

55. Pertile, "Lettura dei sonetti CLXXXI–CCX," 153 (translation ours).

56. Zygmunt G. Barański, "The Ethics of Literature: The *Fiore* and Medieval Traditions of Rewriting," in *The Fiore in Context*, 224.

for all those who today are eating bread
could not keep me from wandering off the straight path,
for I am more desirous of this than a dog is of fat.[57]

Barański suggests that *Falsembiante*'s words not only refer to his anti-clerical beliefs, but also describe Durante's views on the rewriting of the *Rose* and on his attempt to situate the text within the historical and cultural environment of his day.[58] By transforming the text through the use of sound and verse which were humble and simple, *umili* and *piane*, the Italian author also transmutes the form of the *Rose* into an Italian poem, made up of sonnets and hendecasyllables. Here, recalling the view of Gianfranco Folena,[59] Barański cites *Purgatory* 11: "Worldly renown is nothing other than / a breath of wind that blows now here, now there, / and changes name when it has changed its course" (vv. 100–102).[60] He argues that the verbs *mutare-transmutare* refer to the act of translation in Dante and thus to the act of rewriting, as we can see in sonnet 103, "I go about changing both tone and verse" (v. 9).[61]

In support of the complexity of the Italian text, other observations are necessary. The structure of the stages describing the conquest of the flower in the *Fiore* is the same as that in the *Rose*, but the differences and omissions in the Italian text demonstrate the work of a sophisticated author.[62] In the Italian text, the woman and the general subject of love are presented according to their erotic aspects, and the glorification of aristocratic emotions is contrasted with and juxtaposed to that of the earthly senses. The courtly tradition is quickly overturned and challenged in the third sonnet of the *Fiore*, when the author changes the month of May to January:

In the month of January, and not in May,
it was, when I took Love to be my lord
and placed myself completely in his power,
and swore homage to him.

57. Barański, "Il *Fiore* e la tradizione delle *translationes.*"

58. For a recent study on medieval *translatio,* see Rita Copeland, *Rhetoric, Hermeneutics, and Translation in the Middle Ages: Academic Traditions and Vernacular Texts* (Cambridge: Cambridge University Press, 1991).

59. Gianfranco Folena, *Volgarizzare e tradurre* (Turin: Einaudi, 1991).

60. The English translations of the *Comedy* are taken from Dante Alighieri, *The Divine Comedy of Dante Alighieri,* trans. Allen Mandelbaum, 3 vols. (New York: Bantam Books, 1982–1984–1986).

61. Barański, "Il *Fiore* e la tradizione delle *translationes,*" 31–33; Folena, *Volgarizzare e tradurre,* 34–36.

62. For the textual relationship between the *Roman de la Rose* and the *Fiore,* see *"Il Fiore" e "Il Detto d'Amore,"* ed. Claudio Marchiori (Genoa: Tilgher, 1983).

This seasonal variation provided by the month of January with the adversative conjunction *e non* ("and not") confirms the author's conscious intent to change the literary tradition which associated love with springtime, and particularly with the month of May. Claudio Marchiori notes that in using the generic image of a "flower" and not the specific one of a "rose," the author of the *Fiore* underscores the precious nature of the only flower that blooms in the month of January, a flower without rival.[63] The Italian poet "adopts and adapts" an image from Guillaume,[64] but, by eliminating the rose, he rejects the strong literary and cultural association attached to this flower and replaces this tradition with a version which is uniquely his own. The archetypal image of the rose is incorporated and transferred into a flower through a synthesis of dependence and separation:[65]

> With his bow the God of Love pierced me
> while I was gazing at a Flower that pleased me. . . (1.1–2)

Through the dependence of the metonymical association of the flower with the rose, the Italian author evokes the French text, but denies it at the same time. Indeed, he separates himself from the French *topos* of the rose and invents a flower that is without thorns, and thus without obstacles for the lover.

The author of the *Fiore* certainly brings *translatio* into question in sonnet 230 with the metaphor of deflowering in verse 9:

> Time and again I failed to stick it in,
> since it wouldn't fit in there in any way;
> and my moneybag that was hanging from my staff,
> I continued banging it down below,
> thinking thus to ease my staff inside;
> but nothing worked for me.
> However, in the end I shook it so much
> that I finally got it to go inside:

63. Marchiori, "*Il Fiore,*" 10. On this particular point, see also Castets, *Il Fiore,* 10; Aldo S. Bernardo, "Sex and Salvation in the Middle Ages: From the *Romance of the Rose* to the *Divine Comedy,*" *Italica* 67 (1990), 305–318; Roger Dragonetti, "Specchi d'amore: il *Romanzo della Rosa* e il *Fiore,*" *Paragone* 374 (1981), 3–22; and Robert Pogue Harrison, "The Bare Essential: The Landscape of *Il Fiore,*" in *Rethinking the "Romance of the Rose,"* 289–303.

64. For the concept of medieval "mental archetype," see Douglas Kelly, *Medieval Imagination: Rhetoric and the Poetry of Courtly Love* (Madison and London: University of Wisconsin Press, 1978); "*Translatio Studii:* Translation, Adaptation, and Allegory in Medieval French Literature," *Philological Quarterly* 57 (1978), 287–310; Margaret F. Nims, "*Translatio:* 'Difficult Statement' in Medieval Poetic Theory," *University of Toronto Quarterly* 43 (1974), 215–230.

65. See Barański, "Lettura dei sonetti I–XXX," 19.

thus I succeeded in deflowering the Flower,
and with the seed that I had carried,
after the plowing, so came the sowing.
The seed of the Flower had descended;
I mixed the two of them together
such that much good fruit has issued forth.

In verse 9 ("sì ch'io allora il fior tutto sfogl[i]ai"), the author represents not only the deflowering of the flower/woman, but also the stripping away of the original text by the author that was foreshadowed in the last tercet of sonnet 222:

and then we'll certainly take the Flower,
and have it deflowered in such a way
that it will no longer be off limits to any one.

By removing the doctrinal passages of the *Rose* and transforming the remainder into more accessible imagery, the Italian author rewrites the text in a popular vein so that it will be comprehensible to a different and wider audience. The verb *arare* ("to plow") of sonnet 230.11 ("quand' eb[b]i arato, sì·lla seminai") appears only twice in the text;[66] given its agricultural association, it can allude to coital movement. We know from a variety of literary sources that "ploughing fields" and "sowing seeds" are replete with sexual connotations, as, for example, in Cielo d'Alcamo's *contrasto*, "Rosa fresca aulentissima":[67]

Se di meve trabàgliti, follia lo ti fa fare.
Lo mar potresti arompere, a venti asemenare. . . (6–7)[68]

However, the verb *arare* can also be associated with the act of writing. The image provided in sonnet 230.11 of the *Fiore*—"after the plowing, so came the sowing"—recalls that of the *Indovinello veronese*, a riddle associated with the act of writing:[69]

66. See sonnet 65.13.

67. *Poeti del Duecento*, ed. Gianfranco Contini, 2 vols. (Milan and Naples: Ricciardi, 1960), 1:177–185.

68. "If you torment yourself for me, folly makes you do it. / The sea you could plough, and sow seed to the winds. . . ." (Translation ours.)

69. The text of the *Indovinello veronese* follows that in *Early Italian Texts*, ed. Carlo Dionisotti and Cecil Grayson, 2nd ed. (Oxford: Basil Blackwell, 1965), 1–3; see also Arrigo Castellani, *I più antichi*

Se pareba boves, alba pratalia araba,
et albo versorio teneba, et negro semen seminaba.[70]

Critics have associated this riddle with a European folk tradition in which the various elements deployed in writing—the fingers of the hand, the paper or parchment, the pen and the ink—are represented respectively by the oxen driven by the farmer, the field he is ploughing, the plough he guides and the seed he plants.

If we keep in mind the sexual connotation from Cielo d'Alcamo's *contrasto* and the meaning of the verb *arare* from the *Indovinello veronese*, then the verb *sfogliare* ("to deflower") from sonnet 230 would seem to encompass two images: (1) sexual penetration, and (2) the stripping away of one text (the original) and the writing of a new one, as proposed in the last tercet of sonnet 222. Thus, the seemingly contradictory dependence on and separation from the *Rose*, and the simultaneous evoking and denying of the French model are reaffirmed. For the Italian text incorporates both the old text of the *Rose* and the new text of the *Fiore*, thus representing, at the same time, a continuation of the old and a break with it. Moreover, the verb *sfogliare* has an additional meaning: the leafing through or scanning of pages in a book or manuscript. Although this meaning is not documented until after Dante, the Florentine poet himself used the word *foglio* to refer to the "leaves" in a manuscript book: "I do admit that, if one were to search / our volume leaf by leaf, he might still read / one page with . . ." (*Par.* 12.121–123).[71] Moreover, the word *folium* in reference to the pages of a book was used by many late medieval Latin authors and can be found in contemporary dictionaries, as, for example, in Papia:

> *Folia*—graece fylla dicuntur, unde ad nos derivatur. Folia ramorum discipulos apostulorum significant, vel laudes sine sermone doctrinae. Folia librorum dicta a similitudine foliorum arborum.[72]

---

testi italiani, 2nd ed. (Bologna: Pàtron, 1976). For studies on the *Indovinello,* see Vincenzo De Bartholomaeis, "Ciò che veramente sia l'antichissima 'cantilena' *Boves se pareba," Giornale storico della letteratura italiana* 90 (1927), 197–204; Pio Rajna, "Un indovinello volgare scritto alla fine del secolo VIII o al principio del IX," *Speculum* 3 (1928), 291–313; and Gabriele Erasmi, "Toward a New Interpretation of the *Indovinello veronese," Canadian Journal of Italian Studies* 1 (1977–78), 108–114. For a different view, see Francesca Guerra d'Antoni, "A New Perspective on the Veronese Riddle," *Romance Philology* 36 (1982), 185–200.

70. "He yoked the oxen, / ploughed white fields, / and held a white plough, / and sowed black seeds." (Translation ours.)

71. Here Dante alludes to the individual members of the Franciscan Order as though they were the individual leaves that formed one great book.

72. Papia, *Papia vocabulista* (Turin: Bottega d'Erasmo, 1966 [reprinted from the Venetian edition of 1496]): "The word leaf derives from the greek 'fylla.' The leaves of the branches mean the dis-

Returning to sonnet 230, then, *la semenza* recalls both the semen implicitly indicated in the *contrasto*'s "a venti aseminare" ("sow seed to the winds") and the *Indovinello*'s ink, that "negro semen seminaba" ("sowed black seeds"). Just as *Amante* deflowers the flower, so does the author strip away the old text in order to rewrite the new. This image continues in the last tercet where "the seed of the Flower," referring both to the woman's seed and to the idea of the scanning of pages, was mixed together—both by the lover and the author respectively—in order to permit the birth of "much good fruit":[73]

> The seed of the Flower had descended;
> I mixed the two of them together
> such that much good fruit has issued forth.

The "much good fruit," presumed to mean the continuation of the species, can then also refer to the writing of a new and better text and to the establishment of a new Italian literary tradition. The idea of rewriting the text can be supported with the appearance of the three *sì*'s (< Latin *sic*) in the last two tercets of sonnet 230: "Sì ch'io allora . . . sì·lla seminai . . . sì·lle mescolai." Specifically, we would suggest the following interpretation: First, I stripped the old text by correcting the *cattiva erba*, then I mixed my correction with my new ink, and thus I was able to produce *buon'erba*. In other words, the Italian author is expressing a critical judgment on the French text because, as far as he is concerned, not all the *erba* in the French text is *buon'erba*. In the first quatrain of sonnet 231, the Italian author thanks his benefactors:

> When I saw myself in such an exalted state,
> I thanked all my benefactors,
> and I love them more today than ever before,
> for they worked hard to make my pleasure possible.

In these verses, the author of the *Fiore* is referring to those who have assisted him in plucking the Flower. But he is also thanking those past authors who have provided him with a tradition from which he can both draw his inspiration and material and distinguish himself. Thus, the author evokes the metaphors, symbols and erotic subject matter of the courtly tradition,

ciples of the apostles or the praises without words of the doctrine. The pages of books are called in this way through their similarity to the leaves of the trees." (Translation ours.)

73. These verses recall Matthew 13:3–11, where Christ compares the sowing of good seeds to the spreading of the Word of God. "And others fell upon good ground: and they brought forth fruit, some an hundredfold, some sixtyfold, and some thirtyfold." (Douay translation.)

as portrayed in the *Romance of the Rose*, but he also rewrites the poem using his own strategies and a new poetic style and vernacular.

Rewriting the *Rose:* Omission and *Textus Interruptus*

The fact that the Italian author has intentionally set out to rewrite the text of the *Rose* can be seen in the tercets of sonnet 5, verses which are absent from the *Rose*. Here the God of Love tells Lover to disregard the Gospels and, by extension, all writing with theological content:

> With much humility and patience I promised Love
> that I would suffer his pain
> and that my every limb and vein
> were prepared to do his will.
> And my mind is set to serve him and him alone
> and will never cease to do so:
> "As long as I live and breathe,
> I will never depart from this promise."
> And Love then said to me: "My friend,
> your pledge is better than any written promise:
> be sure to worship me, for I am your god;
> and set aside every other belief:
> do not believe Luke or Matthew,
> Mark or John." And then he departs.

By coming perilously close to renouncing the Evangelists of the Bible, is the Italian author situating his text within the cultural and literary tradition of the comic-realistic poets? Why should Lover not listen to the Evangelists? Our interpretation follows Brownlee's view that the *Fiore* questions the French *translatio* by concealing its direct link to French literature.[74] By adding verses not present in the *Rose*, the Italian author intended to reject the primacy attributed to Holy Scripture that Jean de Meun set forth in the didactic and philosophical digressions of the *Rose* and specifically in the sections on Nature and Genius.

These digressions occupy some 5,000 verses (15,891–20,710) and represent the ideological and poetic core of Jean's continuation of the *Rose*. The

74. Brownlee, "The Practice of Cultural Authority."

omission of the characters of Genius and Nature represents an important distinguishing element in the *Fiore*'s rewriting. The poet's silence on these two important characters implicitly suggests that he was well aware of their role in their original context. By eliminating them, the author is able to concentrate on representing the conflicting forces that characterize eros: sexual pleasure and the need to continue the species. In fact, the author of the *Fiore* refers to Nature only as the legitimizing factor for pleasure. In the debate between Reason and Lover in the Italian text (sonnets 39–40) the author recalls the concepts of generative love expressed by Jean:

> I know very well [. . .] that whoever lies with a woman ought to wish [. . .] to continue his divine self and to maintain himself in his likeness in order that the succession of generations might never fail, since all such likenesses are subject to decay. Nature wills, since father and mother disappear, that children rise up to continue the work of generation, and that one's life may be regained by means of another. For this purpose Nature has implanted delight in man because she wants the workman to take pleasure in his task in order that he might neither flee from it nor hate it, for there are many who would never make a move toward it if there were no delight to attract them. Thus nature uses this subtle means of gaining her end. Now understand that no one who desires only his pleasure in love travels the right road or has a right intention. Do you know what they do who go seeking delight? They give themselves up, like serfs or foolish wretches, to the prince of all vices; to seek delight is the root of all evil, as Tully concludes in the book that he wrote *On Old Age,* which he praises and desires more than youth. (4403–4432)[75]

Following the speech by Reason (*Raison*), Lover (*Amaint*) is unable to answer *Raison*'s defense of the continuation of the species, for he states:

75. Mes je sai bien, pas nou devin, / continuer l'estre devin / a son poair voloir deüst / quiconques a fame geüst, / et soi garder an son senblable, / pour ce qu'il sunt tuit corrunpable, / si que ja par succession / ne fausist generacion; / quar puis que pere et mere faillent, / Nature veust que li filz saillent / pour recontinuer ceste euvre, / si que par l'un l'autre requeuvre. / Pour ce i mist Nature delit, / pur ce veust que l'en si delit / que cist ovrier ne s'en foïssent / et que ceste euvre ne haïssent, / quar maint n'i treroient ja tret, / se n'iert deliz qui les atret. / Ainsinc Nature i sotiva. / Sachiez que nus a droit n'i va / ne n'a pas entencion droite / qui, sanz plus, delit i couvoite; / car cil qui va delit querant, / sez tu qu'i se fet? Il se rant / conme sers et chetis et nices / au prince de trestouz les vices, / car c'est de touz maus la racine, / si com Tulles le determine / ou livre qu'il fist *de Viellece,* / qu'il loe et veust plus que Jeunece. (4373–4402)

Thus Reason preached to me. But Love prevented anything from being put into practice, although I heard the whole matter word for word, for Love drew me strongly and hunted through all my thoughts like a hunter whose course lies everywhere. He kept my heart constantly under his wing, and when I was seated for the sermon, he kept watch over me, outside of my head, with a shovel. Whenever Reason cast a word into one ear, he threw one into the other, with the result that she wasted all her efforts and only filled me with anger and wrath. Then, filled with ire, I said to her: "Lady, you wish to betray me. Should I now hate people? Shall I despise everyone? If love were not good, I would never love with refined love, but live always in hatred. Then I would be a mortal sinner, in fact worse, by God, than a sneak thief; I couldn't help sinning. I have to get out of this difficulty by one of two ways: either I love or I hate. But perhaps I should pay more in the end for hatred, even though love weren't worth a penny. You would have given me good advice, then, you who have kept on preaching to me that I should renounce Love. He who wants to believe you is a fool. (4629–4662)[76]

Raison's position,[77] which declares sensual satisfaction to be sinful, is dialectically surpassed in the *Fiore* by Lover (*Amante*) and compels her Italian sister, Reason (*Ragione*), to admit that Nature, in order to realize her end, has made the sexual act pleasurable, as seen in sonnet 39:

"It is not my intention to keep you from loving,"
said Reason, "nor do I want to discourage you from it,
for I want you to love dearly the whole world,
reinforcing your belief in Jesus Christ.

76. Ainsint Reson me preescheit, / mes Amors tout enpeescheit / que riens a euvre n'en meïsse, / ja soit ce que bien entendisse / mot a mot toute la matire; / car Amor, qui forment m'atyre, / qui par trestouz mes pensers chace / con cil qui par tout a sa chace, / et toujor tient mon queur souz s'ele, / hors de ma teste, a une pele, / quant au sarmon seant m'aguiete, / par l'une des oreilles giete / quan que Reson en l'autre boute, / si qu'ele i pert sa peine toute / et m'enple de corroz et d'ire. / Lors li pris touz iriez a dire: / "Dame, bien me voulez traïr. / Doi je donques les genz haïr? / Donc harré je toutes persones? / Puis qu'amors ne sunt mie bones, / ja mes n'ameré d'amors fines, / ainz vivrai toujorz en haïnes? / Lors si seré mortex pechierres, / voire, par Dieu, pires que lierres! / A ce ne puis je pas faillir, / par l'un me couvient il saillir: / ou j'ameré ou je harré. / Mes espoir que je conparré / plus la haïne au dasrenier, / tout ne vaille amors un denier. / Bon conseill m'avez or doné, / qui toujors m'avez sermoné / que je daie d'amor retraire! / Or est fols qui ne vos velt craire!" (4599–4632)

77. For a study on Reason in the *Rose,* see John V. Fleming, *Reason and the Lover* (Princeton: Princeton University Press, 1984).

And if you give your love to someone,
I don't want you to love her only for pleasure
or for delight, but to draw fruit from the relationship,
because whoever wishes a different end falls into sin.
It's true that there is great delight in that act,
which Nature put there as a lure,
in order for men to go to bed with women more often.
And if it were not so, we well know
that few people would engage
in the labor that Adam first began."

Reason's speech in the above sonnet is reinforced by Lover's answer in sonnet 40. In this sonnet, Lover defends his right to enjoy sexual pleasure through natural instinct and uses Nature only as the legitimizing factor for pleasure, seen as an end in itself. In this way he totally eliminates the philosophical and theological arguments set forth by Nature and Genius in the *Rose:*

I said to her: "Reason, since Nature placed
delight in that labor, you may be sure
that she did not put it there
for no reason at all, for she is not so foolish,
but in order that the human race continue;
indeed, Nature wants man to take delight in many ways
in order to return gladly to these encounters,
for it's through pleasure that his seed produces fruit.
You keep saying that I should not take my pleasure,
but I cannot for the life of me understand
why anyone would undertake that labor
without pleasure; thus, I am resolute in my desire.
Don't dissuade me from taking pleasure with the Flower!
Then let God do what he wishes with the Flower!"

Lover warns Reason not to try to prevent him from loving the Flower. Lover's pleasure is a valid end in itself, and the "spiritual" destiny of the Flower is ultimately God's concern. It is interesting to note that the last tercet in this sonnet evokes the portion of the text known as "Nature's Confession" in the *Rose*—a text which has been omitted by the Italian author. Here, Nature, after cataloguing all of creation beneath the sphere of the moon and digressing on the Virgin Mary and Christ's redemption, condemns man for ignoring Nature's laws, especially those of procreation. Of man she states:

> He is a proud, murderous thief, cruel, covetous, miserly and treacherous. He is desperate, greedy, slanderous, hateful, and spiteful; unfaithful and envious, he lies, perjures himself, and falsifies; he is foolish, boastful, inconstant, and senseless; he is a quarrelsome idolater, a traitorous, false hypocrite, and a lazy sodomite; in short he is such a stupid wretch that he is slave to all the vices, and harbors them all within himself. (19225–19232)[78]

After having condemned man, Nature relinquishes all of her authority to God:

> Of course, I leave to God all the sins with which the wretch is stained; let God take care of them and punish when He pleases. (19323–19324)[79]

She then sends "Genyus, li bien anpalez" (19305), the one who has "the gift of speech," to the God of Love, and Genius excommunicates the enemies of procreation, and encourages the others to procreate:

> By the authority of Nature, who has the care of the whole world, as vicar and constable of the eternal emperor, who sits in the sovereign tower of the noble city of the world, of which he made Nature the minister; Nature who administers all good things through the influence of the stars, for they ordain everything according to the imperial justice that Nature executes; Nature who has given birth to all things since this world came into being, who gives them their allotted time for growth and increase, and who never for nothing made anything under the heaven that continues without delay to turn around the earth, as high below as above, and never stops, night or day, but turns always without rest—by the authority of Nature, let all those disloyal apostates, of high rank or low, who hold in despite the acts by which Nature is supported, be excommunicated and condemned without any delay. And let him who strives with all his force to maintain Nature, who struggles to love well, without any base thought, but with lawful labor, go off to paradise decked with flowers. [. . .] Move, skip, leap; don't let

78. Orgueilleus est, murtriers et lierres, / fel, couvoiteus, avers, trichieres, / desesperez, gloz, mesdisanz, / et haïneus et despisanz, / mescreanz, anvieus, mantierres, / parjurs, fausaires, fos, vantierres, / et inconstanz et foloiables, / ydolatres, desagraables, / traïstres et faus ypocrites, / et pareceus et sodomites: / briefmant tant est chetis et nices / qu'il est sers a tretouz les vices / et tretouz an soi les herberge. (19195–19207)

79. San faille, de touz les pechiez / don li chetis est antechiez, / a Dieu les les, bien s'an chevisse. (19293–19295)

yourself get cold or let your limbs become tepid. Put all your tools to work; he who works well keeps warm enough. Plow, for God's sake, my barons, plow and restore your lineages. Unless you think on plowing vigorously, there is nothing that can restore them. (19505–19539, 19698–19703)[80]

Now if we return to the last tercet of sonnet 40 in the *Fiore,* we see that Lover relinquishes the responsibility he feels toward the Flower by ironically ceding his conquest to God in much the same way that Nature relinquishes her power to God. In this sonnet, Durante evokes the sub-text both of "Nature's Confession" and of "Genius' Solution" by denying their power, and thus their recurring *topoi*; at the same time, however, he evokes their global narrative structure.[81] The denial of these two characters is crucial to the rewriting of the *Fiore*, for Durante as protagonist-author takes charge of his text. In other words, he redefines and subjugates the dominant text, the *Rose*, by translating it into Italian literary terms.

The Relationship to Alan of Lille

One of the sub-texts that influenced the creation of Nature and Genius in the *Rose* is *De planctu Naturae* by Alan of Lille.[82] Alan's work[83] represented a

80. De l'auctorité de Nature, / qui de tout le monde a la cure / conme vicaire et connestable / a l'ampereeur pardurable / qui siet en la tour souveraine / de la noble cité mondaine, / don il fist Nature ministre, / qui touz les biens i amenistre / par l'influence des esteles, / car tout est ordené par eles / selonc les droiz anperiaus / don Nature est officiaus, / qui toutes choses a fet nestre / puis que cist mondes vint an estre, / et leur dona terme ansemant / de grandeur et d'acroissemant, / n'onques ne fist riens por noiant / souz le ciel qui va tournoiant / entour la terre san demeure, / si hauz desouz comme deseure, / ne ne cesse ne nuit ne jour, / mes tourjorz tourne san sejour, / saient tuit esconmenié / li delleal, li renié / et condampné san nul respit, / qui les euvres ont en despit, / soit de grant gent soit de menue, / par cui Nature est soutenue. / Et cil qui, de toute sa force, / de Nature garder s'efforce / et qui de bien amer se peine / sanz nule pansee vileine, / mes qui leaument i travaille, / floriz en paradis s'an aille. [. . .] Remuez vos, tripez, sailliez, / ne vos lessiez pas refredir / par trop voz mambres antedir! / Metez touz voz ostiz en euvre: / assez s'eschaufe qui bien euvre. / Arez, por Dieu, baron, arez, / et vos lignages reparez. / Se ne pansez formant d'arer, / n'est riens qui les puist reparer. (19475–19508, 19666–19674)

81. For medieval *topoi* in general, see Paolo A. Cherchi, "Tradition and *Topoi* in Medieval Literature," *Critical Inquiry* 3 (1976), 281–294.

82. All English passages from *De planctu Naturae* come from Alan of Lille, *Plaint of Nature,* trans. and commentary by James J. Sheridan (Toronto: Pontifical Institute of Mediaeval Studies, 1980).

83. For major works on the *Planctu,* see Winthrop Wetherbee, "The Function of Poetry in the *De planctu Naturae* of Alain De Lille," *Traditio* 25 (1969), 87–127, and *Platonism and Poetry in the Twelfth Century* (Princeton: Princeton University Press, 1972); Cesare Vasoli, "Studi recenti su Alano di Lilla (1950–1960)," *Bullettino dell'istituto storico italiano per il medio evo e archivio muratoriano* 72 (1960), 35–89, *La filosofia medioevale* (Milan: Feltrinelli, 1961), and "*Ars grammatica* e *translatio* teologica in alcuni testi di Alano di Lilla," in *Arts libéraux et philosophie au moyen âge: Actes du quatrième congrès international de philosophie médiévale* (Montréal and Paris: Institut d'Études Médiévales and J. Vrin, 1969), 805–813.

medieval reworking of the philosophy of nature developed by Plato, Aristotle, Plotinus, Macrobius, Boethius and Bernardus Silvestris.[84] Before Alan, Bernandus Silvestris in the *Megacosmus and Microcosmus* postulated a philosophy which placed Nature in control of all animal and plant life. Within this domain, Nature placed man, the master of all things. Alan of Lille, instead, extended the power of Nature to include the human moral order. In his perspective, humans are the only beings possessing free will and the power to contravene the natural laws imprinted in their hearts:

> That man, in whose case a simple conversion in an Art causes Nature's laws to come to naught, is pushing logic too far. He hammers on an anvil which issues no seeds. The very hammer itself shudders in horror of its anvil. He imprints on no matter the stamp of a parent-stem: rather his ploughshare scores a barren strand.[85]

In this passage, Alan represents man as a being capable of dismantling the order of nature. Specifically, he (man) hammers on an anvil which produces no seeds. Thus, ironically, Alan through an anvil, which in the ancient world represented any kind of formative work, illustrates both the dismantling of procreation and writing. Furthermore, the author develops a view of creation, in which God is the creator with Nature appointed as his delegate to guide the laws of procreation. However, in a lapse of judgment Nature assigns this power to Venus, who allows the practice of unnatural sexual habits:

> Alas! Where has Nature with her fair form betaken herself? Where have the pattern of morals, the norm of chastity, the love of modesty gone? Nature weeps, moral laws get no hearing, modesty, totally dispossessed of her ancient high estate, is sent into exile. The active sex shudders in disgrace as it sees itself degenerate into the passive sex. A man turned woman blackens the fair name of his sex. The witchcraft of Venus turns him into a hermaphrodite. He is subject and predicate: one and the same term is given a double application. Man here extends too far the laws of grammar. Becoming a barbarian in grammar, he disclaims the manhood given him by nature. Grammar does not

84. For a survey of the figure of Nature in medieval literature, see George D. Economou, *The Goddess Natura in Medieval Literature* (Cambridge, Mass.: Harvard University Press, 1972).

85. *Plaint of Nature,* 69. Meter I.25–30: Hic nimis est logicus per quem conuersio simplex / Artis nature iura perire facit. / Cudit in incude que semina nulla monetat. / Horret et incudem malleus ipse suam. / Nullam materiem matricis signat idea / Sed magis in sterili litore uomer arat.

find favour with him but rather a trope. This transposition, however, cannot be called a trope. The figure here more correctly falls into the category of defects. [. . .] The one who has used the dactylic measure of Venus fares ill in iambics where a long syllable cannot be followed by a short. [. . .] Why do so many kisses lie fallow on maidens' lips while no one wishes to harvest a crop from them? If these kisses were but once planted on me, they would grow honey-sweet with moisture, and grown honey-sweet, they would form a honeycomb in my mouth. My life breath, concentrating entirely on my mouth, would go out to meet the kisses and would disport itself entirely on my lips so that I might thus expire and that, when dead myself, my other self might enjoy in her a fruitful life. [. . .] Yet the man who sells his sex for love of gain makes a miserable return to Nature for her gift to him. Men like these, who refuse Genius his tithes and rites, deserve to be excommunicated from the temple of Genius.[86]

In this passage, Alan of Lille discourses on the interrelationship of sexual and grammatical perversions, and depicts man as sinning against Nature through his "unnatural" practices, the most notable of which is homosexuality characterized by the prevention of procreation. Yet homosexuality seems to be secondary, when compared to the laws of Nature governing heterosexual love. Lawful coition occurs within the state of marriage,[87] and the author underscores the analogy between the laws of reproduction governing the proper regeneration of natural species and the laws of grammar mandating the proper use of language. Thus, as a consequence of the lapse into verbal and sexual perversions described in the *Planctus*, Nature retaliated by enlisting Genius to outlaw and ban those indulging in these vices. In fact, Genius shares a long kinship with Nature, and at the end of the treatise, he proclaims:

86. *Plaint of Nature*, 67–72. Meter I.11–24, 31–32, 43–50, 57–60: Heu, quo Nature secessit gracia, morum / Forma, pudicitie norma, pudoris amor? / Flet Natura, silent mores, proscribitur omnis / Orphanus a ueteri nobilitate pudor. / Actiui generis sexus se turpiter horret / Sic in passiuum degenerare genus. / Femina uir factus sexus denigrat honorem, / Ars magice Veneris hermafroditat eum. / Predicat et subicit, fit duplex terminus idem. / Gramatice leges ampliat ille nimis. / Se negat esse uirum Nature, factus in arte / Barbarus. Ars illi non placet, immo tropus. / Non tamen ista tropus poterit translatio dici. / In uicium melius ista figura cadit. [. . .] Sic pede dactilico Veneris male iambicat usus / In quo non patitur sillaba longa breuem. [. . .] Virginis in labiis cur basia tanta quiescunt, / Cum reditus in eis sumere nemo uelit? / Que michi pressa semel mellirent oscula succo, / Que mellita darent mellis in ore fauum. / Spiritus exiret ad basia, deditus ori / Totus et in labiis luderet ipse sibi, / Vt dum sic moriar, in me defunctus, in illa / Felici uita perfruar alter ego. [. . .] Sed male Nature munus pro munere donat / Cum sexum lucri uendit amore suum. / A Genii templo tales anathema merentur / Qui Genio decimas et sua iura negant.

87. Economou, *The Goddess Natura*, 87.

O Nature, it is not without the divine breath of interior inspiration that there has come from your balanced judgement this imperial edict, to the effect that all who strive to make our laws obsolete by misuse and desuetude, by not keeping holiday on our solemn days of rest, should be struck with the sword of anathema.

Since this legitimately promulgated law is not at variance with the law of justice and your studied and balanced judgement agrees with the results of my own judicious inquiry, I am eager to reinforce with all haste the directions issued by you. For, although my mind, straitened by man's disgusting vices, travels down to the hell of gloom and knows not the paradise of joy, yet the seedlings of delightful joy are sending me their fragrance because I see that you join in my sighs of longing for due punishment. Nor is it surprising that I find a melody and harmony in the agreement and union of our wills since the conceptive exemplar of one idea brought us to birth and existence, since our status as administrators of one office brings us into accord, since it is no hypocritical love that joins us by a superficial bond of attachment but, rather, it is a pure and modest love that dwells in the deeper recesses of the soul.[88]

In a long closing speech, Genius then excommunicates all of those who have acted against Nature's laws:

By the authority of the super-essential Usia and his eternal Idea, with assent of the heavenly army, with the combined aid and help of Nature and the other recognised virtues, let everyone who blocks the lawful path of Venus, or courts the shipwreck of gluttony or the nightmares of drunkenness, or indulges the fire of thirsty avarice, or scales the shadowy heights of insolent arrogance, or submits to the death

88. *Plaint of Nature,* 219–220. XVIII, Prose 9.119–134: O natura, non sine interne inspirationis afflatione diuina a tue discretionis libra istud inperiale processit edictum, ut omnes, qui abusiua dissuetudine nostras leges obsoletas reddere moliuntur, non in nostre sollempnitatis feria feriantes, anathematis gladio feriantur.

Et quia lex huius promulgationis legitime legem iusticie non oppugnat tuique examinali libra iudicii mee discretionis sedet examini, tue editionis maximam ocius roborare maturo. Quamuis enim mens mea, hominum uiciis angustiata deformibus, in infernum tristicie peregrinans, leticie nesciat paradisum, tamen in hoc amenantis gaudii odorat primordia, quod te mecum uideo ad debite uindicte suspirare suspiria.

Nec mirum si in nostrarum uoluntatum unione conformi concordie reperio melodiam, cum unius idee exemplaris notio nos in natiuum esse produxerit, unius officialis administrationis conformet conditio, cum nostras mentes non superficiali dilectionis uinculo amor iungat ypocrita sed penitiora animorum nostrorum latibula casti amoris pudor inhabitet.

> of the heart in envy, or makes a companion of the hypocritical love of flattery—let every such be separated from the kiss of heavenly love as his ingratitude deserves and merits, let him be demoted from Nature's favour, let him be set apart from the harmonious council of the things of Nature.
>
> Let him who makes an irregular exception to the rule of Venus be deprived of the seal of Venus. Let him who buries himself in the abyss of gluttony be punished by a shameful impoverishment. Let him who benumbs himself in the Lethe-flood of drunkenness be harassed by the fires of perpetual thirst. Let him who has a burning thirst for gain be assailed by the wants of unceasing poverty.
>
> Let him who has raised himself to the top of the precipice of avarice and belches forth his wind of exaltation come down in ruination to the valley of humiliation and dejection. Let him who in envy gnaws the riches of another's happiness with the worm of detraction be the first to discover that he is his own enemy. Let him who hunts for paltry gifts from the rich by his hypocritical flattery be cheated by a reward of deceptive worth.[89]

As we can see, Genius' speech in the *Rose* recalls that of the *Planctus*, and even though homosexuality is the only explicit sexual vice, the term is polyvalent, as it is in the *Planctus*, thus referring to any unnatural sexual activity which does not serve Nature's purpose to continue the species.[90]

In the text of both the *Planctus* and the *Rose*, we note that the authors cite idolatry among the examples of irrational sensuality. Thus, as a violation against nature, idolatry can also represent an inordinate love of letters, for, as we have seen from Alan's text, in the twelfth century, grammar was repre-

89. *Plaint of Nature,* 220–221. XVIII, Prose 9.141–158: Auctoritate superessentialis Vsye eiusque Notionis eterne, assensu celestis milicie, coniuncte Nature etiam ceterarumque officialium uirtutum ministerio suffragante, a superne dilectionis osculo separetur ingratitudinis exigente merito, a Nature gracia degradetur, a naturalium rerum uniformi concilio segregetur omnis qui aut legitimum Veneris obliquat incessum aut gulositatis naufragium aut ebrietatis sentit insomnium aut auaricie sicientis experitur incendium aut insolentis arrogantie umbratile ascendit fastigium aut precordiale patitur liuoris exicium aut adulationis amorem comitatur ficticium.

Qui a regula Veneris exceptionem facit anomalam, Veneris priuetur sigillo. Qui gulositatis mergitur in abisso, mendicitatis erubescentia castigetur. Qui ebrietatis leteo flumine soporatur, perpetuate sitis uexetur incendiis. Ille, in quo sitis incandescit habendi, perpetuatas paupertatis egestates incurrat. Qui in precipicio arrogantie exaltatus spiritum elationis eructuat, in uallem deiecte humilitatis ruinose descendat. Qui aliene felicitatis diuicias tinea detractionis inuidendo demordet, primo se sibi hostem inueniat. Qui adulationis ypocrisi a diuitibus uenatur munuscula, sophistici meriti fraudetur in premio.

90. On the subject of unnatural sexuality in the *Rose,* see Kelly, *Internal Difference,* 113–114.

sented as a major discipline which followed the law of Nature.[91] Alan stresses the relationship between nature and grammar in Prose 5 of the *Planctus* where Nature instructs Venus on lawful propagation using grammatical metaphors:

> Since the plan of Nature gave special recognition, as the evidence of Grammar confirms, to two genders, to wit, the masculine and feminine (although some men, deprived of a sign of sex, could, in my opinion, be classified as of neuter gender), I charged the Cyprian, with secret warnings and mighty, thunderous threats, that she should, as reason demanded, concentrate exclusively in her connections on the natural union of masculine and feminine gender.
>
> Since, by the demands of the conditions necessary for reproduction, the masculine joins the feminine to itself, if an irregular combination of members of the same sex should come into common practice, so that appurtenances of the same sex should be mutually connected, that combination would never be able to gain acceptance from me either as a means of procreation or as an aid to conception. For if the masculine gender, by a certain violence of unreasonable reason, should call for a gender entirely similar to itself, this bond and union will not be able to defend the flaw as any kind of graceful figure but will bear the stain of an outlandish and unpardonable solecism.
>
> Moreover, my command instructed the Cyprian that in her unions she should observe the regular procedure in matters of subjacent and superjacent and should assign the role of subjacent to the part characteristic of the female sex and should place that part that is a specific mark of the male sex in the prestigious position of superjacent in such a way that the superjacent cannot go down to take the place of the subjacent nor the subjacent pass over to the demesne of the superjacent. Since each requires the other, the superjacent with the characteristic of an adjective is attracted by the law of urgent need to the subjacent which appropriates the special characteristics of a noun.[92]

91. Economou, *The Goddess Natura,* 87.

92. *Plaint of Nature,* 156–158. X, Prose 5.43–65: Cum enim, attestante gramatica, duo genera specialiter, masculinum uidelicet et femininum, ratio nature cognouerit, quamuis et quidam homines, sexus depauperati signaculo, iuxta meam oppinionem possint neutri generis designatione censeri, tamen Cypridi sub intimis ammonitionibus minarumque immensis iniunxi tonitruis, ut in suis coniunctionibus ratione exigentie naturalem constructionem solummodo masculini femininique generis celebraret.

Cum enim masculinum genus suum femininum exigentia habitudinis genialis adsciscat, si eorundem generum constructio anomale celebretur, ut res eiusdem sexus sibi inuicem construantur,

In this passage, we see how Venus must control the natural union between the masculine and female gender, for if she does not, it will result in confusion of gender, as is the case in grammar. Furthermore, Nature, using the metaphor of noun / adjective, advises Venus to make sure that the noun—the feminine gender—and the adjective—the male gender—always keep their proper relationship: the order of language is juxtaposed to the social order of procreation. If this order is disrupted, it will result, respectively, in unnatural sexual practices and idolatry of undue letters. Thus, we can see an equation between idolatry and sexual perversion in medieval poetics. Drawing on the work of André Pézard, Eugene Vance states that it was the parable of Matthew 13 that gave rise in the Middle Ages to daring analogies between speaking and the ejaculation of semen.[93]

In the *Fiore* Durante, by silencing Nature and Genius, eliminates any possible complications that may arise in the defloration of the Flower. Furthermore, during the Middle Ages, the character of Genius was interpreted as the reproductive power of the *paterfamilias*, the *animus*, the rational soul and a moral guide. If we consider Genius's various innate implications, as they appeared to the medieval mind, then the author of the *Fiore*, by omitting all reference to Genius and his power, refuses to embrace the ideological content of the French text and emphasizes the primacy of sexual pleasure.[94] In other words, he returns to Venus all of her creative power and, in so doing, eliminates the tension that exists between sexual and grammatical perversion expressed in the *Planctus*:

> For the human race, fallen from its high estate, adopts a highly irregular (grammatical) change when it inverts the rule of Venus by introducing barbarisms in its arrangement of genders. Thus man, his sex changed by a ruleless Venus, in defiance of due order, by his arrangement

---

illa equidem constructio nec euocationis remedio uel conceptionis suffragio apud me ueniam poterit promereri. Si enim genus masculinum genus consimile quadam irrationabilis rationis deposcat iniuria nulla figure honestate illa constructionis iunctura uicium poterit excusare sed inexcusabili soloecismi monstruositate turpabitur.

Preterea Cipridi mea indixit preceptio, ut ipsa in suis constructionibus, suppositiones appositionesque ordinarias obseruando, rem feminini sexus caractere presignitam suppositionis destinaret officio, rem uero specificatam masculini generis intersignis sede collocaret appositi, ut nec appositum in uicem suppositi ualeat declinare nec suppositum possit in regionem appositi transmigrare. Et cum utrumque exigatur ab altero, appositum sub adiectiua proprietate, supposito substantiue proprietatis proprium retinenti, exigentie legibus inuitatur.

93. Eugene Vance, *Mervelous Signals: Poetics and Sign Theory in the Middle Ages* (Lincoln: University of Nebraska Press, 1986), 239.

94. For the meaning of Genius in Antiquity and the Middle Ages, see Jane Chance Nitzsche, *The Genius Figure in Antiquity and the Middle Ages* (New York: Columbia University Press, 1975).

changes what is a straightforward attribute of his. Abandoning in his deviation the true script of Venus, he is proved to be a sophistic pseudographer. Shunning even a resemblance traceable to the art of Dione's daughter, he falls into the defect of inverted order.[95]

In returning Venus to power, Durante rewrites both the *Planctus* and the *Rose*. In the sequence of sonnets where Venus lays siege to the castle in order to free the Flower, the Italian author reinstates both to Venus and to humans the liberty they need to exercise their free will and thereby to engage in all manner of sexual practices, even unnatural ones. For example, in sonnet 219 Venus says to her son Love:

> "My son, you will make a pledge,
> and I will make one too:
> namely, that I will never let chastity remain
> in any woman who has common sense,
> and you should do the same with any man you like.
> And I say to you that I will go to work
> with my torch, and I'll heat them up
> so much that each one will obey our command."
> In order to make these vows, they brought—
> in the place of relics and a missal—
> torches and bows and arrows; and so they swore
> on these objects, declaring them to be equally valid.
> All those in the army of Love were in agreement,
> for each one of them knew the Decretals.

Durante not only recasts Jean de Meun's lines, but also those of Alan of Lille. In fact, by excluding both Nature and Genius from the *Rose*, the Italian author reshapes Alan's text and, in Alan's words, "adopts a highly irregular (grammatical) change." Specifically, Durante follows Venus's rule and introduces "barbarisms in its arrangement of genders." The sonnet recalls lines 15,796–15,860, where Venus and *Amaint* make their oath to the army of Love. However, if we look carefully at lines 6–8 of the above sonnet—"Ed i' te dico ben ch' i' lavorròe / col mi' brandone: sì gli scalderòe / che ciaschedun

95. *Plaint of Nature*, 133–134. VIII, Prose 4.55–61: Humanum namque genus, a sua generositate degenerans, in constructione generum barbarizans, Venereas regulas inuertendo nimis irregulari utitur metaplasmo. Sic homo, Venere tiresiatus anomala, directam predicationem per compositionem inordinate conuertit. A Veneris ergo orthographia deuiando recedens sophista falsigraphus inuenitur. Consequentem etiam Dionee artis analogiam deuitans, in anastrophen uiciosam degenerat.

verrà a comandamento" ("And I say to you that I will go to work / with my torch, and I'll heat them up/so much that each one will obey our command")—we realize that these verses are missing in the *Rose*. Moreover, these lines admit to a double meaning: for Durante transforms Venus into a hermaphrodite and allows her to disrupt and invert both grammatical and sexual rules. With the verses "col mi' brandone: sì gli scalderòe / che ciaschedun verrà a comandamento," Durante suggests that if man denies all of the strict laws of reproduction that must govern the proper regeneration of the natural species, then he also denies the laws of grammar. Specifically, through Venus's *brandone* ("torch," and a word very close to Lover's *bordon*), which can also refer to male genitalia, the Italian author claims his authority as author, for he is free to invent and change, through False Seeming's humble and simple words, as Barański has noted, both sound and verse.[96] Through this sonnet, the author abandons any loyalty to other authors and hides his craftiness as an artist under the veil of his simple and humble style. In so doing, the author extends the laws of grammar into new territory, allowing him both to evoke and to deny the French text and to rewrite it within his own cultural, literary and linguistic environment.

Note on the Translation

We have intended this translation to be as literal as possible, so that comparisons may be easily made with the original text. We have consistently translated the proper names of the allegorical characters with one and only one word, although we recognize the dangers of limiting their "meaning" to a single English word. For the commentary we have benefited from the extensive notes and critical apparatus provided in the editions of Parodi, Marchiori, Contini and Rossi, and acknowledge this debt here. We have noted succinctly the textual parallels between the *Fiore* and the *Roman de la Rose*, following the edition of Félix Lecoy. For questions concerning language, etymology, and codicological matters, we refer the reader to the editions of Contini and Rossi.

96. For a study of the image and meaning of Venus, seen as creative power in Dante's works, see Giuseppe Mazzotta, "The Light of Venus and the Poetry of Dante: *Vita Nuova* and *Inferno* XXVII," in *Dante,* ed. Harold Bloom (New York, New Haven, and Philadelphia: Chelsea House Publishers, 1986), 189–204, as well as chapter 3 ("The Light of Venus") of *Dante's Vision and the Circle of Knowledge* (Princeton: Princeton University Press, 1993), 56–74.

Guide to the Characters

(in alphabetical order in English)

Angel-Like: *Angelicanza*
Bad Mouth: *Mala-Bocca*
Beauty: *Bieltà*
Boldness: *Ardimento*
Chastity: *Castità*
Courage: *Sicurtà*
Courtesy: *Cortesia*
Deceit: *Baratto*
Delight: *Diletto*
Extravagance: *Troppo-Donare*
Fair Appearance: *Bel-Sembiante*
Fair Welcome: *Bellacoglienza*
False Seeming: *Falsembiante*
Fear: *Paura*
Forced Abstinence: *Costretta-Astinenza*
Fortune: *Fortuna*
Friend: *Amico*
Generosity: *Larghezza*
God of Love / Love: *Dio d'Amore / Amore*
Good Hope: *Buona Speranza*
Happiness: *Letezza*
Honor: *Onore*
Humility: *Umilitate*
Hypocrisy: *Ipocresia*
Jealousy: *Gelosia*
Joyfulness: *Giolività*
Leisure: *Oziosa*
Lover: *Amante*
Mercy: *Pietà, Pietate, Pietanza*
Modesty: *Vergogna*
Nature: *Natura*
Noble Heart: *Nobiltà-di-Cuore*
Old Woman: *La Vecchia*
Pain: *Dolore*
Patience: *Pacienza*
Pleasure: *Piacere*
Poverty: *Povertà*

Prodigality: *Folle Larghezza*
Reason: *Ragione*
Resistance: *Schifo*
Sincerity: *Franchezza / Franchigia*
Social Grace: *Compagnia*
Solace: *Solazzo*
Sweet Glance: *Dolze Riguardo*
Venus: *Venusso*
Wealth: *Ricchezza*
Well-Hidden: *Ben-Celare*
Youth: *Giovanezza*

(in alphabetical order in Italian)
Amante: Lover
Amico: Friend
Angelicanza: Angel-Like
Ardimento: Boldness
Baratto: Deceit
Bellacoglienza: Fair Welcome
Bel-Sembiante: Fair Appearance
Ben-Celare: Well-Hidden
Bieltà: Beauty
Buona Speranza: Good Hope
Castità: Chastity
Compagnia: Social Grace
Cortesia: Courtesy
Costretta-Astinenza: Forced Abstinence
Diletto: Delight
Dio d'Amore/Amore: God of Love / Love
Dolore: Pain
Dolze-Riguardo: Sweet Glance
Falsembiante: False Seeming
Folle Larghezza: Prodigality
Fortuna: Fortune
Franchezza / Franchigia: Sincerity
Gelosia: Jealousy
Giolività: Joyfulness
Giovanezza: Youth
Ipocresia: Hypocrisy
Larghezza: Generosity

Letezza: Happiness
Mala-Bocca: Bad Mouth
Natura: Nature
Nobiltà-di-Cuore: Noble Heart
Onore: Honor
Oziosa: Leisure
Pacienza: Patience
Paura: Fear
Piacere: Pleasure
Pietà, Pietate, Pietanza: Mercy
Povertà: Poverty
Ragione: Reason
Ricchezza: Wealth
Schifo: Resistance
Sicurtà: Courage
Solazzo: Solace
Troppo-Donare: Extravagance
Umilitate: Humility
La Vecchia: Old Woman
Venusso: Venus
Vergogna: Modesty

The Fiore

1

Lo Dio d'Amor con su' arco mi trasse
Perch'i' guardava un fior che m'abellia,
Lo quale avea piantato Cortesia
Nel giardin di Piacer; e que' vi trasse

Sì tosto c[h]' a me parve ch'e' volasse,
E disse: "I' sì ti tengo in mia balìa".
Alló·gli pia[c]que, non per voglia mia,
Che di cinque saette mi piagasse.

La prima à non' Bieltà: per li oc[c]hi il core
Mi passò; la seconda, Angelicanza:
Quella mi mise sopra gran fredore;

La terza Cortesia fu, san' dottanza;
La quarta, Compagnia, che fe' dolore;
La quinta apella l'uon Buona Speranza.

1[1]

With his bow the God of Love pierced me[2]
while I was gazing at a Flower that pleased me,[3]
the Flower that Lady Courtesy had planted
in the garden of Pleasure.[4] Love came

so quickly that it seemed to me he flew,
and said: "I have you in my power."
Then as was his pleasure, and no desire of mine,
he wounded me with five arrows.[5]

The first, named Beauty, passed my eyes
and transfixed my heart; the second, Angel-Like,
gave me a bitter chill;[6]

the third without doubt was Courtesy;
the fourth, Social Grace, caused pain;
the fifth is called Good Hope.

1. Cf. *Roman de la Rose*, 928–979, 1679–1878.

2. The first-person narrator of the poem is referred to as *Amante* (Lover) in the text.

3. As the figure of the beloved woman, the rose of the *Roman de la Rose* has here become a generic flower.

4. In the *Romance of the Rose* there is no reference to the planting of the flower by Lady Courtesy in Pleasure's garden.

5. The situation is similar to that in many lyric poems of the Middle Ages, in which the God of Love, armed with bow and arrow, wounds the potential Lover. In the *Rose* (vv. 928–1979), the arrows are called *Biautez* (Beauty), *Simpleice* (Simplicity), *Franchise* (Openness), *Compaignie* (Company) and *Bel-Samblant* (Fair Seeming). There are discrepancies in the naming of the arrows between the *Rose* and the *Fiore*. For example, the Italian author has substituted Courtesy for *Franchise*, perhaps because the textual tradition of the *Rose* is ambiguous in this area. According to Castets and Gorra, the third arrow, *Franchise*, was originally *Courtoysie* (Courtesy) in the *Rose*, but commentators have been unable to account for the substitution of *Simpleice* with *Angelicanza*. It should be noted that the five additional arrows that appear in the *Rose*—*Orguelx* (Pride), *Vilennie* (Villainy), *Honte* (Shame), *Desesperance* (Despair) and *Noviaus-Pensers* (New Thought)—are not found in the *Fiore*.

6. *Angelicanza* refers to the moral and spiritual qualities (those of an angel) and recalls the terminology the poets of the "Sweet New Style" (*Dolce Stil Nuovo*)—Guido Guinizzelli, Dante, Cino da Pistoia—used to describe the beloved woman, who becomes in their poetry a *donna angelicata* ("angelicized lady").

2

L'Amante e Amore

Sentendomi ismagato malamente
Del molto sangue ch'io avea perduto,
E non sapea dove trovar aiuto,
Lo Dio d'Amor sì venne a me presente,

E dissemi: "Tu·ssaï veramente
Che·ttu mi se' intra·lle man caduto
Per le saette di ch'i' t'ò feruto,
Sì ch'e' convien che·ttu mi sie ubidente".

Ed i' risposi: "I' sì son tutto presto
Di farvi pura e fina fedeltate,
Più ch'asses[s]ino a·Veglio o a Dio il Presto".

E quelli allor mi puose, in veritate,
La sua boc[c]a a la mia, sanz'altro aresto,
E disse: "Pensa di farmi lealtate".

2

Lover and Love[1]

When I felt myself so drained
because of all the blood I'd lost
and did not know where to find help,
in a flash the God of Love was there

and said: "You surely know
that you have fallen into my hands
thanks to the arrows with which I wounded you;
thus, you must obey me."

And I replied: "I'm ready
to give you my true and noble loyalty,
greater than the assassin's to the Veglio or Prester John's to God."[2]

And then, in truth, he put his lips
to mine and said without a pause:
"Be loyal to me."[3]

1. Cf. *Rose*, 1882–1923.

2. The Lover's reference to the *Veglio* has no correspondence in the *Romance of the Rose*. The faithfulness of the "Assassin" to the "Old Man" is well known in Italy (see, among others, the last tale in the *Novellino*, the *Detto del gatto lupesco*, and Guido delle Colonne's poem, "Gioiosamente canto"). According to the legend, these bodyguards of the Old Man of the Mountain were so devout that they would willingly kill themselves by jumping from high places on command. The figure of Prester John—the legendary Christian king-priest of India, known in the West through the French translation of the apocryphal letter written by "Prestre John"—is another medieval commonplace (cf. the first tale in the *Novellino*).

3. The kiss is the final act in the ceremony of fealty.

3

L'Amante e Amore

Del mese di genaio, e non di mag[g]io,
Fu quand'i' presi Amor a signoria,
E ch'i' mi misi al tutto in sua baglìa
E saramento gli feci e omaggio;

E per più sicurtà gli diedi in gaggio
Il cor, ch'e' non avesse gelosia
Ched'i' fedel e puro i' no·gli sia,
E sempre lui tener a segnó·maggio.

Allor que' prese il cor e disse: "Amico,
I' son segnor assà' forte a servire;
Ma chi mi serve, per certo ti dico

Ch'a la mia grazia non può già fallire,
E di buona speranza il mi notrico
Insin ch'i' gli fornisca su' disire".

3

Lover and Love[1]

In the month of January, and not in May,[2]
it was, when I took Love to be my lord
and placed myself completely in his power,
and swore homage to him.

And as further assurance, I gave him my heart
as a pledge, so that he would not worry
that I might not be true and loyal to him
and always hold him as my lord and master.[3]

Then he took my heart and said: "Friend,
I am a very exacting lord to serve;
but truly I say unto you that the one who serves me

will never fail to win my favor,
and I will nourish him with good hope
until I satisfy his desire."

1. Cf. *Rose*, 2041–2770.

2. The temporal situation provided by the month of January confirms the author's conscious wish to change the literary tradition which associated love with the month of May. Moreover, the harshness of the season suggests the difficulties the Lover will need to overcome in his amorous quest.

3. As is well known, the courtly lyric drew upon feudal terminology to describe the relationship between man and woman, whereby the lady became the feudal lord—*midons* ("my lord")—and her lover the vassal.

4

L'Amante e Amore

Con una chiave d'or mi fermò il core
L'Amor, quando così m'eb[b]e parlato;
Ma primamente l'à nett'e parato,
Sì c[h]'ogn'altro pensier n'à pinto fore.

E po' mi disse: "I' sì son tu' signore,
E tu sì se' di me fedel giurato:
Or guarda che 'l tu' cuor non sia 'mpacciato
Se non di fino e di leal amore.

E pensa di portar in pacïenza
La pena che per me avrà' a sofrire
Inanzi ch'io ti doni mia sentenza;

Ché molte volte ti parrà morire:
Un'ora gioia avrai, altra, doglienza;
Ma poi dono argomento di guerire".

4

Lover and Love[1]

With a golden key Love locked my heart,
after he had spoken to me in that way;
but before all this he purified and prepared it well
so that he drove out every other thought.[2]

And then he said to me: "Just as I am your Lord,[3]
so are you my liege man:[4]
now be sure your heart's not occupied
with anything but noble and true love.

And remember to bear patiently
the pain you will suffer because of me,
before I give you my verdict.

For many times you'll think you're dying:
one hour you'll be happy, another sad,
but then I'll give you a remedy to get well."[5]

1. Cf. *Rose*, 1997–2040.

2. For the notion of the purified/perfected heart, cf. Guinizzelli's sonnet "Io voglio del ver la mia donna laudare," especially the eighth verse: "medesmo Amor per lei rafina meglio" (*Poeti del Duecento*, 2:472).

3. For a similar statement, see Dante, *Vita nuova* 3.3: "Ego dominus tuus."

4. The term *fedel giurato* is used in courtly love poetry to describe the lover's pledge to the beloved.

5. Love was viewed as a sickness in the Middle Ages. For an extensive study, see Mary F. Wack, *Lovesickness in the Middle Ages: The "Viaticum" and Its Commentaries* (Philadelphia: University of Pennsylvania Press, 1990).

5

L'Amante e Amore

Con grande umilitate e pacienza
Promisi a Amor a sofferir sua pena,
E c[h]'ogne membro, ch'i' avea, e vena
Disposat'era a farli sua voglienza;

E solo a lui servir la mia credenza
È ferma, né di ciò mai nonn-alena:
"Insin ched i' avrò spirito o lena,
I' non farò da·cciò giamà' partenza".

E quelli allor mi disse: "Amico meo,
I' ò da·tte miglior pegno che carte:
Fa che m'adori, ched i' son tu' deo;

Ed ogn'altra credenza metti a parte,
Né non creder né Luca né Matteo
Né Marco né Giovanni". Allor si parte.

5

Lover and Love[1]

With much humility and patience I promised Love
that I would suffer his pain
and that my every limb and vein
were prepared to do his will.

And my mind is set to serve him and him alone
and will never cease to do so:
"As long as I live and breathe,
I will never depart from this promise."

And Love then said to me: "My friend,
your pledge is better than any written promise:
be sure to worship me, for I am your god;[2]

and set aside every other belief:
do not believe Luke or Matthew,
Mark or John."[3] And then he departs.

1. Cf. *Rose*, 2041–2748.

2. The establishment of a cult of Love, in which secular and religious elements are confused, is typical of the medieval erotic tradition (see sonnet 219).

3. The last four verses in this sonnet appear to be an invention of the Italian poet, since they have no source in the *Rose*.

6

L'Amante e lo Schifo

Partes'Amor [le] su' ale battendo
E 'n poca d'or sì forte isvanoìo
Ched i' no'l vidi poi, né no·ll'udìo,
E·llui e 'l su' soccorso ancor atendo.

Allor mi venni forte ristrignendo
Verso del fior, che·ssì forte m'ulìo,
E per cu' feci homag[g]io a questo dio,
E dissi: 'Chi mi tien, ched i' no'l prendo?';

Sì ch'i' verso del fior tesi la mano,
Credendolo aver colto chitamente;
Ed i' vidi venir un gran villano

Con una maz[z]a, e disse: "Or ti ste' a mente
Ch'i' son lo Schifo, e sì son ortolano
D'esto giardin; i' ti farò dolente".

6

Lover and Resistance[1]

Love departs with a flutter of wings,
and in a moment he disappeared so rapidly
that I no longer saw or heard him;
yet still I wait for him and his assistance.

Then I moved closer and closer
to the Flower whose fragrance bewitched me
and for whom I had pledged my fealty to this god.
I said: "Who keeps me from plucking it?"

And so I stretched my hand toward the Flower,
thinking I would be able to pluck it freely.[2]
But I saw a big uncouth man[3] approaching

with club in hand, saying: "Now keep in mind
that I am Resistance,[4] and that I am the keeper
of this garden. I'll make you suffer."

1. Cf. *Rose*, 2749–2926.

2. The overtly sexual connotations of the flower are present from the beginning of the text. In the Italian lyric tradition the flower often appears as a highly erotic element, as, for example, in Cielo d'Alcamo's *contrasto* "Rosa fresca aulentissima," Bonagiunta da Lucca's sonnet "Tutto lo mondo si mantien per fiore" (*Poeti del Duecento*, 1:271), and Guido Cavalcanti's ballata "Fresca rosa novella" (*Poeti del Duecento*, 2:491–492).

3. In the courtly tradition, we find the usual contrast between *villano* (the coarse, rustic man) and *cavaliere* (the courtly knight). Thus, Resistance's role in the poem is in direct opposition to that of Lover.

4. This is the character represented by *Dangier* in the *Rose*.

7

L'Amante

Molto vilmente mi buttò di fora
Lo Schifo, crudo, fello e oltrag[g]ioso,
Sì che del fior non cred'esser gioioso,
Se Pietate e Franchez[z]a no·ll'acora;

Ma prima, credo, conver[r]à ch'eo mora,
Perché 'l me' cor [i]stà tanto doglioso
Di quel villan, che stava là nascoso,
Di cu' no·mmi prendea guardia quell'ora.

Or m'à messo in pensero e in dottanza
Di ciò ched i' credea aver per certano,
Sì c[h]'or me ne par essere in bilanza.

E tutto ciò m'à fatto quello strano;
Ma di lui mi richiamo a Pietanza,
Che venga a·llui collo spunton i·mmano.

7

Lover[1]

With much rudeness he threw me out,
that cruel, vicious and abusive Resistance did,
so that I think I'll not have pleasure with the Flower,
unless Mercy and Sincerity do away with him.

But before that happens I think I'll die,
since my heart is in so much pain
because of that uncouth man, who was hiding there
and against whom I took no precaution at that crucial moment.

Now this has made me worried and fearful,
for what I thought I had for certain
now seems to me to be at risk.

And all this that savage one[2] did to me!
But I will appeal to Mercy about him,
so that she may confront him with spear[3] in hand.

1. Cf. *Rose*, 2927–2934.

2. The term *strano* refers to those people who are outsiders, who do not belong to the courtly world and thus are unable to understand the Lover's desires.

3. Mercy will use this spear to assist Sincerity in the battle against Resistance (see sonnets 79 and 208).

8

L'Amante

Se mastro Argus[so], che fece la nave
In che Giason andò per lo tosone,
E fece a conto regole e ragione
E le diece figure, com'on save,

Vivesse, gli sareb[b]e forte e grave
Multiplicar ben ogne mia quistione
C[h]'Amor mi move, sanza mesprigione;
E di ciascuna porta esso la chiave,

Ed àllemi nel cor fermate e messe
Con quella chiavicella ch'i' v'ò detto,
Per ben tenermi tutte sue promesse:

Per ch'io a·ssue merzé tuttor mi metto;
Ma ben vor[r]è' che, quando gli piacesse,
E' m'alleg[g]iasse il mal che·ssì m'à stretto.

8

Lover[1]

If Master Argus,[2] who built the ship
that Jason used to seek the Golden Fleece,
and who invented the rules and rationale for computation
and the ten numerical signs,[3] as everyone knows,

if he were alive, it would be difficult for him
to calculate all the problems
that Love gives me, without mistakes.
Yet, for every door Love has the key,

and with this little key[4] that I just mentioned to you[5]
he has placed and locked them in my heart
in order to keep all his promises to me.

For this reason I am always ready to do his bidding;
however, I would like for him—whenever he would like—
to ease the pain that has so conquered me.

1. Cf. *Rose*, 2935–2954.

2. The Italian poet conflates the story of Jason and the Argonauts with the ninth-century geographer and astronomer Muhammad ibn Musa al-Khuwarizmi, in whose book (*Kitab al-giabr wa'l muqabalah*) the word *algebra* appears for the first time.

3. Arabic numbers.

4. See sonnet 4 where Lover tells the reader that Love has locked his heart with a golden key.

5. The author addresses his audience directly with the "voi" form, a technique common to the oral presentational mode, as, for example, in the *cantari* that were presented in the town square by jongleurs. See also 16.4.

9

L'Amante e Ragione

Dogliendomi in pensando del villano
Che·ssì vilmente dal fior m'à 'lungiato,
Ed i' mi riguardai dal dritto lato,
E sì vidi Ragion col viso piano

Venir verso di me, e per la mano
Mi prese e disse: "Tu·sse' sì smagrato!
I' credo che·ttu à' troppo pensato
A que' che·tti farà gittar in vano,

Ciò è Amor, a cui dat'ài fidanza.
Ma·sse m'avessi avuto al tu' consiglio,
Tu non saresti gito co·llui a danza:

Ché, sie certano, a cu' e' dà di piglio,
Egli 'l tiene in tormento e malenanza,
Sì che su' viso nonn-è mai vermiglio".

9

Lover and Reason[1]

While thinking sadly about that savage one
who so savagely chased me from the Flower,
I looked on my right side and saw
Reason,[2] who, with tranquil face,

was coming towards me. She took me by the
hand and said: "You have become so thin!
I believe that you have thought too much
about that one who'll make you work in vain:[3]

that person is Love, to whom you've given loyalty.
But if you had listened to my advice,
you would not have gone with him to dance.[4]

For you can be sure the one he seizes
he'll keep in torment and in sorrow,
such that his face will never be red."[5]

1. Cf. *Rose*, 2955–3056.

2. The figure of Reason—the personification of rational thought, sober reflection and the power of the mind over emotions—opposes Love. The contrast between these two sides of the human personality is central to medieval discussions of love.

3. The Italian phrase *gittar in vano* has several possible meanings. One refers to a game of dice, in which a particular throw would result in no gain. Another possible meaning is that of sowing seeds and not reaping any fruit, both agriculturally and erotically. The phrase recalls the biblical parable of the sower (Matthew 13:3–8; Mark 4:3–8; Luke 8:5–8). The erotic connotation of the act of sowing seeds is well documented: see, for example, the *contrasto* of Cielo d'Alcamo, "Rosa fresca aulentissima" (v. 7): "Lo mar potresti arompere, a venti asemenare . . ." (*Poeti del Duecento*, 1:177).

4. The idea of going with someone to dance seems to come from the courtly traditions in which it would signify the establishment of a close and intimate relationship.

5. The colors red (*vermiglio*) and white, in the Provençal lyric tradition were considered to be those of beauty and love. In the Middle Ages good health was indicated by a ruddy complexion.

10

L'Amante

Udendo che Ragion mi gastigava
Perch'i' al Die d'Amor era 'nservito,
Di ched i' era forte impalidito,
E sol perch'io a·llui troppo pensava,

I' le dissi: "Ragion, e' no·mi grava
Su' mal, ch'i' ne sarò tosto guerito,
Ché questo mio signor lo m'à gradito",
E ch'era folle se più ne parlava;

"Chéd i' son fermo pur di far su' grado,
Perciò ch'e' mi promise fermamente
Ched e' mi mettereb[b]e in alto grado

Sed i' 'l servisse bene e lealmente":
Per che di lei i' non pregiava un dado,
Né su' consiglio i' non teneva a mente.

10

Lover[1]

Hearing that Reason was scolding me
for my enslavement to the God of Love,
for which I had become so pale,
and only because of my thinking of him too much,

I said to her: "Reason, the pain he inflicts does not weigh
on me, because I will soon be healed,
for this master of mine has promised it to me"
—and that Reason was crazy if she continued to discuss it.

"For I am set only on pleasing him,
since he gave me firm promises
that he would put me in a high place,

if I would serve him well and faithfully."
Therefore, I did not care about her at all,
nor did I remember or follow her advice.

1. Cf. *Rose*, 3057–3079.

11

L'Amante e Amico

Ragion si parte, udendomi parlare,
E me fu ricordato ch'i' avea
Un grande amico, lo qual mi solea
In ogne mio sconforto confortare;

Sì ch'i' no'l misi guari a ritrovare,
E dissigli com'e' si contenea
Lo Schifo ver' di me, e ch'e' parea
Ch'al tutto mi volesse guer[r]eggiare.

E que' mi disse: "Amico, sta sicuro,
Ché quello Schifo si à sempre in usanza
Ch'a·cominciar si mostra acerbo e duro.

Ritorna a·llui e non ab[b]ie dottanza:
Con umiltà tosto l'avrà' maturo,
Già tanto non par fel né san' pietanza".

11

Lover and Friend[1]

Upon hearing me speak, Reason departs,
and I remembered that I had
a loyal friend, who usually comforted me
whenever I experienced discomfort.

I found him rather quickly
and told him how Resistance was behaving
towards me, and that it seemed
he wanted nothing better than to war with me.

And that one said to me: "Friend, don't worry,
for it is Resistance's custom
to be bitter and harsh in the beginning.

Go back to him and have no fear:
by showing humility, you will soon soften him,[2]
no matter how cruel and pitiless he may seem."

1. Cf. *Rose*, 3080–3129.

2. In Dante's *Divine Comedy*, unripeness, bitterness, and a lack of maturity (*maturo*) and thus a lack of softness, denote pride and reflect the incomplete state of sinners in Hell (cf. *Inf.* 14.48 and 25.18). Humility is the virtue that counters the vice of pride (*superbia*) (cf. *Purg.* 10–12).

12

L'Amante

Tutto pien d'umiltà verso 'l giardino
Torna'mi, com'Amico avea parlato,
Ed i' guardai, e sì eb[b]i avisato
Lo Schifo, con un gran baston di pino,

Ch'andava riturando ogne camino,
Che dentro a forza non vi fosse 'ntrato;
Sì ch'io mi trassi a lui, e salutato
Umilemente l'eb[b]i a capo chino,

E sì gli dissi: "Schifo, ag[g]ie merzede
Di me, se 'nverso te feci alcun fallo,
Chéd i' sì son venuto a pura fede

A tua merzede, e presto d'amendarlo".
Que' mi riguarda, e tuttor si provede
Ched i' non dica ciò per ingan[n]arlo.

12

Lover[1]

Full of meekness[2] I turned back
towards the garden, as Friend had said I should,
and I looked and so I saw
Resistance, with a large club made of pine,[3]

who was blocking off every passageway,
so that I could not go inside.
Thus, I approached and greeted him
meekly with my head bowed down,

and said to him: "Resistance, have mercy
on me, if I have done you any wrong,
for I have come in good faith

to ask your mercy, and am ready to make amends."
He stares at me and, as he does, tries to determine
if I'm saying this to deceive him.

1. Cf. *Rose*, 3130–3186.

2. Humility is one of the standard virtues that lovers in the courtly tradition must have. This same concept returns in the eighth verse with the adverb *umilemente* and the reverential position of the lover with his head bowed down (*a capo chino*: cf. *Vita nuova* 9.10).

3. The rough-hewn club is the standard weapon for a "savage" in medieval literature.

13

Franchezza

Sì com'i' stava in far mia pregheria
A quel fellon ch'è sì pien d'arditez[z]a,
Lo Dio d'Amor sì vi man[dò] Franchez[z]a,
Co·llei Pietà, per sua ambasceria.

Franchez[z]a cominciò la diceria,
E disse: "Schifo, tu·ffaï stranez[z]a
A quel valletto ch'è pien di larghez[z]a
E prode e franco, sanza villania.

Lo Dio d'Amor ti manda ch'e' ti piaccia
Che·ttu non sie sì strano al su' sergente,
Ché gran peccato fa chi lui impaccia;

Ma sòffera ch'e' vada arditamente
Per lo giardino, e no'l metter in caccia,
E guardi il fior che·ssì gli par aolente".

13

Sincerity[1]

While I was pleading my case
to that cruel one who is so rash,
the God of Love sent Sincerity and with her Mercy
on a special mission to that place.

Sincerity began her speech,
saying: "Resistance, you are most unkind
to that young vassal who is so generous
and valiant and brave, and certainly not vulgar.

The God of Love wants to let you know
that you should not be so unkind to his servant,
because whoever hinders him commits a great sin;

but allow him to go freely
into the garden—don't chase him out!—
and let him gaze upon the Flower that seems to him so fragrant."

1. Cf. *Rose*, 3231–3268.

14

Pietà

Pietà cominciò poi su' parlamento,
Con lagrime bagnando il su' visag[g]io,
Dicendo: "Schifo, tu faresti oltrag[g]io
Di non far grazia al meo domandamento.

Pregar ti fo che·tti si'a piacimento
Ch'a quel valletto, ch'è·ssì buon e saggio,
Tu non sie verso lui così salvaggio,
Ché sai ch'e' non à mal intendimento.

Or avén detto tutto nostr'affare
E la cagion per che no' siàn venute:
Molt'è crudel chi per noi non vuol fare!

Ancor ti manda molte di salute
Il lasso cu' ti pia[c]que abandonare:
Fa che nostre preghiere i sian valute!".

14

Mercy[1]

Mercy then began her speech
with tears streaming down her face,
saying: "Resistance, you would commit a great offence
if you were not to grant my request.

I beg you that you may find it in your heart
to not be so cruel toward that young vassal,
who is so good and wise,
for you know that he does not have bad intentions.

Now, we have told you our concerns,
and the reason why we have come:
cruel is he who will not do what we ask!

The poor fellow whom you delighted in abandoning
sends you many greetings:
may our prayers help him in this time of need!"

1. Cf. *Rose*, 3269–3300.

15

Lo Schifo

Lo Schifo disse: "Gente messag[g]iere,
Egli è ben dritto ch'a vostra domanda
I' faccia grazia, e ragion lo comanda:
Ché voi non siete orgogliose né fiere,

Ma siete molto nobili parliere.
Venga il valetto e vada a sua comanda,
Ma non ched egli al fior sua mano ispanda,
Ch'a·cciò no·gli varrian vostre preghiere;

Perciò che·lla figl[i]uola Cortesia,
Bellacoglienza, ch'è dama del fiore,
Sì 'l mi por[r]eb[b]e a gran ricredentia.

Ma fate che·lla madre al Die d'Amore
Faccia a Bellacoglienza pregheria
Di lui, e che·lle scaldi un poco il core".

15

Resistance[1]

Resistance replied: "Noble messengers,
it is proper that I accede to your request
and reason orders it,
for you are neither vain nor proud,

but you are very noble orators.[2]
The young man may come and go at will,
but on condition that he not try to touch the Flower,
because your prayers will not help him in that at all.

For this the daughter of Lady Courtesy,
Fair Welcome, who is in charge of the Flower,
would think my manners rude.

But let the mother of the God of Love[3]
make a plea to Fair Welcome on his behalf,
so that her heart may be warmed a little."

1. Cf. *Rose*, 3301–3308.

2. Rhetoric and rhetorical skills were very important in Italian and particularly in Florentine political life, and the literature of the period contains numerous rhetorical manuals, both original treatises and translations of earlier works.

3. That is, Venus.

16

L'Amante e lo Schifo

Quand'i' vidi lo Schifo sì adolzito,
Che solev'esser più amar che fele
Ed i' 'l trovà' vie più dolce che mele,
Sap[p]iate ch'i' mi tenni per guerito.

Nel giardin me n'andai molto gichito
Per dotta di misfar a quel crudele,
E gli giurai a le sante guagnele
Che per me non sareb[b]e mai marrito.

Allor mi disse: "I' vo' ben che·ttu venghi
Dentr'al giardin[o] sì com'e' ti piace,
Ma' che lungi dal fior le tue man tenghi.

Le buone donne fatt'ànno far pace
Tra me e te: or fa che·lla mantenghi,
Sì che verso di me no sie fallace".

16

Lover and Resistance[1]

When I saw how Resistance was mollified,
he who usually was more bitter than gall
but whom I found much sweeter than honey,
you should know that I considered myself as good as healed.

I passed into the garden in very subdued state
for fear of offending that cruel one,
and I swore to him on the holy gospels
that, because of me, he would never be distressed.

Then he said to me: "I truly want you to come
inside the garden, since you find it pleasant,
provided you keep your hands far away from the Flower.

The good women[2] have established peace
between me and you: now make sure you keep it,
so that you do not betray my trust."

1. Cf. *Rose*, 3335–3390.
2. Sincerity and Mercy.

17

Venùs

Venusso, ch'è socorso degli amanti,
Ven[n]'a Bellacoglienza col brandone,
E sì·recava a guisa di penone
Per avampar chiunque l'è davanti.

A voler racontar de' suo' sembianti
E de la sua tranobile faz[z]one,
Sareb[b]e assai vie più lungo sermone
Ch'a sermonar la vita a tutti i santi.

Quando Bellacoglienza sentì 'l caldo
Di quel brandon che così l'avampava,
Sì tosto fu 'l su' cuor col mïo saldo;

E Venusso, ch'a·cciò la confortava,
Si trasse verso lei col viso baldo,
Dicendo che ve·me troppo fallava.

17

Venus[1]

Venus, who comes to the aid of lovers,
came to Fair Welcome with a torch,
which she held like a lance
to set on fire all those she meets.[2]

If one were to describe her appearance
and her very noble disposition,
it would take much longer to tell
than to tell the lives of all the Saints.

When Fair Welcome felt the heat
of that torch which was setting her ablaze,
immediately her heart was joined with mine;[3]

and Venus, who was urging her to this,
moved close to her with a powerful look
and told her she was greatly at fault in my regard.

1. Cf. *Rose,* 3402–3423, 3455–3460.

2. Among the many attributes associated with Venus, the torch or firebrand is very common, just as her chariot drawn by her favorite birds, doves, in sonnet 217.

3. The image of fire as the amorous spark that rapidly becomes the raging flame of passion is a commonplace in the literary tradition.

18

Venùs e Bellacoglienza

"Tu falli trop[p]o verso quell'amante",
Disse Venus[so], "che cotanto t'ama;
Néd i' non so al mondo sì gran dama
Che di lui dovess'es[s]er rifusante,

Ch'egli è giovane, bello e avenante,
Cortese, franco e pro', di buona fama.
Promettili un basciar, e a·tte 'l chiama,
Ch'e' non à uon nel mondo più celante".

Bellacoglienza disse: "I' vo' che vegna,
E basci il fior che tanto gli è ['n] piacere,
Ma' ched e' sag[g]iamente si contegna;

Ché siate certa che no·m'è spiacere".
"Or gli ne manda alcuna buona 'nsegna",
Disse Venùs, "e fagliele a·sapere".

18

Venus and Fair Welcome[1]

Venus said: "You are making a big mistake
with that lover who loves you so much;
I do not know any great lady in the world
who would reject him:

for he is young, beautiful and charming,
courteous, loyal, bold and well respected.
Promise him a kiss and call him to you,
for no one in the world is more discreet[2] than he."

Fair Welcome said: "I want him to come
and kiss the Flower that he loves so much,
on condition that he behave wisely;

for you should know that this does not displease me."
Venus then said: "Now send him
a good sign and let him know this."

1. Cf. *Rose*, 3424–3454.

2. The importance of secrecy and discretion (*più celante*) is part of the *fin'amors* tradition. It was common in the early Romance lyric for the poet to conceal the true identity of the lady by means of a *senhal*, i.e., a code name. Here we note that the lover is praised for his discretion and the term used—*celante*—refers specifically to the notion of concealment.

19

L'Amante

Per Bel-Sembiante e per Dolze-Riguardo
Mi mandò la piacente ch'i' andasse
Nel su' giardin e ch'io il fior bascias[s]e,
Né non portasse già lancia né dardo:

Ché lo Schifo era fatto sì codardo
Ch'e' [no] mi bisognava ch'i' 'l dottasse;
Ma tuttor non volea ched i' v'entrasse,
Sed e' non fosse notte ben a tardo.

"Perciò che Castità e Gelosia
Sì ànno messo Paura e Vergogna
In le' guardar, che non faccia follia;

Ed un villan che truov'ogne menzogna
La guarda, il qual fu nato i·Normandia,
Mala-Boc[c]a, que' c[h]'ogne mal sampogna".

19

Lover

By means of Fair Appearance and Sweet Glance
the beautiful one informed me that I should enter
her garden and kiss the Flower,
but that I should bring neither spear nor arrow:[1]

for Resistance had become so cowardly
there was no need for me to fear him;
but nevertheless she did not want me to enter there
unless it were very late at night.

"Since Chastity and Jealousy
have entrusted Fear and Modesty with guarding her,
let's hope she doesn't do anything foolish.

Moreover, there watches over her an uncourtly one,
who invents a pack of lies, Bad Mouth[2] is he,
the one born in Normandy,[3] who is the source of all evil."[4]

1. Throughout the *Fiore* martial and erotic imagery are joined: the struggle to obtain love is described as a battle between two opposing forces, or armies. Fortifications are put in place; strategies and stratagems are presented and employed, and the weapons of war are, by and large, phallic in form. Thus, Lover "should bring neither spear nor arrow" for this is intended to be a chaste, platonic, nonsexual love, consisting only of a kiss.

2. Bad Mouth is the traditional figure of the slanderer, the *malparliere*, in Romance lyric. He may also have a connection to *Malacoda* (Evil Tail) and the *Malebranche* (Evil Claws) in the fifth ditch of the eight circle of Hell—*Malebolge* (Evil Ditches). The action of *Inf.* 21–23 turns on the lie told by *Malacoda* (*Inf.* 21.106–114).

3. In the *Rose* his place of origin is the same.

4. Literally, the one who "sounds the bagpipes," i.e., who proclaims things noisily. The reference to the *sampogna* also recalls the strange sound—the *diversa cennamella* (*Inf.* 22.10) in reference to the trumpet blast with which *Inferno* 21 ended—that announces the movement of the *Malebranche* in *Inferno* 22.

20

L'Amante e Bellacoglienza

Udendo quella nobile novella
Che que' genti messag[g]i m'aportaro,
Sì fortemente il cuor mi confortaro
Che di gioia perdé' quasi la favella.

Nel giardin me n'andà' tutto 'n gonella,
Sanz' armadura, com'e' comandaro,
E sì trovai quella col viso chiaro,
Bellacoglienza; tosto a·ssé m'apella,

E disse: "Vien avanti e bascia 'l fiore;
Ma guarda di far cosa che mi spiaccia,
Ché·ttu ne perderesti ogne mio amore".

Sì ch'i' alor feci croce de le braccia,
E sì 'l basciai con molto gran tremore,
Sì forte ridottava suo minaccia.

20

Lover and Fair Welcome[1]

Hearing that noble tale
brought to me by those courteous messengers,
I felt such great comfort in my heart
that out of joy I almost lost the power of speech.

Into the garden I went in my gonella,[2]
without any weapons, as they had commanded.
There I found that one with the resplendent face,
Fair Welcome, who immediately called me to her

and said: "Step forward and kiss the Flower;
but don't do anything that would displease me,
because you would lose all my love."

Thus I crossed my arms,[3]
and kissed the Flower with great trembling,
so fearful was I of her menacing words.

1. Cf. *Rose*, 3455–3460.

2. In the Middle Ages a *gonella* is a kind of outer-garment, like a tunic, open in the front and showing the clothing underneath.

3. The crossing of the arms suggests an attitude of supplication.

21

L'Amante

Del molto olor ch'al cor m'entrò basciando
Quel prezioso fior, che tanto aulia,
Contar né dir per me non si poria;
Ma dirò come 'l mar s'andò turbando

Per Mala-Boc[c]a, quel ladro normando,
Che se n'avide e svegliò Gelosia
E Castità, che ciascuna dormia;
Per ch'i' fu' del giardin rimesso in bando.

E sì vi conterò de la fortez[z]a
Dove Bellacoglienza fu 'n pregione,
Ch'Amor abatté poi per su' prodez[z]a;

E come Schifo mi tornò fellone
E lungo tempo mi ten[n]e in distrez[z]a,
E come ritornò a me Ragione.

21

Lover[1]

Of the great fragrance that entered my heart
when I kissed the precious and sweet-smelling Flower,
I am unable to speak or tell;
but I will tell how the sea became tempestuous[2]

because of Bad Mouth, that Norman thief,[3]
who saw the event and awakened Jealousy
and Chastity, for they were sleeping;
for this reason I was again cast out of the garden.

And now I will tell you of the fortress
where Fair Welcome was imprisoned,
the one that Love destroyed with his strength.

I will also tell how Resistance became hostile towards me
and kept me in distress for a very long time,
and how Reason returned to me.

1. Cf. *Rose*, 3459–3526.

2. The link between love and seafaring is common in medieval literature (see sonnets 33, 35 and 48).

3. *Mala-Bocca* was born in Normandy (see sonnet 19).

22

Castità

Castità, che da Veno è guer[r]eggiata,
Sì disse a Gelosia: "Perdio, merzede!
S'a questo fatto l'uon non ci provede,
I' potrè' bentosto es[s]ere adontata.

Vergogna e Paura m'ànno abandonata;
In quello Schifo foll'è chi si crede,
Ch'i' son certana ch'e' non ama a fede,
Po' del giardin sì mal guardò l'entrata;

Donde vo' siete la miglior guardiana
Ch'i' 'n esto mondo potes[s]e trovare.
Gran luogo avete in Lombardia e 'n Toscana.

Perdio, ched e' vi piaccia il fior guardare!
Che se que' che 'l basciò punto lo sgrana,
non fia misfatto ch'uon poss'amendare".

22

Chastity[1]

Chastity, against whom Venus wages war,
said thus to Jealousy: "In the name of God, have mercy!
If one does not attend to this matter,
I could soon suffer shame.

Modesty and Fear have abandoned me;
foolish is the one who trusts in that Resistance,
for I am certain that he does not love faithfully,
since he guarded the entrance of the garden so badly.

As a result, you are the best guardian
that I could ever find in this world.
You are well known in Lombardy and Tuscany.[2]

In the name of God, please guard the Flower!
If the man who kissed the Flower should despoil it even slightly,[3]
such a great misdeed can never be remedied."

1. Cf. *Rose*, 3527–3534.

2. These place names, which do not appear in the *Rose*, represent, respectively, the northern and central regions of Italy.

3. The verb used here—*sgranare*—is an agricultural term that refers to the "degraining" of wheat, corn, etc. This sort of imagery signals the ultimate "deflowering" of the flower.

23

Gelosia

Gelosia disse: "I' prendo a me la guarda,
Ch'a ben guardar il fior è mia credenza
Ch'i' avrò gente di tal provedenza
Ched i' non dotto già che Veno gli arda".

Al giardin se n'andò fier'e gagliarda,
Ed ivi sì trovò Bellacoglienza
E dis[s]ele: "Tu à' fatta tal fal[l]enza
Ch'i' ti tengo per folle e per musarda.

Ed a voi dico, Paur'e Vergogna,
Che chi di fior guardar in voi si fida,
Certa son ch'e' non à lett'a Bologna.

E quello Schifo che punt'or non grida,
Gli var[r]ia me' ch'e' fosse in Catalogna,
Sed e' non guarda ben ciò ch'egli à 'n guida".

23

Jealousy[1]

Jealousy replied: "I assume the responsibility
of guarding the Flower,
for I believe my associates are so wise
that I have no fear that Venus will enflame them."

To the garden she went, proud and strong,
and, finding Fair Welcome there,
she said to her: "You have made such a mistake
that I consider you to be senseless and foolish.

And to you, Fear and Modesty, I say
that whoever relies on you to guard the Flower
I'm sure that he has not studied in Bologna.[2]

And as for Resistance, who now does not boast at all,
it would be better for him to be in Catalonia,[3]
if he cannot protect that which is in his care."

1. Cf. *Rose,* 3583–3619.

2. Bologna is the seat of the oldest European university, and the name of the city has come to signify a place of great learning. There is debate over the meaning of this verse. Some critics (Marchiori) believe that *leggere* referred to teaching in the universities, but others (Contini, Rossi) view the term as indicating study.

3. Catalonia is here used to suggest a distant land.

24

Vergogna

Vergogna contra terra il capo china,
Ché ben s'avide ch'ella avea fallato,
E d'un gran velo il viso avea velato;
E sì disse a Paura sua cugina:

"Paura, no' siàn messe nell'aìna
Di Gelosia, e ciò ci à procacciato
Lo Schifo, perch'egli à corteseg[g]iato
Al bel valetto ch'i' vid'ier mattina.

Or andiàn tosto e troviàn quel villano,
E gli dirén com'e' fia malbalito
Se Gelosia gli mette adosso mano;

Ch[ed] egli à 'n ben guardar troppo fallito,
Ch'e' sì dé es[s]er a ciascuno strano,
E 'l diavol si·ll'à ora incortesito".

24

Modesty[1]

Modesty bows her head toward the ground,
for she knew that she had made a mistake,
and covered her face with a large veil.
And in this way she spoke to her cousin, Fear:

"Fear, we find ourselves hated
by Jealousy, and this has been done to us
by Resistance, because he was courteous
to that handsome lad whom I saw yesterday morning.

Now let's go quickly to find that uncouth one,
and we'll tell him how badly he'll be treated,
if Jealousy gets her hands on him;

for he has not kept guard the way he should have,
since he should be hostile to everyone;
but the devil has now made him so refined!"

1. Cf. *Rose*, 3620–3650.

25

Vergogna e Paura

Per lo Schifo trovar ciascun'andava,
Per dirli del misfatto molto male;
E que' s'avëa fatto un capez[z]ale
D'un fascio d'erba e sì son[n]iferava.

Vergogna fortemente lo sgridava;
Paura d'altra parte sì·ll'assale,
Dicendo: "Schifo, ben poco ti cale
Che Gelosïa sì forte ne grava,

E ciò ci avien per te, quest'è palese.
Quando tu, per la tua malaventura,
Tu vuogli intender or d'es[s]er cortese

(Ben sa' ch'e' non ti move di natura!),
Con ciaschedun dé' star a le difese
Per ben guardar questa nostra chiusura".

25

Modesty and Fear[1]

Everyone was looking for Resistance
to blame him for his bad mistake;
and that one had made himself a bed
from a bundle of grass, and there he fell asleep.

Modesty was reprimanding him very harshly;
in her turn Fear assails him,
saying: "Resistance, you don't care at all
that Jealousy is so upset with us!

And this happens to us because of you, it's clear.
Whenever you, for your misfortune,
wish to seem or to be courteous

(you well know that it's not your nature!),
you must be, as we all are, on the defensive,
in order to protect this enclosed place of ours."

1. Cf. *Rose,* 3651–3712.

26

Lo Schifo

Lo Schifo, quando udìo quel romore,
Conob[b]e ben ched egli avea mispreso,
Sì disse: "Il diavol ben m'avea sorpreso,
Quand' io a nessun uon mostrav'amore.

Ma s'i', colui che ven[n]e per lo fiore,
I' 'l posso nel giardin tener mai preso,
I' sia uguanno per la gola impeso
Sed i' no'l fo morir a gran dolore".

Allor ricigna il viso e gli oc[c]hi torna,
E troppo contra me tornò diverso:
Del fior guardar fortemente s'atorna.

A[h]i lasso, c[h]'or mi fu cambiato il verso!
In poca d'or sì 'l fatto mi bistorna
Che d'abate tornai men ch'a converso.

26

Resistance[1]

When Resistance heard that reproach,
he knew very well that he had made a mistake.
Thus he said: "The devil has deceived me,
when I showed kindness to someone.

But if I can catch the one who came for the Flower,
and if I can keep him prisoner,
may I be hanged by my neck
if I don't make him die with great pain."

Then he squints and rolls his eyes
and became quite horrible towards me:
he prepares to guard the Flower resolutely.

Alas! How things have changed for me!
In such a short time my situation has so changed
that from abbot I fell to being less than the lowest brother.[2]

1. Cf. *Rose*, 3713–3748.
2. Note the proverbial character of this line.

27

Gelosia

Gelosïa, che stava in sospeccione
Ch'ella del fior non fosse baratata,
Sì fe' gridar per tutta la contrata
Ch'a·llei venisse ciascun buon maz[z]one,

Ch' ella volea fondar una pregione
Dove Bellacoglienza fia murata;
Ché 'n altra guardia non fie più lasciata,
Po' ch'ella l'à trovata i·mesprigione:

"Ché la guardia del fior è perigliosa,
Sì saria folle se 'llei mi fidasse
Per la bieltà ch'à 'n lei maravigliosa".

E se Venùs' ancor la vicitasse,
Di ciò era certana, e non dottosa,
Ch'e' conver[r]eb[b]e ch'ella il fior donasse.

27

Jealousy[1]

Jealousy, who was afraid
of being cheated out of the Flower,
had it announced throughout the countryside
that all good masons should come to her,

because she wanted to build a prison
where they could imprison Fair Welcome.
She will not be left with another guardian,
since Jealousy found her guilty of malfeasance.

"Since guarding the Flower is dangerous,
it would be a mistake to put my trust in her
for all her marvelous beauty."

And if Venus should come again to visit her,
she was sure and had no doubt
of what would happen: that she would give up the Flower.

1. Cf. *Rose,* 3592–3610, 3779–3783.

28

L'Amante

Gelosia fece fondar un castello
Con gran fossi d'intorno e barbacani,
Ché molto ridottava uomini strani,
sì facev'ella que' di su' ostello;

E nel miluogo un casser fort'e bello,
Che non dottava as[s]alto di villani,
Fece murare a' mastri più sovrani
Di marmo lavorato ad iscarpello;

E sì vi fece far quat[t]ro portali
Con gran tor[r]i di sopra imbertescate,
Ch'unque nel mondo non fur fatte tali;

E porte caditoie v'avea ordinate,
Che venian per condotto di canali:
L'altr'eran tutte di ferro sprangate.

28

Lover[1]

Jealousy had a castle built
with large moats and fortifications all around,
because she greatly feared outsiders,
just as much as she did those within her castle.

And in the middle she had the greatest craftsmen
construct an impressive tower
with finely chiseled marble,
which feared no assault from uncouth men.

She then had four portals made
that were surmounted with lofty crenelated towers:
never had the world seen anything like them.

She ordered movable gates
that opened and closed hydraulically;
the other gates were all reinforced with iron.

1. Cf. *Rose*, 3784–3819.

29

L'Amante

Quando Gelosia vide il castel fatto,
Sì si pensò d'avervi guernimento,
Ch[ed] e' non era suo intendimento
Di renderlo per forza néd a patto.

Per dare a' suo' nemici mal atratto,
Vi mise dentro gran saettamento,
E pece e olio e ogn' altro argomento
Per arder castel di legname o gatto,

S'alcun lo vi volesse aprossimare:
Ché perduti ne son molti castelli
Per non prendersi guardia del cavare.

Ancor fe' far traboc[c]hi e manganelli
Per li nemici lungi far istare
E servirli di pietre e di quadrelli.

29

Lover[1]

On seeing that the castle was complete,
Jealousy had it stocked with arms,
for she did not wish to surrender it
either through battle or treaty.

In order to give her enemies a bad reception
she placed inside a great store of projectiles,
and tar and oil and everything else
that would ignite a war machine or battering ram,

if any one of these would approach too close.
For many castles have been lost
by those who failed to note their enemies' ploys.[2]

Jealousy had still other weapons made,
such as catapults that would keep the enemies far away
by pelting them with stones and darts.

1. Cf. *Rose*, 3835–3848.

2. The suggestion here is that enemy troops may attempt to gain entrance to a besieged castle by digging around its perimeter or by tunneling underneath it.

30

L'Amante

Quand' el[l]'eb[b]e il castel di guernigione
Fornito sì com'egli era mestiere,
Ad ogne porta mise su' portiere,
De' più fidati c[h]'avea in sua magione:

E perch'ella dottava tradigione,
Mise lo Schifo in sul portal primiere,
Perch'ella il sentia aspro cavaliere;
Al secondo, la figlia di Ragione,

Ciò fu Vergogna, che fe' gran difensa;
La terza porta sì guardò Paura,
Ch'iera una donna di gran provedenza;

Al quarto portal, dietro da le mura,
Fu messo Mala-Boc[c]a, la cui 'ntenza
Ferm'iera a dir mal d'ogne criatura.

30

Lover[1]

As soon as she had the castle supplied
with weapons as was necessary,
she put watchmen at every door:
these were the most trusted in her household.

And since she feared betrayal,
she placed Resistance at the main door,
because she knew he was a determined knight.
At the second gate she put Reason's daughter—

Modesty—who provided great defense;
the third gate was guarded by Fear,
a lady famous for her shrewdness;

and at the fourth gate, behind the wall,
Bad Mouth stood: his constant purpose
was to say evil things about everyone.

1. Cf. *Rose,* 3849–3873.

31

L'Amante

Bellacoglienza fu nella fortez[z]a
Per man di Gelosia mess'e fermata.
Ad una vec[c]hia l'eb[b]e acomandata
Che·lla tenesse tuttor in distrez[z]a;

Ch'ella dottava molto su' bellez[z]a,
Che Castità à tuttor guer[r]eg[g]iata,
E Cortesia, di cu' era nata,
No·lle facesse far del fior larghez[z]a.

Ver è ched ella sì 'l fece piantare
Là 've Bellacoglienza era 'n pregione,
Ch'altrove no'l sapea dove fidare.

Lassù non dottav'ella tradigione,
Ché quella vec[c]hia, a cu' 'l diede a guardare,
Sì era del lignag[g]io Salvagnone.

31

Lover[1]

Fair Welcome was put and enclosed
inside the fortress by Jealousy,
who charged an old woman
to keep her always under lock and key.

Jealousy greatly feared her beauty,
which Chastity has always defended,
and that Lady Courtesy, who is her mother,[2]
might make her give away the Flower.

And so it is true that she had it planted
there where Fair Welcome was imprisoned,
for she knew of no other safe place.

There on top she feared no betrayal,
for that old woman, to whom she gave it for safekeeping,
was a descendant of Salvagnone.[3]

1. Cf. *Rose*, 3893–3908j.
2. Fair Welcome is the daughter of Lady Courtesy.
3. While Salvagnone does not appear in the *Rose*, he is featured in some Old French romances and in some Italian poems (e.g., the *Cantare dei Cantari*) and poets (Cecco Angiolieri and Pietro dei Faitinelli). In this tradition Salvagnone was a well-known thief, and thus the reference here suggests that because of this lineage the old woman is well-versed in the ways of criminals—i.e., those who might attempt to "steal" the flower.

32

L'Amante

Gelosia andava a proveder le porte,
Sì trovava le guardie ben intese
Contra ciascuno star a le difese
E per donar e per ricever morte;

E Mala-Bocca si sforzava forte
In ogne mi' sacreto far palese:
Que' fu 'l nemico che più mi v'afese,
Ma sopra lui ricad[d]or poi le sorte.

Que' non finava né notte né giorno
A suon di corno gridar: "Guarda, guarda!";
E giva per le mura tutto 'ntorno

Dicendo: "Tal è putta e tal si farda,
E la cotal à troppo caldo il forno,
E l'altra follemente altrù' riguarda".

32

Lover[1]

Jealousy went to check the doors
and found the guards alert and ready
to ward off all attacks,
as well as to give and to suffer death.

Bad Mouth was trying very hard
to make me reveal all my secrets:
he was the enemy who gave me the most trouble,
but it was he instead who received the most harm.

All day and night to the sound of his horn
that one kept on shouting: "Look, look!"
And he circled all around the walls,

saying: "That one is a whore, and that one paints her face;
that other one has a really hot oven,[2]
and that other one casts her rash and roving eye on men."

1. Cf. *Rose*, 3874–3892, 3910–3919.

2. The rather obvious metaphoric language used here to refer to sexual desire and genital organs will recur frequently in the poem (see sonnets 221–222).

33

L'Amante

Quand' i' vidi i marosi sì 'nforzare
Per lo vento a Provenza che ventava,
C[h]'alberi e vele e ancole fiac[c]ava,
E nulla mi valea il ben governare,

Fra me medesino comincià' a pensare
Ch'era follïa se più navicava,
Se quel maltempo prima non passava
Che dal buon porto mi facé' alu[n]giare:

Sì ch'i' allor m'ancolai a una piag[g]ia,
Veg[g]endo ch'i' non potea entrar in porto:
La terra mi parea molto salvaggia.

I' vi vernai co·molto disconforto.
Non sa che mal si sia chi non asaggia
Di quel d'Amor, ond'i' fu' quasi morto.

33

Lover[1]

When I saw the waves rise ever higher,
because of the wind that blew from Provence,[2]
such that masts and sails and anchors broke,
and my good steering was to no avail,

I began to think in my heart of hearts
that it was madness to pursue my course,
until that bad weather passed,
which was keeping me far from the good harbor.[3]

Thus, I anchored myself upon a beach,
seeing that I could not enter the harbor;
the land seemed very inhospitable to me.

There I passed the winter in much discomfort.
He does not know what pain is who has not experienced
the pain of Love, because of which I almost died.

1. The material contained in this sonnet and the next has no direct antecedent in the *Rose*. These two sonnets provide a sort of transition between the end of Guillaume's part of the *Rose* and the beginning of Jean's part.

2. This is perhaps the strong, northerly cold wind known as the Mistral.

3. Sea imagery was commonly used in the Middle Ages to refer to the difficulties and uncertainties encountered in amorous relationships. See also sonnets 21, 35, 48 and 56.

34

L'Amante

Pianto, sospiri, pensieri e afrizione
Eb[b]i vernando in quel salvag[g]io loco,
Ch'pena de·ninferno è riso e gioco
Ver' quella ch'i' soffersi a la stagione

C[h]'Amor mi mise a tal distruzione
Ch'e' no·mi die' sog[g]iorno as[s]à' né poco:
Un'or mi tenne in ghiaccio, un'altra 'n foco.
Molto m'atten[n]e ben sua promessione,

Ma non di gioia né di nodrimento:
Ch'e' di speranza mi dovea nodrire
Insin ched e' mi desse giug[g]iamento.

Digiunar me ne fece, a ver vo dire;
Ma davami gran pez[z]e di tormento,
Con salsa stemperata di languire.

34

Lover

With weeping, sighs, thoughts and affliction
I passed the winter in that harsh place,
for the pain of Hell is laughter and play
compared to that which I suffered that season

when Love put me in such distress
and gave me no truce, neither little nor great:
one moment he kept me cold as ice, another on fire:
Love certainly kept the promise he made to me,

but not his promise of joy or nourishment!
He should have nourished me with hope,
at least until he pronounced his verdict.

To tell you the truth he made me fast,
while giving me large servings of torment,
with a piquant sauce of anguish.

35

L'Amante e Ragione

Languendo lungiamente in tal manera,
E non sapea ove trovar socorso,
Ché 'l tempo fortunal che m'era corso
M'avea gittato d'ogne bona spera,

Allor tornò a me, che lungi m'era,
Ragion la bella, e disse: "Tu·sse' corso,
Se·ttu non prendi i·me alcun ricorso,
Po' che Fortuna è 'nverso te sì fera.

Ed i' ò tal vertù dal mi' Segnore
Che mi crïò, ch'i' metto in buono stato
Chiunque al mi' consiglio ferma il core;

E di Fortuna che·tt'à tormentato,
Se vuogli abandonar il Die d'Amore,
Tosto t'avrò co·llei pacificato".

35

Lover and Reason[1]

While I was languishing for a long time in this way,
and not knowing where to find assistance,
for the stormy times I'd suffered
had deprived me of any hope,

beautiful Reason, who was far away from me,
then returned and said: "You may have gone too far,
if you do not seek help from me,
since Fortune is so cruel toward you.

But from the Lord who created me
I have such power that I can put in a good state
anyone who follows my advice faithfully.

As to Fortune who has tormented you,
if you want to abandon the God of Love,
I'll quickly reconcile you with her."

1. The material in sonnets 35–40 presents a summary of vv. 4191–5764 in the *Rose*.

36

L'Amante

Quand'i' udì' Ragion che 'l su' consiglio
Mi dava buon e fin, sanza fallacie,
Dicendo di trovarmi acordo e pace
Con quella che m'avea messo 'n asiglio,

I' le dissi: "Ragion, vec[c]o ch'i' piglio!
Ma non ch'i' lasci il mi' signor verace,
Ched i' son su' fedel, e sì mi piace
Tanto ch'i' l'amo più che padre figlio.

Onde di ciò pensar non è mestero
Né tra no' due tenerne parlamento,
Ché non sareb[b]e fatto di leg[g]iero

perciò ch'i' falseria mi' saramento.
Megli'amo di Fortuna es[s]er guer[r]ero
Ched i' a·cciò avesse pensamento".

36

Lover

When I heard the good and fine advice
of Reason who said, without deception, that she would
reestablish me in peace and concord
with that one who had put me in torment,

I said to her: "Reason, of course I will comply!
Provided that I do not have to leave my true lord;[1]
for I am his faithful servant, and he gives me such pleasure
that I love him more than a son loves his father.

For this reason it is unthinkable
and unnecessary for us to talk about it,
for this would not be easily done,

since I would be violating my pledge.
I prefer to be an enemy of Fortune[2]
than to worry about this."

1. That is, the God of Love.

2. For the concept of Fortune and her various attributes in the Middle Ages, see, among others, Howard R. Patch, *The Goddess Fortuna in Mediaeval Literature* (Cambridge, Mass.: Harvard University Press, 1927).

37

Ragione

"Falsar tal saramento è san' pec[c]ato,
Poi te' ciascun, secondo Dicretale,
Che, se l'uon giura di far alcun male,
S'e' se ne lascia, non è pergiurato.

Tu mi proposi che tu se' giurato
A questo dio, che·tt'à condotto a tale
C[h]'ogne vivanda mangi sanza sale,
sì fortemente t'à disavorato.

E sì si fa chiamar il Die d'Amore:
Ma chi così l'apella fa gran torto,
Ché su' sornome dritto sì è Dolore.

Or ti parti da·llui, o tu se' morto,
Né no'l tener giamà' più a signore,
E prendi il buon consiglio ch'i' t'aporto".

37

Reason[1]

"To violate such a pledge does not constitute sin,
since everyone knows, according to the Decretals,[2]
that if a man vows to commit a crime,
and then abstains from doing it, it is not perjury.

You say to me that you have sworn allegiance
to this god, who has guided you to such a point
that you eat all foods without salt,
so has he made you lose the sense of taste.

And so he has people call him the God of Love,
but whoever calls him this makes a great mistake,
for his proper name is Pain.[3]

Now separate yourself from him, or you will die,
and no longer keep him as your lord,
and take the good advice I am giving you!"

1. Cf. *Rose*, 4570–4584.

2. When referring to the Decretal(s), scholars sometimes make a distinction between the singular and plural form of the proper noun. In its plural form, the term would refer to the collection of papal letters and decrees that were assembled by Pope Gregory IX in 1234 and became a major part of canon law (*Corpus iuris canonici*). In its singular form, the term would refer to the *Decretum*, a collection of similar writings made by Gratian around 1140, which serves as a sort of basic textbook of canon law. See also sonnet 219.

3. In the Middle Ages the play on words and names was common and often followed the principle of *nomina sunt consequentia rerum*, by which the nature of something could be determined by its name. Thus, the word for love, *amore*, was linked with *amaro* ("bitter"), *mare* ("sea") and *morte* ("death"); moreover, because of its rhyme, it was associated with *dolore* ("pain," "sadness").

38

L'Amante

"Ragion, tu sì mi vuo' trar[e] d'amare
E di' che questo mi' signor è reo,
E ch'e' non fu d'amor unquanche deo,
Ma di dolor, secondo il tu' parlare.

Da·llui partir non credo ma' pensare,
Né tal consiglio non vo' creder eo,
Chéd egli è mi' segnor ed i' son seo
Fedel, sì è follia di ciò parlare.

Per ch'e' mi par che 'l tu' consiglio sia
Fuor di tu' nome troppo oltre misura,
Ché sanza amor nonn-è altro che nuìa.

Se Fortuna m'à tolto or mia ventura,
Ella torna la rota tuttavia,
E quell'è quel che molto m'asicura".

38

Lover

"Reason, you want to keep me from loving,
and you say that this lord of mine is harmful
and that, according to your word, he never was
the God of Love, but of Pain.

I would never think of departing from him,
nor do I want to follow your advice,
because he is my Lord and I am his
faithful servant; thus, it's madness to speak of such things.

For this reason it seems to me that your advice goes
beyond the bounds of your name,[1]
because to be without love is nothing but a burden.

If Fortune has taken away my good luck,
she will continue to turn her wheel,[2]
and that is what gives me assurance."

1. That is, Reason's advice is unreasonable.

2. Among Fortune's several attributes, the wheel is probably the most common and familiar. Illustrations of the wheel of Fortune traditionally present four figures positioned in such a way as to convey their varying degrees of prosperity. In some manuscript illuminations these figures are also accompanied by a pertinent Latin phrase. For example, in an illustration to canto 7 of Dante's *Divine Comedy* (MS Magl. Conv. C.3.1266 in the Biblioteca Nazionale of Florence), where the concept of fortune is presented, we see and read the following figures and legends: the man enthroned and crowned on top of the wheel says *regno* ("I reign"), in contrast to the one dispossessed and overturned at the bottom of the wheel, who laments *sum sine regno* ("I am without possessions"); the figure ascending on the left remarks *regnabo* ("I shall reign"), and this image is countered by that of the man who descends on the right and says *regnavi* ("I reigned"). The ever-turning wheel is intended to be both monitory and consolatory: on the one hand, it is a reminder of the transitory nature of earthly things, warning those in positions of power and prosperity that their time at the top is limited; on the other hand, the image provides a message of hope to those who, out of favor, languish at the bottom of the wheel, reminding them that the wheel will eventually turn and they will escape their misery. Here Lover is referring to the message of hope. For the manuscript illumination, see Peter Brieger, Millard Meiss and Charles S. Singleton, *Illuminated Manuscripts of the Divine Comedy*, 2 vols. (Princeton: Princeton University Press, 1969), 2:109.

39

Ragione

"Di trareti d'amar nonn-è mia 'ntenza",
Disse Ragion, "né da ciò non ti butto,
Ch'i' vo' ben che·ttu ami il mondo tutto,
Fermando in Gesocristo tu' credenza.

E s'ad alcuna da' tua benvoglienza,
Non vo' che·ll'ami sol per lo didutto
Né per diletto, ma per trarne frutto,
Ché chi altro ne vuol cade in sentenza.

Ver è ch'egli à in quel[l]'opera diletto,
Che Natura vi mise per richiamo,
Per più sovente star con esse in letto:

Che se ciò non vi fos[s]e, ben sap[p]iamo
Che poca gente por[r]eb[b]e già petto
Al lavorio che cominciò Adamo".

39

Reason[1]

"It is not my intention to keep you from loving,"
said Reason, "nor do I want to discourage you from it,
for I want you to love dearly the whole world,
reinforcing your belief in Jesus Christ.

And if you give your love to someone,
I don't want you to love her only for pleasure
or for delight, but to draw fruit from the relationship,
because whoever wishes a different end falls into sin.

It's true that there is great delight in that act,
which Nature[2] put there as a lure,
in order for men to go to bed with women more often.

And if it were not so, we well know
that few people would engage
in the labor that Adam first began."[3]

1. For this and the following sonnet, cf. *Rose,* 4368–4390.

2. For the importance of Nature in the Middle Ages, see George D. Economou, *The Goddess Natura in Medieval Literature* (Cambridge, Mass.: Harvard University Press, 1972).

3. The word "labor" (*lavorio*) is usually used to refer to sexual intercourse in the poem.

40

L'Amante

I' le dissi: "Ragion, or sie certana,
Po' che Natura diletto vi mise,
In quel lavor, ched ella no'l v'asise
Già per niente, ché non è sì vana,

Ma per continüar la forma umana;
sì vuol ch'uon si diletti in tutte guise
Per volontier tornar a quelle asise,
Ché 'n dilettando sua semenza grana.

Tu va' dicendo ch'i' no·mi diletti,
Mad i' per me non posso già vedere
Che sanza dilettar uon vi s'asetti,

A quel lavor, per ch'io ferm'ò volere;
Di dilettar col fior no·me ne getti.
Faccia Dio po' del fiore su' piacere!".

40

Lover

I said to her: "Reason, since Nature placed
delight in that labor, you may be sure
that she did not put it there
for no reason at all, for she is not so foolish,

but in order that the human race continue;
indeed, Nature wants man to take delight in many ways
in order to return gladly to these encounters,
for it's through pleasure that his seed produces fruit.[1]

You keep saying that I should not take my pleasure,
but I cannot for the life of me understand
why anyone would undertake that labor

without pleasure; thus, I am resolute in my desire.
Don't dissuade me from taking pleasure with the Flower!
Then let God do what he wishes with the Flower!"

1. The verb *granare* (modern *granire:* "to seed," "to bear grain," "to produce fruit"), like the related *sgranare* (sonnet 22), is an agricultural term that has sexual connotations.

41

Ragione

"Del dilettar non vo' chiti tua parte",
Disse Ragion, "né che sie sanz'amanza,
Ma vo' che prendi me per tua 'ntendanza:
Ché·ttu non troverai i·nulla parte

Di me più bella (e n'ag[g]ie mille carte),
Né che·tti doni più di dilettanza.
Degna sarei d'esser reina in Franza;
Sì fa' follïa, s' tu mi getti a parte:

Ch'i' ti farò più ric[c]o che Ric[c]hez[z]a,
Sanza pregiar mai rota di Fortuna,
Ch'ella ti possa mettere in distrez[z]a.

Se be·mi guardi, i·me nonn-à nes[s]una
Faz[z]on che non sia fior d'ogne bellez[z]a:
Più chiara son che nonn-è sol né luna".

41

Reason[1]

"I don't want you to give up your pleasure,"
said Reason, "nor for you to be without a lover,
but I want you to take me for your lady;
for you will not find anywhere

a woman more beautiful than I
(even if you search in many books),
or one who will give you more pleasure.
I would be worthy to be the Queen of France;[2]
thus, you would be foolish to toss me aside,

for I will make you richer than Wealth herself,
without concern that the wheel of Fortune
may put you in a sorry state.

If you look at me clearly, you will not find in me any
feature that is not the best of every beauty;
I am more radiant than the sun and the moon."

1. Cf. *Rose,* 5765–5808.

2. This is a standard expression in medieval literature to indicate great wealth, dignity and high station.

42

L'Amante

"Ragion, tu sì mi fai larga proferta
Del tu' amor e di te, ma i' son dato
Del tutto al fior, il qual non fia cambiato
Per me ad altr'amor: di ciò sie certa.

Né non ti vo' parlar sotto coverta:
Che s'i' mi fosse al tutto a·tte gradato,
Certana sie ch'i' ti verrè' fallato,
Che ch'i' dovesse aver, o prode o perta.

Allora avrè' fallato a·llui e te,
E sì sarei provato traditore,
Ched i' gli ò fatto saramento e fé.

Di questo fatto non far più sentore,
Ché 'l Die d'Amor m'à·ssì legato a·ssé
Che·tte non pregio e lui tengo a signore".

42

Lover[1]

"Reason, you make me such a generous offer
of your love and yourself, but I am totally
committed to the Flower, which I will not exchange
for another love: of this you may be certain.

Nor do I want to speak with you in unclear terms:
if I were everything you wanted,
then you may be sure that I would not be loyal to you,
no matter what I would have in return, either gain or loss.

Then I would have deceived both him and you,
and I would be a traitor for sure,
because I swore and pledged him loyalty.

Of this matter don't say another word,
because the God of Love has so bound me to him
that you I value very little and him I consider as my lord."

1. Cf. *Rose,* 6871–6897.

43

Ragione

"Amico, guarda s' tu fai cortesia
Di scondir del tu' amor tal damigella
Chente son io, che son sì chiara e bella
Che nulla falta i·me si troveria.

Nel mi' visag[g]io l'uon si spec[c]hieria,
Sì non son troppo grossa né tro' grella,
Né troppo grande né tro' pic[c]iolella:
Gran gioia avrai se m'ài in tua balia.

Ched i' sì·tti farò questo vantag[g]io,
Ch'i' ti terrò tuttor in ricco stato,
Sanz'aver mai dolor nel tu' corag[g]io.

E così tenni Socrato beato;
Ma mi credette e amò come sag[g]io,
Di che sarà di lui sempre parlato.

43

Reason[1]

"Consider, my friend, if you're acting courteously
by refusing to love a woman
such as myself, who am so resplendent and beautiful
that no flaw can be found in me!

One could see his reflection in my face,
and I am neither too fat nor too thin,
neither too big nor too small:[2]
you will have great joy if you have me in your power.

For I will grant you this favor:
I will keep you always in a prosperous state,
and you will never have any pain in your heart.

In this matter I kept Socrates in a blessed state;
but he, as a wise man, believed and loved me,
for which reason he will always be remembered."

1. Cf. *Rose,* 2962–2979, 5803–5806, 6341–6347, 6857–6862.

2. This description would suggest that Reason embodies the Aristotelian golden mean, the *aurea mediocritas,* according to which excess is to be avoided and moderation followed in all things; thus, Reason would present the perfect model to imitate.

44

Ragione

"Quel Socrato dond'i' ti vo parlando,
Sì fu fontana piena di salute,
Della qual derivò ogne salute,
Po' ched e' fu del tutto al me' comando.

Né mai Fortuna no'l gì tormentando:
Non pregiò sue levate né cadute;
Suo' gioie e noie per lui fur ricevute,
Né ma' su' viso nonn-andò cambiando.

E bene e mal mettea in una bilanza
E tutto la facea igual pesare,
Sanza prenderne gioia né pesanza.

Per Dio, ched e' ti piaccia riguardare
Al tu' profitto, e prendim'ad amanza!
Più alto non ti puo' tu imparentare.

44

Reason[1]

"That Socrates of whom I speak to you
was a veritable fountain of happiness,
from which all happiness has derived,
after he was completely under my command.

Fortune never tormented him;
he gave no heed to her ups and downs.
He accepted her joys and troubles,
and never did his face change expression.

On a scale he put both good and evil,
and since he gave them equal weight,
he had no joy or sadness.

In the name of God, please reconsider
for your profit, and take me as your lover!
You can affiliate with no one more noble than I."

1. Cf. *Rose*, 5817–5838.

45

Ragione

"Ancor non vo' t'incresca d'ascoltarmi:
Alquanti motti ch'i' voglio ancor dire
A ritenere intendi e a udire,
Ché non potresti aprender miglior' salmi.

Tu sì à' cominciato a biasimarmi
Perch'i' l'Amor ti volea far fug[g]ire,
Che fa le genti vivendo morire:
E tu 'l saprai ancor se no·lo spalmi!

Sed i' difendo a ciaschedun l'ebrez[z]a,
Non vo' che 'l ber per ciò nes[s]un disami,
Se non se quello che la gente blez[z]a.

I' non difendo a·tte che·ttu non ami,
Ma non Amor che·tti tenga 'n distrez[z]a,
E nella fin dolente te ne chiami".

45

Reason[1]

"I don't want you to tire of listening to me:
please try to hear and remember
the few things I still want to say,
for you can not learn better psalms.[2]

You have begun to blame me
because I wanted you to flee from Love,
who makes people die even as they live,
and one day this you'll learn if you don't free yourself from him![3]

If I forbid someone from drinking excessively,
I don't want people to hate drinking for this reason,
except for that variety that causes harm to people.

I do not forbid you from loving,
but I do want to stop Love from keeping you in distress,
and, in the end, to stop you from calling yourself wretched."

1. Cf. *Rose,* 5695–5721.
2. That is, "sayings," "speeches."
3. Literally, to "undo a handshake," that is, to remove oneself from an agreement that had been confirmed by a handshake.

46

L'Amante

Quando Ragion fu assà' dibattuta
E ch'ella fece capo al su' sermone,
I' sì·lle dissi: "Donna, tua lezione
Sie certa ch'ella m'è poco valuta,

Perciò ch'i' no·ll'ò punto ritenuta,
Ché no·mi piace per nulla cagione;
Ma, cui piacesse, tal amonizione
Sì gli sareb[b]e ben per me renduta.

Chéd i' so la lezion tratutta a mente
Pe·ripètall'a gente cu' piacesse,
Ma già per me nonn-è savia niente:

Ché fermo son, se morir ne dovesse,
D'amar il fior, e 'l me' cor vi s'asente,
O 'n altro danno ch'avenir potesse".

46

Lover[1]

When Reason had ceased with her impassioned plea
and brought her sermon to an end,
I said to her: "Lady, you may be sure
your lesson has had little value for me,

since I have not believed any of it,
and I do not like it at all.
However, if anyone would like to have such warnings,
I would gladly pass them on to him.

For I know the whole lesson by heart,
and I can repeat it to those people who would appreciate it,
but for me it contains no wisdom at all.

I am determined, even if I should die from it,
to love the Flower, and my heart is in complete agreement,
even if death or any other harm would result from it."

1. Cf. *Rose,* 4329–4340.

47

L'Amante e Amico

Ragion si parte, quand'ella m'intese,
Sanza tener più meco parlamento,
Ché trovar non potea nullo argomento
Di trarmi de·laccio in ch'Amor mi prese.

Allor sì mi rimisi a le difese
Co' mie' pensieri, e fu' i·mag[g]ior tormento
Assà' ched i' non fu' al cominciamento:
No·mmi valea coverta di pavese.

Allor sì pia[c]que a Dio che ritornasse
Amico a me per darmi il su' consiglio.
Sì tosto ch'e' mi vide, a me sì trasse

E disse: "Amico, i' sì mi maraviglio
Che ciascun giorno dimagre e apasse:
Dov'è il visag[g]io tu' chiaro e vermiglio?".

47

Lover and Friend[1]

When she heard my words, Reason leaves
without speaking to me any longer,
for she could not find any other argument
to free me from the snare in which Love had me.

Thus, once more I began to deal with my thoughts
and found myself in much greater torment
than I was in the beginning:
no large shield could help me in this state.

And so it pleased God that Friend
returned to me to give me his advice.
As soon as he saw me, he drew close

and said: "Friend, I am amazed
to see you becoming thinner and paler with each passing day:
where is your shining, red face?"

1. Cf. *Rose*, 7199–7211.

48

L'Amante

"Non ti maravigliar s'i' non son grasso,
Amico, né vermiglio com'i' soglio,
Ch'ogne contrario è presto a ciò ch'i' voglio,
Così Fortuna m'à condotto al basso.

Ira e pensier m'ànno sì vinto e lasso
Ch'e' non è maraviglia s'i' mi doglio,
Chéd i' sì vo a fedir a tale iscoglio,
S'Amor non ci provede, ch'i' son casso.

E ciò m'à Mala-Boc[c]a procacciato,
Che svegliò Castitate e Gelosia
Sì tosto com'i' eb[b]i il fior basciato.

Allor fos[s]'egli stato i·Normandia,
Nel su' paese ove fu strangolato,
Ché sì gli pia[c]que dir ribalderia!".

48

Lover[1]

"Friend, don't be amazed if I am not as fat,
or red, as I used to be,
for the opposite of what I desire always occurs,
so Fortune has brought me to this low state!

Sadness and worry have so conquered and exhausted me
that it's no wonder I'm in such pain;
for I will run aground and destroy myself on such a reef,
if Love does not assist me.

And this end Bad Mouth has secured for me
when he awakened Chastity and Jealousy
as soon as I had kissed the Flower.

Would that he had been in Normandy,
there in his country where he was hanged,
for indeed he delighted in saying defamatory things."

1. Cf. *Rose*, 7213–7215, 7230–7250.

49

L'Amante e Amico

Com' era gito il fatto eb[b]i contato
A motto a motto, di filo in aguglia,
Al buono Amico, che non fu di Puglia;
Che m'eb[b]e molto tosto confortato,

E disse: "Guarda che n[on] sie ac[c]et[t]ato
Il consiglio Ragion, ma da te il buglia,
Ché ' fin'amanti tuttor gli tribuglia
Con quel sermon di che·tt'à sermonato.

Ma ferma in ben amar tutta tua 'ntenza,
E guarda al Die d'Amor su' [o]manag[g]io,
Ché tutto vince lungia soferenza.

Or metti a me intendere il corag[g]io,
Chéd i' ti dirò tutta la sentenza
Di ciò che dé far fin amante sag[g]io.

49

Lover and Friend[1]

I told the tale as it had happened,
word for word, leaving nothing out,
to my good Friend, who was not from Apulia.[2]
After having consoled me,

he said: "Make sure you do not accept
Reason's advice, but keep it far removed from you,
because Reason always troubles courtly lovers
with that sermon she has preached to you.

But put all your desire in loving properly,
and keep your pledge to the God of Love,
for long suffering can conquer everything.

Now give me your full attention,
for I will tell you the entire story
of what a wise refined lover must do."

1. Cf. *Rose*, 7253–7276.

2. The reference to Apulia is generally taken to indicate the southern part of Italy and the betrayal of Manfred (Emperor Frederick II's natural son) by barons who shifted their allegiance to Charles of Anjou during the battle of Benevento in 1266. Thus, the association of this region with treacherous acts.

50

Amico

"A Mala-Bocca vo' primieramente
Che·ttu sì no gli mostri mal sembiante;
Ma se gli passe o dimore davante,
Umile gli ti mostra ed ubidente.

Di te e del tuo gli sie largo offerente
E faccia di te come di su' fante:
Così vo' che lo 'nganni, quel truante
Che si diletta in dir mal d'ogne gente.

Col braccio al collo sì die on menare
Il su' nemico, insin che si' al giubetto,
Co·le lusinghe, e po' farlo impiccare.

Or metti ben il cuor a·cciò c[h]'ò detto:
Di costù' ti convien così ovrare
Insin ch'e' sia condotto al passo stretto.

50

Friend[1]

"First of all I don't want you to give
Bad Mouth any angry looks,
but when you pass by or stop in front of him,
show yourself to be humble and obedient.

Be generous and offer him your person and possessions,
and let him treat you like his servant.
In this way I want you to deceive that rascal,
who takes pleasure in bad-mouthing everyone.

With your arm around his shoulder and with pleasant words
you must lead your enemy to the gallows,
where then you'll have him hanged.

Now pay attention to what I've said:
with this one you must behave like this
until he has been led to that narrow pass."[2]

1. Cf. *Rose*, 7303–7368.
2. That is, to death.

51

Amico

“Impresso vo’ che·ttu ag[g]ie astinenza
Di non andar sovente dal castello,
Né non mostrar che·tti sia guari bello
A riguardar là ov’è Bellacoglienza:

Ché·tti convien aver gran provedenza
Insin che Mala-Boc[c]a t’è ribello,
Ché·ttu sa’ ben ch’egli è un mal tranello
Che giorno e notte grida e nogia [e] tenza.

De l’altre guardie non bisogna tanto
Guardar com’e’ ti fa di Mala-Boc[c]a,
Ch’elle starian volontier da l’un canto;

Ma quel normando incontanente scoc[c]a
Ciò ched e’ sa, ed in piaz[z]a ed a santo,
E contruova di sé e mette in coc[c]a.

51

Friend[1]

"After this I want you to refrain
from going often to the castle,
and do not show that you like
to gaze at the place where Fair Welcome resides.

For you must be very careful,
as long as Bad Mouth is hostile towards you,
since you know that he is a terrible person
who screams and shouts and argues day and night.

You don't have to be as careful with the other guards
as you do with Bad Mouth,
for they would gladly stay off to one side;

but that Norman immediately shoots off his mouth
about everything he knows, both in the squares and in the churches;
he concocts his tales and readies them for delivery."[2]

1. Cf. *Rose*, 7278–7288, 7340–7346.

2. The image is that of an archer (*Mala-Bocca*) who prepares to shoot (*scocca*) an arrow by placing its notch in the bowstring (*cocca*).

52

Amico

"La Vec[c]hia che Bellacoglienz'à 'n guarda,
Servi ed onora a tutto tu' podere:
Che s'ella vuol, troppo ti può valere,
Chéd ella nonn-è folle né musarda.

A Gelosïa, che mal fuoco l'arda,
Fa 'l somigliante, se·lla puo' vedere:
Largo prometti a tutte de l'avere,
Ma 'l pagamento il più che puo' lo tarda.

E se·llor doni, dona gioeletti,
Be' covriceffi e reti e 'nt[r]ecciatoi
E belle ghirlanduz[z]e e ispil[l]etti

E pettini d'avorio e riz[z]atoi,
Coltelli e paternostri e tessutetti:
Ché questi non son doni strug[g]itoi.

52

Friend[1]

"Serve and honor with all your might
the Old Woman who guards Fair Welcome;
if she wishes, she can be very useful to you,
because she is neither silly nor foolish.

With Jealousy—may an evil fire burn her!—
do the same, if you succeed in seeing her.
Promise all of them generous compensation,
but delay payment as much as possible.

And if you give gifts, give jewels,
beautiful hats and bonnets and silk ribbons
and beautiful garlands and pins,

and ivory combs and barrettes,
knives and rosaries and cloths;
for these are inexpensive gifts."

1. Cf. *Rose*, 7369–7372, 7401–7411, 7415–7417.

53

Amico

"Se non ài che donar, fa gran pro[m]essa
Sì com'i' t'ò contato qui davanti,
Giurando loro Idio e tutti i santi,
Ed anche il sacramento della messa,

Che ciascuna farai gran baronessa,
Tanto darai lor fiorini e bisanti:
Di pianger vo' che faccie gran semb[i]anti,
Dicendo che non puo' viver sanz'essa.

E se·ttu non potessi lagrimare,
Fa che·ttu ag[g]ie sugo di cipolle
O di scalogni, e farànolti fare;

O di scialiva gli oc[c]hi tu·tte 'molle,
S'ad altro tu non puo' ricoverare.
E così vo' che ciascheduna bolle.

53

Friend[1]

"If you have nothing to give, make great promises,
just as I have told you now,
pledging to them by God and all the Saints
and even on the sacrament of the mass,

that you will make each of them a great baroness,
and in the meantime you will give them florins and *bisanti*.[2]
I want you to pretend to weep,
saying that you cannot live without her.

And if you should be unable to shed any tears,
make sure that you have some juice from onions
or scallions, and this will make you cry;

or dampen your eyes with saliva,
if you cannot find anything else.
And in this way I want you to deceive them all."

1. Cf. *Rose*, 7415–7440.
2. Gold coins of a certain value minted at Byzantium.

54

Amico

"Se·ttu non puo' parlar a quella ch'ami,
Sì·lle manda per lettera tu' stato,
Dicendo com'Amor t'à·ssì legato
Ver' lei, che ma' d'amarla non ti sfami.

E le' dirai: 'Per Gesocristo, tra'mi
D'esti pensier', che m'ànno sì gravato!';
Ma guarda che·llo scritto sia mandato
Per tal messag[g]io che non vi difami.

Ma nella lettera non metter nome;
Di lei dirai 'colui', di te 'colei':
Così convien cambiar le pere a pome.

Messag[g]io di garzon' ma' non farei,
Chéd e' v'à gran periglio, ed odi come:
Nonn-à fermez[z]a in lor; perciò son rei.

54

Friend[1]

"If you cannot speak to the one you love,
then let her know your state by letter,
saying how Love has so bound you
to her that you will never get enough of loving her.

And you will say to her: 'In the name of Jesus Christ, free me
from these thoughts that have oppressed me!'
But make sure that the letter is delivered
by a messenger who will not harm your reputation.

But don't use any names in the letter;
for 'her' you will say 'him' and for 'you' 'her':[2]
Thus are pears changed into apples.

I would never use a boy as a messenger,
for there is great danger, and here's why:
there's no constancy in them; thus, they are no good."

1. Cf. *Rose*, 7457–7478.

2. The use of pronouns that invert the gender of the individual hides the identity of the protagonists, and this reflects the convention of maintaining secrecy in amorous affairs.

55

Amico

"E se·lla donna prende tu' presente,
Buon incomincio avrà' di far mercato;
Ma·sse d'un bascio l'avessi inarrato,
Saresti poi certan del rimanente.

E s'ella a prender non è conoscente,
Anzi t'avrà del tutto rifusato,
Sembianti fa che sie forte crucciato,
E pàrtiti da·llei san' dir nïente.

E poi dimora un tempo san' parlarne,
E non andar in luogo ov'ella sia,
E fa sembiante che nonn-ài che farne.

Ell'enterrà in sì gran malinconia
Che no·lle dimorrà sopr'osso carne;
Sì·ssi ripentirà di sua follia.

55

Friend [1]

"And if the Lady takes your gift,
you'll have a good beginning for your dealings;
but if you had obtained the promise of a kiss from her,
you would then be sure of having the rest.

And if she does not have the courtesy to accept,
but indeed has totally refused you,
pretend that you are very upset,
and leave her without saying anything.

And then don't speak to her for a while,
and don't go to those places where she might be,
and pretend you don't know how you'll manage.

She will then become so sad [2]
that she will no longer have any meat on her bones;
and thus she will repent of her folly."

1. Cf. *Rose*, 7487–7518.

2. The term is *malinconia* and refers specifically to the black bile that was considered in medieval medicine to be one of the four humors. An imbalance in these humors produced sickness and, in this particular case, great sadness.

56

Amico

"Il marinaio che tuttor navicando
Va per lo mar, cercando terra istrana,
Con tutto si guid'e' per tramontana,
Sì va e' ben le sue vele cambiando

E per fug[g]ire da terra e apressando,
In quella guisa c[h]'allor gli è più sana:
Così governa mese e settimana
Insin che 'l mar si va rabonacciando.

Così dé far chi d'Amor vuol gioire
Quand'e' truova la sua donna diversa:
Un'or la dé cacciar, altra fug[g]ire.

Allor sì·lla vedrà palida e persa,
Ché sie certan che le parrà morire
Insin che no·lli cade sotto inversa.

56

Friend[1]

"The sailor who continues to sail
over the sea, looking for an unknown land,
even though he sets his course by the North star,
still he adjusts his sails

to move away from the coast or to approach it,
thus doing what is best for him at that moment:
in this way he sails for months and weeks,
until the sea becomes calm.[2]

Whoever desires Love's joy must act in this way,
if he discovers his lady to be cruel:
now he must hunt her, and now flee from her.

When he'll see her pale and pallid,
he'll know she'll think it forever
until she's flat on her back beneath him."

1. Cf. *Rose*, 7519–7528.
2. See also sonnet 33.

57

Amico

"Quando fai ad alcuna tua richesta,
O vec[c]hia ch'ella sia o giovanzella,
O maritata o vedova o pulzella,
Sì convien che·lla lingua tua sia presta

A·lle' lodar suo' oc[c]hi e bocca e testa
E dir che sotto 'l ciel non à più bella:
'Piacesse a Dio ch'i' v'avesse in gonella
Là ov'io diviserei, in mia podesta!'.

Così le déi del tutto andar lodando,
Ché e' nonn-è nes[s]una sì atempata
Ch'ella non si diletti in ascoltando,

E credes'esser più bella che fata;
E 'mmantenente pensa a gir pelando
Colui che prima tanto l'à lodata.

57

Friend[1]

"When you make your amorous request to a woman,
whether she be old or young,
married or widowed or virgin,
your tongue must be ready

to praise her eyes and mouth and head,
and to say that there's no more beautiful woman on earth:
'Would to God that I could have you in your *gonella,*[2]
wherever I would like, and in my power!'

You must praise them all this way,
for no woman is so old that she
does not delight to hear these things,

and think herself to be more beautiful than a fairy.
And immediately she begins to think of ways to skin
the man who's just given her such praise."[3]

1. Cf. *Rose*, 9905–9932.

2. A *gonella* is a slip or loose-fitting tunic. Thus, the sense is that the woman would only be partially clothed (see sonnet 20).

3. The verb *pelare* ("to skin") recurs often in the poem to describe the action of women in exploiting their lovers to obtain material goods.

58

Amico

"Le giovane e le vec[c]hie e le mez[z]ane
Son tutte quante a prender sì 'ncarnate
Che nessun puote aver di lor derate
Per cortesïa, tanto son villane:

Ché quelle che si mostran più umane
E non prendenti, dànno le ghignate.
Natur'è quella che·lle v'à 'fetate,
Sì com'ell'à 'fetato a caccia il cane.

Ver è c[h]'alcuna si mette a donare;
Ma ella s'è ben prima proveduta
Ch'ella 'l darà in luogo d'adoppiare.

I·llor gioei non son di gran valuta,
Ma e' son esca per uccè' pigliare.
Guardisi ben chi à corta veduta!

58

Friend[1]

"All women—young, old, middle-aged—
are so naturally disposed[2] to taking
that no one can have their wares
for free, so uncourtly are they:

for those who show themselves to be more charitable
and not greedy make fun of you.
Nature is the one who has taught them
just as she has taught the dog to hunt.

It's true that some are disposed to give,
but only if they've first made sure
that what they give will come back twofold.

Their jewels are not of great value,
but they're the bait to snare the pigeons.
May the short-sighted ones beware!"

1. Cf. *Rose*, 8251–8272, 9939–9944.
2. The word *'ncarnate* could also mean "eager" or "avid."

59

Amico

"Se quella cu' richiedi ti rifiuta,
Tu sì non perdi nulla in su' scondetto,
Se non se solo il motto che·ll'ài detto:
Dello scondir sarà tosto pentuta.

Una nel cento non fu mai veduta
(Ed ancor più, che 'l miglià' ci ti metto)
Femina cu' piacesse tal disdetto,
Come ch'ella t'asalga di venuta.

Richiè', c[h]'almen n'avrà' su' ben volere,
Con tutto ti vad'ella folleg[g]iando,
Ché·ttu no·le puo' far mag[g]ior piacere.

Ma di ciò non dé gir nessun parlando
Se 'n averla non mette su' podere,
Chéd ella se ne va dapoi vantando.

59

Friend[1]

"If the one you desire rejects you,
you don't lose anything because of her rejection,
except for the words you've said to her:
she'll soon regret her rejection.

One woman in a hundred has never been seen
(or even better, I'll bet one in a thousand)
who liked to make such a refusal,
even though she may attack you at the beginning.

Make your amorous request, for at least you'll have her favor,
even though she may say crazy things about you,
for you can't do her any bigger favor.

But no one must say anything about this,
if he fails in his quest to have her,
for afterwards she will go around raving about it."

1. Cf. *Rose*, 7532–7578.

60

Amico

"E quando tu·ssarai co·llei soletto,
Prendila tra·lle braccia e fa 'l sicuro,
Mostrando allor se·ttu·sse' forte e duro,
E 'mantenente le metti il gambetto.

Né no·lla respittar già per su' detto:
S'ella chiede merzé, cheg[g]ala al muro.
Tu·lle dirai: 'Madonna, i' m'assicuro
A questo far, c[h]'Amor m'à·ssì distretto

Di vo', ched i' non posso aver sog[g]iorno;
Per ch'e' convien che vo' ag[g]iate merzede
Di me, che tanto vi son ito intorno;

Ché·ssiate certa ched i' v'amo a fede,
Né d'amar voi giamai no·mmi ritorno,
Ché per voi il me' cor salvar si crede'.

60

Friend[1]

"And when you are all alone with her,
take her in your arms and do it boldly,
revealing then that you are strong and hard,
and immediately trip her up.[2]

Don't give her respite no matter what she says:
if she asks for mercy, let her ask in vain.
You'll tell her: 'Lady, I dare
to do this, for Love has so taken me

with you, that I can have no peace;
therefore, you must have mercy
on me, who have courted you so much.

For you may be sure that I love you loyally,
and that I will never stop loving you,
for my heart believes it can have salvation only from you'."[3]

1. Cf. *Rose*, 7639–7676.

2. As other phrases in this sonnet, the expression *le metti il gambetto* has obvious sexual connotations—something like "put your little leg in her."

3. The idea that the lover (or his heart) can achieve salvation from the lady is common in thirteenth-century Italian poetry: e.g., Giacomo da Lentini's canzone "Meravigliosamente" and Guinizzelli's sonnet "Io voglio del ver la mia donna laudare."

61

Amico

"E se·ttu ami donna ferma e sag[g]ia,
Ben sag[g]iamente e fermo ti contieni,
C[h]'avanti ch'ella dica: 'Amico, tieni
Delle mie gioie', più volte t'asag[g]ia.

E se·ttu ami femina volaggia,
Volag[g]iamente davanti le vieni
E tutt'a la sua guisa ti mantieni;
Od ella ti terrà bestia salvaggia,

E crederà che·ttu sie un papalardo,
Che sie venuto a·llei per inganarla:
Chéd ella il vol pur giovane e gagliardo.

La buona e·ssaggia ma' di ciò non parla,
Anz'ama più l'uon fermo che codardo,
Ché non dotta che que' faccia blasmarla.

61

Friend[1]

"And if you love a constant and wise woman,
behave wisely and constantly;
for before she'll say: 'Friend, take
my jewels,' she'll put you to the test many times.[2]

And if you love a fickle woman,
come before her in a fickle fashion,
and behave just as she does;
if you don't, she'll consider you to be a wild beast,

and believe you to be a hypocrite,[3]
who's come to deceive her;
for she wants someone who's young and hardy.

A good and wise woman never speaks of this;
indeed, she loves a determined man more than a coward,
because she does not fear that he would bring her shame."

1. Cf. *Rose*, 7707–7730.

2. Note the sexual innuendos in the play (*translatio*) on the "jewels," which are thinly veiled allusions to parts of the female anatomy.

3. Two words for "hypocrite" appear in the poem: *pappalardo* and *ipocrita*. The word *pappalardo* (< *pappare* + *lardo*: "to devour fat") derives from the practice of hypocritical religious who would consume prohibited foods during times of fasts.

62

Amico

"Ancor convien che·ttu sacci' alcun'arte
Per governar e te e la tu' amica:
Di buon' morsei tuttor la mi notrica,
E dàlle tuttavia la miglior parte.

E s'ella vuol andar i·nulla parte,
Sì·lle dì: 'Va, che Dio ti benedica';
In gastigarla non durar fatica,
Sed al su' amor non vuo' tagliar le carte.

E se·lla truovi l'opera faccendo,
Non far sembiante d'averla veduta:
In altra parte te ne va fug[g]endo.

E se·lle fosse lettera venuta,
Non t'intrametter d'andar incheg[g]endo
Chi·ll'à recata né chi la saluta.

62

Friend[1]

"Still it's better that you know some rules
in order to govern both yourself and your friend:
nourish her with tender morsels,
and always give her the best part.

And if she wants to go somewhere,
tell her: 'Go, and may God bless you.'
Don't waste your time in reprimanding her,
unless you want to end the relationship.

And if you discover her making love,
don't let on that you saw her,
and go off somewhere else.

And if she were to receive a love letter,
don't bother to go ask her
who brought it or who is sending her greetings."

1. Cf. *Rose*, 8177–8188, 9667–9695.

63

Amico

"S'a scac[c]hi o vero a·ttavole giocassi
Colla tua donna, fa ch'ag[g]ie il pig[g]iore
Del gioco, e dille ch'ell'è la migliore
Dadi-gittante che·ttu mai trovassi.

S'a coderon giocaste, pigna ambassi,
E fa ched ella sia là vincitore:
Della tua perdita non far sentore,
Ma che cortesemente la ti passi.

Falla seder ad alti, e·ttu sie basso,
E sì·ll'aporta carello o cuscino:
Di le' servir non ti veg[g]hi mai lasso.

S'adosso le vedessi un buscolino,
Fa che glie·levi, e se vedessi sasso
Là 'v'ella dé passar, netta 'l camino.

63

Friend[1]

"If you should play chess or backgammon
with your lady, make sure that
you lose and tell her that she's the best
thrower of dice you've ever seen.

And if you should play coderon,[2] throw snake eyes,
and make sure she's the winner:
don't make a fuss over your loss,
but handle it in a courtly manner.

Have her sit in a high place, and you down low,
and bring her a cushion[3] and a pillow;
don't ever let her see you weary of serving her.

If you should see a little speck on her,
make sure that you brush it off, and if you should see a stone
where she must walk, brush off the path."

1. Cf. *Rose*, 7737–7760.
2. Another kind of dice game.
3. The *carello* may be either a square cushion or a small upholstered stool.

64

Amico

"A sua maniera ti mantien tuttora:
Che s'ella ride, ridi, o balla, balla;
O s'ella piange, pensa a consolalla,
Ma fa che pianghe tu sanza dimora.

E se con altre don[n]e fosse ancora
Che giocas[s]ero al gioco della palla,
S'andasse lungi, corri ad aportalla:
A·lle' servir tuttor pensa e lavora.

E se vien alcun'or ch'ella ti tenza,
Ch'ella ti crucci sì che·ttu le dài,
Imantenente torna ad ubidenza;

E giurale che ma' più no'l farai;
Di quel ch'ài fatto farai penitenza;
Prendila e falle il fatto che·tti sai.

64

Friend[1]

"Always behave the way she does:
if she laughs, you laugh, or if she dances, you dance;
and if she cries, attempt to console her,
but make sure that you cry without delay.

And if she should be playing a game of ball
with other women, and the ball
should go far away, run and bring it back to her:
always think and work to serve her.

And if the time comes when she argues with you,
or when she angers you so much that you strike her,
immediately return to obey her,

and swear to her that you'll never do it again;
you will do penance for what you did.
Grab her and do to her what you do best!"[2]

1. Cf. *Rose*, 7689–7706, 9725–9732.
2. Note the thinly veiled erotic innuendo.

65

Amico

"Sovr'ogne cosa pensa di lusinghe,
Lodando sua maniera e sua faz[z]one,
E che di senno passa Salamone:
Con questi motti vo' che·lla dipinghe.

Ma guarda non s'aveg[g]a che·tt'infinghe,
Ché non v'andresti mai a processione;
Non ti var[r]eb[b]e lo star ginoc[c]hione:
Però quel lusingar fa che tu 'l tinghe.

Chéd e' n'è ben alcuna sì viziata
Che non crede già mai ta' favolelle,
Perc[h]'altra volta n'è stata beffata;

Ma queste giovanette damigelle,
Cu' la lor terra nonn-è stata arata,
Ti crederanno ben cotà' novelle.

65

Friend[1]

"Above all, think about flattery,
praising her manners and her appearance,
and how she passes Solomon in wisdom:
with these words I want you to describe her.

But be careful she doesn't notice you're pretending,
because you would never go there in procession,[2]
nor would it serve you to kneel in front of her:
therefore, be sure to disguise your flattery well.

There's always a woman so clever
she never believes such tales,
because she was once deceived by them.

But these young ladies,
whose field has never been plowed,
will certainly believe such stories from you."[3]

1. Cf. *Rose*, 7453–7456.

2. That is, to ask for forgiveness and pardon.

3. For the sexual imagery associated with plowing and related activities, see Introduction and sonnets 9 and 230.

66

Amico

"Se·ttu ài altra amica procacciata,
O ver che·ttu la guardi a procac[c]iare,
E sì non vuo' per ciò abandonare
La prima cu' à' lungo tempo amata,

Se·ttu a la novella à' gioia donata,
Sì dì ch'ella la guardi di recare
In luogo ove la prima ravisare
No·lla potesse, ché seria smembrata.

O s'ella ancor ne fosse in sospez[z]one,
Fa saramenta ch'ella t'ag[g]ia torto,
C[h]'unque ver' lei non fosti i·mesprigione;

E s'ella il pruova, convien che sie acorto
A dir che forza fu e tradigione:
Allor la prendi e sì·lle 'nnaffia l'orto.

66

Friend[1]

"If you have found another female friend,
or if you are trying to get one,
and you don't want for this reason to abandon
the first woman whom you've loved for some time,

and if you've given a jewel to the new woman,
tell her to be careful not to wear it
in a place where the first woman might see
and recognize it, for she would be cut into pieces.

Now, if the first woman were still suspicious,
swear that she's wrong about you,
that you would never misbehave in her regard.

And if she can prove it, you must be quick
to say it happened by force and treachery:
then grab her and water her garden."[2]

1. Cf. *Rose*, 9745–9820.
2. Note the continuation of the highly sexual image.

67

Amico

"E se·ttua donna cade i·mmalatia,
Sì pensa che·lla faccie ben servire,
Né·ttu da·llei giamai non ti partire;
Dàlle vivanda c[h]'a piacer le sia;

E po' sì·lle dirai: 'Anima mia,
Istanotte ti tenni i·mmio dormire
intra·lle braccia, sana, al me' disire:
Molto mi fece Idio gran cortesia,

Che mi mostrò sì dolze avisïone'.
Po' dica, ch'ella l'oda, come sag[g]io,
Che per lẹi farà' far gran processione,

O·ttu n'andrà' in lontan pellegrinag[g]io,
Se Gesocristo le dà guerigione.
Così avrai il su' amor e 'l su' corag[g]io".

67

Friend[1]

"And if your lady becomes ill,
make sure that she's served well,
and never leave her side:
give her food that she likes;

and then you'll say to her: 'My soul,
last night in my dream I held you
in my arms, completely cured, as I hoped and prayed:
certainly God granted me a great favor,

when he showed me such a sweet vision.'
Then say, as a wise man would, so that she may hear,
that for her you'll have a great ceremony performed,

or that you'll go on a long pilgrimage,
if Jesus Christ heals her.
Thus, you'll have her love and her heart."

1. Cf. *Rose*, 9839–9864.

68

L'Amante e Amico

Quand'eb[b]i inteso Amico che leale
Consiglio mi d[on]ava a su' podere,
I' sì·lli dissi: "Amico, il mi' volere
Non fu unquanche d'esser disleale;

Né piaccia a Dio ch'i' sia condotto a tale
Ch'i' a le genti mostri benvolere
E servali del corpo e dell'avere,
Ch[ed] i' pensas[s]e poi di far lor male.

Ma sòffera ch'i' avante disfidi
E Mala-Bocca e tutta sua masnada,
Sì che neuno i·mme giamai si fidi;

Po' penserò di metterli a la spada".
Que' mi rispuose: "Amico, mal ti guidi.
Cotesta sì nonn-è la dritta strada.

68

Lover and Friend[1]

When I had listened to the faithful counsel
that Friend gave me, to the best of his ability,
I said to him: "Friend, my wish
was never to be disloyal.

Nor may it please God that I be led to such a point
that I show kindness to people
and offer them myself and my possessions,
and then that I would think of doing harm to them.

But first of all let me challenge
Bad Mouth and all his gang,[2]
so that they will know where I stand.

Then I'll find a way to put them to the sword."
Friend answered me: "Friend, you are mistaken:
this is not the right road."

1. Cf. *Rose*, 7765–7788.
2. I.e., Resistance, Shame, and Fear.

69

Amico

"A te sì non convien far disfidaglia,
Se·ttu vuo' ben civir di questa guerra:
Lasciala far a' gran' signor' di terra,
Che posson sof[f]erir oste e battaglia.

Mala-Bocca, che così ti travaglia,
È traditor: chi 'l tradisce non erra;
Chi con falsi sembianti no·ll'aferra,
il su' buon gioco mette a ripentaglia.

Se·ttu lo sfidi o batti, e' griderà,
Chéd egli è di natura di mastino:
Chi più 'l minaccia, più gli abaierà.

Chi Mala-Bocca vuol metter al chino,
Sed egli è sag[g]io, egli lusingherà:
Ché certo sie, quell'è 'l dritto camino".

69

Friend[1]

"You must not make this challenge,
if you want to end this war well.
Let the great lords of the land do it,
those who can afford the army and battles!

Bad Mouth, who so torments you,
is a traitor: whoever betrays him makes no mistake;
whoever does not capture him with false appearances,
puts at risk his own good game.

If you challenge or strike him, he will howl,
for his nature is of that of a watch-dog:
the more he's threatened, the more he'll bark.

Whoever wants to conquer Bad Mouth,
will flatter him, if he's wise,
for certainly that is the proper road."

1. Cf. *Rose*, 7789–7846.

70

L'Amante e Amico

"Po' mi convien ovrar di tradigione
E a·tte pare, Amico, ch'i' la faccia,
I' la farò, come ch'ella mi spiaccia,
Per venir al di su di quel cagnone.

Ma sì·tti priego, gentil compagnone,
Se·ssai alcuna via che·ssia più avaccia
Per Mala-Bocca e' suo' metter in caccia
E trar Bellacoglienza di pregione,

Che·ttu sì·lla mi insegni, ed i' v'andrò
E menerò comeco tal aiuto
Ched i' quella fortez[z]a abatterò".

"E' nonn-à guari ch'i' ne son venuto",
Rispuose Amico, "ma 'l ver ti dirò,
Che·ss'i' v'andai, i' me ne son pentuto.

70

Lover and Friend[1]

"Since it suits my purpose to act treacherously,
and you think, Friend, that I should,
I will do so, even though I find it unpleasant,
in order to overcome that ugly watch-dog.[2]

But I beg you, noble companion,
if you know a quicker route
to chase away Bad Mouth and all his associates[3]
and to release Fair Welcome from prison,

show it to me, and I will go that way
and take with me such powerful help
that I'll bring that fortress down."

"I have just returned from there,"
answered Friend, "but I'll tell you the truth,
that as sure as I went that way, I have regretted it."

1. Cf. *Rose*, 7847–7854, 7869–7872.
2. Note the canine terminology to describe Bad Mouth: *mastino* (sonnet 69, v. 10).
3. Cf. sonnet 68, v. 10.

71

Amico

"L'uom'apella il camin Troppo-Donare;
E' fu fondato per Folle-Larghez[z]a;
L'entrata guarda madonna Ric[c]hez[z]a,
Che non i lascia nessun uon passare,

S'e' nonn-è su' parente o su' compare:
Già tanto nonn-avreb[b]e in sé bellez[z]a,
Cortesia né saver né gentilez[z]a,
Ched ella gli degnasse pur parlare.

Se puo' per quel camin trovar passag[g]io,
Tu·ssì abatterà' tosto il castello,
Bellacoglienza trarà' di servag[g]io.

Non vi varrà gittar di manganello,
Néd a le guardie lor folle musag[g]io,
Porte né mura, né trar di quadrello.

71

Friend[1]

"That road is called Extravagance,
and it was built by Foolish Generosity;
Lady Wealth guards the entrance
and lets no one pass,

if that person is not her relative or friend.
No matter how much beauty he might have,
or how much courtesy or wisdom or nobility,
she would not even deign to speak with him.

If you can find a way to go along that road,
you will quickly demolish the castle
and free Fair Welcome from prison.

A catapult will be of no help there,
nor will their foolish surveillance serve the guards,
not doors or walls or the shooting of darts."

1. Cf. *Rose*, 7866–7867, 7873–7882, 7913–7914.

72

Amico

"Or sì·tt'ò detto tutta la sentenza
Di ciò che·ssag[g]io amante far dovria:
Così l'amor di lor guadagneria,
Sanz'aver mai tra·llor malivoglienza.

Se mai trai di pregion Bellacoglienza,
Sì fa che·ttu ne tenghi questa via,
Od altrimenti mai non t'ameria,
Che ch'ella ti mostrasse in aparenza.

E dàlle spazio di poter andare
Colà dove le piace per la villa;
Pena perduta seria in le' guardare:

Ché·ttu ter[r]esti più tosto un'anguilla
Ben viva per la coda, e fossi i·mmare,
Che non faresti femina che ghilla".

72

Friend[1]

"Now I've summarized for you the main points
of what a wise lover should do:
in this way he will earn their love,
without there ever being enmity among them.

If you succeed in freeing Fair Welcome from prison,
make sure that you keep to this path,
or else she would never love you,
no matter how much she might appear to do so.

And give her freedom to be able to go
wherever she likes in the city;
it would be wasted effort to try to keep tabs on her.

For you could more easily hold
a live eel by the tail, even if you were in the sea,
than you would be able to handle a wily woman."

1. Cf. *Rose*, 8215–8243, 9873–9886, 9957–9962.

73

L'Amante

Così mi confortò il buon Amico,
Po' si partì da me sanza più dire;
Allor mi comincià' fort'a gechire
Ver' Mala-Bocca, il mi' crudel nemico.

Lo Schifo i' sì pregiava men ch'un fico,
Ch'egli avea gran talento di dormire;
Vergogna si volea ben sofferire
Di guer[r]eg[g]iarmi, per certo vi dico.

Ma e' v'era Paura, la dottosa,
C[h]'udendomi parlar tutta tremava:
Quella nonn-era punto dormigliosa;

In ben guardar il fior molto pensava;
Vie più che·ll'altre guardi' era curiosa,
Perciò che ben in lor non si fidava.

73

Lover

In this way my good Friend comforted me;
then he left without another word.
At that point I began to be very humble
towards Bad Mouth, my cruel enemy.

I didn't give a hoot about Resistance,
who had a great desire to sleep;
Modesty truly wanted to abstain
from battling me, I tell you this for sure.

But there was Fear, the fearful one,
who, hearing me speak, trembled all over:
that one was not sleepy at all;

she took great care in guarding the Flower,
and she was more zealous than the other guards,
since she placed no trust in them at all.

74

L'Amante

Intorno dal castello andai cercando
Sed i' potesse trovar quel[l]'entrata
La qual Folle-Larghez[z]a avea fondata,
Per avacciar ciò che giva pensando.

Allor guardai, e sì vidi ombreando
Di sotto un pin una donna pregiata,
Sì nobilmente vestita e parata
Che tutto 'l mondo gia di lei parlando.

E sì avea in sé tanta bel[l]ez[z]a
Che tutto intorno lei aluminava
Col su' visag[g]io, tanto avea chiarez[z]a;

Ed un suo amico co·llei si posava.
La donna sì avea nome Ric[c]hez[z]a,
Ma·llui non so com'altri l'apellava.

74

Lover[1]

All around the castle I went looking
to see if I could find the entrance
that Foolish Generosity had built,
in order to speed up what I was plotting.

Then I looked, and in the shadows
under a pine tree, I saw a worthy lady,
so nobly dressed and adorned
that everyone was speaking about her.

And she was so beautiful
that she illuminated everything around her
with her face, so resplendent it was;

and a friend was resting there with her.
The lady's name was Wealth,
but I do not know what the man's name was.

1. Cf. *Rose*, 9985–10030.

75

L'Amante e Ric[c]hez[z]a

Col capo inchin la donna salutai,
E sì·lla cominciai a domandare
Del camin c[h]'uomo apella Troppo-Dare.
Quella rispose: "Già per me no'l sai;

E se 'l sapessi, già non vi 'nterrai,
Chéd i' difendo a ciaschedun l'entrare
Sed e' nonn-à che spender e che dare,
Sì farai gran saver se·tte ne vai:

C[h]'unquanche non volesti mi' acontanza,
Né mi pregiasti mai a la tua vita.
Ma or ne prenderò buona vengianza:

Ché sie certano, se·ttu m'ài schernita,
i' ti darò tormento e malenanza,
Sì ch'e' me' ti var[r]ia avermi servita".

75

Lover and Wealth[1]

With bowed head I greeted the lady,
and then began to ask her
about the path that's called Extravagance.
She answered: "You'll never know it from me;

and even if you were to know it, you will never enter there,
because I forbid entrance to everyone,
except to those who have the means to spend and spend some more.
So if you're smart, you'll leave,

for you never desired my friendship,
nor have you ever praised me in your life.
But now I'll take my sweet revenge:

for rest assured that just as you scorned me,
so I'll give you such torment and unhappiness,
that it would be better for you to have served me."

1. Cf. *Rose*, 10033–10054.

76

L'Amante e Ric[c]hez[z]a

"Per Dio, gentil madonna, e per merzede",
Le' dissi allor, "s'i' ò ver' voi fallato,
Ched e' vi piaccia ched e' sia amendato
Per me, chéd i' 'l farò a buona fede:

Ch'i' son certan che 'l vostro cuor non crede
Com'io dentro dal mio ne son crucciato;
Ma quando vo' m'avrete ben provato,
E' sarà certo di ciò c[h]'or non vede.

Per ch'i' vi priego che mi diate il passo,
Ched i' potesse abatter il castello
Di Gelosia, che m'à sì messo al basso".

Quella mi disse: "Tu se' mio ribello;
Per altra via andrai, ché sarà' lasso
Innanzi che n'abatti un sol crinello".

76

Lover and Wealth[1]

"For God's sake, gentle lady, and in mercy's name,"
I said to her then, "if I have wronged you,
please grant that I may make amends,
for this I'll do in good faith.

For I am sure your heart does not know
how my own heart is afflicted;
but when you've put me to the test,
your heart will be sure of that which now it does not see.[2]

For this reason I beg you to let me pass,
so that I can bring down the castle
of Jealousy, who has laid me low."

She said to me: "You are my enemy;
along another path you will go, for you will be exhausted
before you knock down a single crenellation on the tower."

1. Cf. *Rose*, 10201–10210.

2. Note the parody of the theological definition of faith as found in Paul's letter to the Hebrews: "Now faith is the substance of things hoped for, the evidence of things not seen" (11:1).

77

L'Amante e Dio d'Amore

Già no·mi valse nessuna preghera
Ched i' verso Ric[c]hez[z]a far potesse,
Ché poco parve che le ne calesse,
Sì la trovai ver' me crudel e fera.

Lo Dio d'Amor, che guar' lungi no·mm'era,
Mi riguardò com'io mi contenesse,
E parvemi ched e' gli ne increscesse;
Sì venne a me e disse: "In che manera,

Amico, m'ài guardato l'omanag[g]io
Che mi facesti, passat'à un anno?".
I' gli dissi: "Messer, vo' avete il gag[g]io

Or, ch'è il core". "E' non ti fia già danno,
Ché tu·tti se' portato come sag[g]io,
Sì avrai guiderdon del grande afanno".

77

Lover and the God of Love[1]

No prayer I made to Wealth
did me any good,
for it seemed she cared very little,
so cruel and heartless I found her towards me.

The God of Love, who was not far from me,
looked to see how I was faring,
and it seemed to me my manner annoyed him.
He came to me and said: "In what way,

friend, have you kept the oath of fealty
you made to me a year ago?"
I said to him: "Sire, you have my pledge,

which is my heart."—"It will be all right,
since you have behaved with wisdom and skill,
you will have reward for your great distress."[2]

1. Cf. *Rose*, 10277–10365, 10539–10632.

2. The term *guiderdone* ("reward") is a key term in the courtly tradition, indicating the compensation that the lover receives from the lady for his faithful service.

78

L'Amante

Lo Dio d'Amor per tutto 'l regno manda
Messag[g]i e lettere a la baronia:
Che davanti da lui ciaschedun sia,
Ad alcun priega e ad alcun comanda;

E ch'e' vorrà far lor una domanda
La qual fornita converrà che·ssia:
D'abatter il castel di Gelosia,
Sì ch'e' non vi dimori inn-uscio banda.

Al giorno ciaschedun si presentò,
Presto di far il su' comandamento:
Dell'armadure ciaschedun pensò,

Per dar a Gelosia pene e tormento.
La baronia i' sì vi nomerò
Secondo ched i' ò rimembramento.

78

Lover[1]

Throughout the kingdom the God of Love sends
messengers and letters to all the barons;
some he entreats and others he commands
that they come to him.

He will wish to make a request of them,
a request that must be fulfilled:
to bring down Jealousy's castle,
so that not one iron band remains on the door.

On the great day, everyone presented himself,
ready to do the God of Love's command:
each one gave thought to the arms

to give Jealousy pain and torment.
I will name the Barons for you
insofar as I remember them.

1. Cf. *Rose*, 10409–10418.

79

La baronia d'Amore

Madonna Oziosa venne la primiera
Con Nobiltà-di-Cuor e con Ric[c]hezza:
Franchigia, Cortesia, Pietà, Larghez[z]a,
Ardimento e Onor, ciaschedun v'era.

Diletto e Compagnia seguian la schiera;
Angelicanza, Sicurtà e Letezza
E Solaz[z]o e Bieltate e Giovanez[z]a
Andavan tutte impresso la bandera.

Ancor v'era Umiltate e Pacïenza;
Giolività vi fue e Ben-Celare
E Falsembiante e Costretta-Astinenza.

Amor si cominciò a maravigliare
Po' vide Falsembiante in sua presenza,
E disse: "Chi·ll'à tolto a sicurare?".

79

The Barons of Love[1]

Lady Leisure was in the first line
with Noble Heart and with Wealth;
Sincerity, Courtesy, Mercy, Generosity,
Boldness and Honor, all of them were there.

Delight and Social Grace followed in the company;
Angel-Like, Safety, and Happiness
and Joy and Beauty and Youth
were all following the banner.

Then came Humility and Patience;
Joyfulness was there and Well-Hidden
and False Seeming and Forced Abstinence.

Love was astonished
to see False Seeming in his presence,
and said: "Who's vouched for him?"

1. Cf. *Rose*, 10419–10430, 10445–10449.

80

Costretta-Astinenza

Astinenza-Costretta venne avanti,
E disse: "E' vien comeco in compagnia,
Ché sanza lui civir no·mmi poria,
Tanto non pregherei né Die né ' santi;

E me e sé governa co' sembianti
Che gli 'nsegnò sua madre Ipocresia.
I' porto il manto di papalardia
Per più tosto venir a tempo a' guanti.

E così tra noi due ci governiamo
E nostra vita dimeniàn gioiosa,
Sanza dir cosa mai che noi pensiamo.

La ciera nostra par molto pietosa,
Ma nonn-è mal nes[s]un che non pensiamo,
Ben paià·noi gente relegïosa".

80

Forced Abstinence[1]

Forced Abstinence came forward
and said: "He comes as my companion,
because without him, I could not provide for myself,
no matter how much I might pray to God and the Saints.

He governs himself and me according to the ways
his mother Hypocrisy taught him.
I wear the mantle of hypocrisy
in order to gain my rewards more quickly.

And thus we look after each other
and lead a happy life,
without ever saying what we really think.

Our appearance seems very pious,
but there's no evil act that we don't conceive,
although we appear to be religious folk."

1. Cf. *Rose*, 10439–10444, 10450–10462.

81

Dio d'Amor e Falsembiante

Lo Dio d'Amor sor[r]ise, quando udìo
Astinenza-Costretta sì parlare,
E disse: "Qui à gente d'alt'affare!
Dì, Falsembiante, se·tt'aiuti Idio,

S'i' ti ritegno del consiglio mio,
Mi potrò io in te punto fidare?".
"Segnor mio sì, di nulla non dottare,
Ch'altro c[h]'a lealtà ma' non pens'io".

"Dunqu'è cotesto contra tua natura".
"Veracemente ciò è veritate,
Ma tuttor vi met[t]ete in aventura!

Mai i·lupo di sua pelle non gittate,
No·gli farete tanto di laidura,
Se voi imprima no·llo scorticate".

81

The God of Love and False Seeming[1]

The God of Love smiled when he heard
Forced Abstinence speak in this way,
and said: "We've got some big shots here!
Tell me, False Seeming, may God help you,

if I keep you on my council,
will I be able to trust you at all?"
"Yes, my Lord, don't worry about a thing,
for I don't think of anything but loyalty."

"Therefore, this is against your nature."
"To be truthful, this is the truth,
but nonetheless you are putting yourself at risk!

No matter how many bad things you do to it,
you'll never remove a wolf from its hide,
unless you skin it first."

1. Cf. *Rose*, 11947–11968.

82

Dio d'Amore

Amor disse a' baroni: "I' v'ò mandato
Perch'e' convien ch'i' ag[g]ia il vostro aiuto,
Tanto che quel castel si' abattuto
Che Gelosia di nuovo à già fondato.

Onde ciascun di voi è mi' giurato:
Sì vi richeg[g]io che sia proveduto
Per voi in tal maniera che tenuto
Non sia più contra me, ma si' aterrato.

Ch'e' pur convien ch'i' soccorra Durante,
Chéd i' gli vo' tener sua promessione,
Ché trop[p]o l'ò trovato fin amante.

Molto penò di tòr[r]elmi Ragione:
Que' come sag[g]io fu sì fermo e stante
Che no·lle valse nulla su' sermone".

82

The God of Love[1]

Love said to the Barons: "I've sent for you
because I need your help
until that castle is brought down,
the one that Jealousy recently built.

Since each one of you is my sworn ally,
I ask you to act
in such a way that the castle
may no longer stand against me, but that it be leveled to the ground.

For I must help Durante,[2]
since I want to keep my promise to him,
for I have found him to be a very refined lover.

Reason tried very hard to take him away from me;
but that one was so wise and tenacious and constant
that Reason's speech had no effect at all."

1. Cf. *Rose*, 10463–10648.

2. This is the first time the name of the poem's character-narrator—the lover, Amante—appears in the text.

83

Il consiglio della baronia

La baronia sì fece parlamento
Per devisar in che maniera andranno
O la qual porta prima assaliranno;
Sì fur ben tutti d'un acordamento,

Fuor che Ric[c]hez[z]a, che fe' saramento
Ch'ella non prendereb[b]e per me affanno,
Néd al castel non dareb[b]e già danno
Per pregheria né per comandamento

Che nessuna persona far potesse,
Perciò ch'i' non volli anche sua contezza:
Sì era dritto ch'i' me ne pentesse.

Ben disse ch'i' le feci gran carezza
Sotto dal pin, ma non c[h]'ancor vedesse
Che Povertà no·m'avesse in distrezza.

83

The Council of the Barons[1]

The Barons met together
to decide how they would proceed,
or which gate they would attack first.
On this they were all in agreement,

except for Wealth, who pledged
that she would neither trouble herself for me,
nor would she do any harm to the castle,
no matter how many prayers or orders

might be given,
because I never wanted her friendship:
it was right that I should repent for that.

Indeed, she allowed that I showed her great respect
under the pine tree, but she still saw
that Poverty had me in the straits.

1. Cf. *Rose*, 10649–10686.

84

L'ordinanze delle battaglie de la baronia

Al Die d'Amor ricordaro il fatto,
E disser ch'e' trovavar d'acordanza
Che Falsembiante e Costretta-Astinanza
Dessono a Mala-Bocca scacco matto;

Larghez[z]a e Cortesia traes[s]er patto
Con quella che·ssa ben la vec[c]hia danza,
E Pietate e Franchez[z]a dear miccianza
A quello Schifo che sta sì 'norsato;

E po' vada Diletto e Ben-Celare,
Ed a Vergogna dean tal lastrellata
Ched ella non si possa rilevare;

Ardimento a Paura dea ghignata,
E Sicurtà la deg[g]ia sì pelare
Ched ella non vi sia ma' più trovata.

84

The Battle Plan of the Barons[1]

They went over the plan with the God of Love
and told him they agreed
that False Seeming and Forced Abstinence
would give Bad Mouth the coup de grace.

Generosity and Lady Courtesy would make a deal
with that one who knows the old dance well,[2]
and Mercy and Sincerity would give problems
to Resistance who is so fierce.

And then Delight and Well-Hidden will advance
and deal a mighty blow to Modesty
so that she cannot get up.

And Boldness will make fun of Fear,
and Safety should flay her so severely
that she'll no longer be found there.

1. Cf. *Rose*, 10689–10708.

2. The reference is to the old woman, the *Vecchia*, who is the guardian of Fair Welcome and who knows the amorous arts.

85

Lo Dio d'Amore

Amor rispuose: "A me sì piace assai
Che l'oste avete bene istabulita;
Ma·ttu, Ric[c]hez[z]a, c[h]'or mi se' fallita,
Sed i' potrò, tu·tte ne penterai.

S'uomini ric[c]hi i' posso tener mai,
Non poss'io già star un giorno in vita,
S'avanti che da me facciar partita
Non recherò a poco il loro assai.

Uomini pover' fatt'ànno lor sire
Di me, e ciaschedun m'à dato il core:
Per ch'a tal don mi deg[g]io ben sofrire.

Se di ric[c]hez[z]a sì come d'amore
I' fosse dio, non possa io ben sentire
Sed i' no·gli mettesse in gran riccore".

85

The God of Love[1]

Love answered: "It pleases me greatly
that you have organized the army so well;
but you, Wealth, since you have failed me,
If I'm able, you'll regret your action.

If I'm ever able to have rich men in my control,
may I not live one more day,
if I don't diminish their possessions from great to small
before they take their leave from me.

Poor men have taken me as their Lord,
and each one has given me his heart;
thus I must be content with such a gift.

If I were the god of riches as I am of love,
I would be unhappy
if I could not make them extremely rich."

1. Cf. *Rose*, 10817–10856.

86

La risposta de la baronia

"S'uomini ric[c]hi vi fanno damag[g]io,
Vo' avete ben chi ne farà vendetta:
Non fate forza s'ella non s'afretta,
Ché no' la pagherén ben de l'oltrag[g]io.

Le donne e le pulzelle al chiar visag[g]io
Gli metteranno ancor a tal distretta,
Ma' che ciascuna largo si prometta,
Che strutto ne sarà que' ch'è 'l più sag[g]io.

Ma Falsembiante trametter non s'osa
Di questi fatti, né sua compagnia,
Ché gra·mmal gli volete: ciò ci posa.

Sì vi priega tutta la baronia
Che·riceviate, e [a]menderà la cosa".
"Da po' che vo' volete, e così sia".

86

The Response of the Barons[1]

"If rich men do you harm,
you certainly have those who will avenge you.
Don't worry if this does not come rapidly,
because we'll pay her[2] back for her offence.

Women and young ladies with radiant faces
will put the wealthy in such distress,
that even the most savvy of them will be destroyed,
provided that each woman exacts extravagant promises for herself.

But False Seeming and his friend[3]
will not dare to take part in these matters,
because you despise them: this displeases us.

Therefore, the assembled barony asks
you to welcome them, and the situation will be put right."
"Since you wish it, so it will be done."

1. Cf. *Rose*, 10857–10897.
2. I.e., Wealth.
3. I.e., Forced Abstinence.

87

Amore

Amor sì disse: "Per cotal convento,
Falso-Sembiante, i·mmia corte enter[r]ai,
Che tutti i nostri amici avanzerai
E metterai i nemici in bassamento.

E sì·tti do per buon cominciamento
Che re de' barattier' tu sì sarai:
Ché pez[z]'à che 'n capitolo il fermai,
Ch'i' conoscëa ben tu' tradimento.

Or sì vo' che·cci dichi in audïenza,
Pe·ritrovarti se n'avrén mestiere,
I·luogo dove tu·ffai residenza,

Né di che servi, né di che mestiere.
Fa che n'ag[g]iàn verace conoscenza;
Ma no'l farai, sì·sse' mal barattiere".

87

Love[1]

Thus Love said: "False Seeming,
on this condition you will enter my court:
you will assist all of our allies
and put our enemies down.

And to begin this business, I confer on you
the title of king of deceivers;
I decided this some time ago in council,
for I was well acquainted with your treacherous ways.

Now I want you to tell us in this hearing
where you dwell
in case we have to find you,

and tell us what you do and how you do it.
Make sure we understand these things well,
and if you don't, you're truly an evil cheat."

1. Cf. *Rose*, 10898–10921.

88

Falsembiante

"Po' ch'e' vi piace, ed i' sì 'l vi diròe",
Diss'alor Falsembiante: "or ascoltate,
Chéd i' sì vi dirò la veritate
De·luogo dov'io uso e dov'i' stoe.

Alcuna volta per lo secol voe,
Ma dentro a' chiostri fug[g]o in salvitate,
Ché quivi poss'io dar le gran ghignate
E tuttor santo tenuto saròe.

Il fatto a' secolari è troppo aperto:
Lo star guari co·lor no·mmi bisogna,
C[h]'a me convien giucar troppo coperto.

Perch'i' la mia malizia mi ripogna,
Vest'io la roba del buon frate Alberto:
Chi tal rob'àe, non teme mai vergogna.

88

False Seeming[1]

"Since it is your pleasure, I'll tell you all you want,"
False Seeming said then. "Now listen,
for I'll tell you the truth
about the place I frequent and where I stay.

Sometimes I mix with the laity,
but I flee to the cloisters for safety,
for there I can be a great mocker
and will always be regarded as a saint.

Lay brothers' work is way too open:
I don't need to associate with them a lot,
for I have to play my game in great secrecy.

In order to hide my wickedness,
I don the habit of the good brother Albert.[2]
Whoever wears that garb never fears shame."

1. Cf. *Rose*, 10969–10992.

2. False Seeming is dressed in the same habit as Albert the Great (ca. 1200–ca. 1280), a philosopher and theologian of the Dominican Order. Albert took an active role in opposing William of St. Amour and his radical views on the mendicant orders (see sonnet 92).

89

Falsembiante

"I' sì mi sto con que' religïosi,
Religïosi no, se non in vista,
Che·ffan la ciera lor pensosa e trista
Per parer a le genti più pietosi;

E sì si mostran molto sofrettosi
E 'n tapinando ciaschedun a[c]quista:
Sì che perciò mi piace lor amista,
C[h]'a barattar son tutti curïosi.

Po' vanno procacciando l'acontanze
Di ric[c]he genti, e van[n]ole seguendo,
E sì voglion mangiar le gran pietanze,

E' prezïosi vin' vanno bevendo:
E queste son le lor grandi astinanze;
Po' van la povertà altrui abellendo.

89

False Seeming[1]

"So I pass my time with those religious—
well, religious only in appearance—
those who make their face seem sad and anguished,
in order to appear more pious to the people.

And they show themselves to be in need,
and through begging each one reaps and profits:[2]
therefore, I like their friendship,
for they are all very eager to deceive.

Then they go seeking friendship
with wealthy people and follow after them,
because they want to eat great delicacies

and drink high quality wines.
This is the way they practice great abstinence!
And then they go about praising poverty to others."

1. Cf. *Rose*, 10993–11017.

2. The Dominicans and Franciscans—the two mendicant orders—both relied on alms for their maintenance.

90

Falsembiante

"E' sì vanno lodando la poverta,
E le ric[c]hez[z]e pescan co' tramagli,
Ed ivi mettor tutti lor travagli,
Tutto si cuoprar e' d'altra coverta.

Di lor non puo' tu trare cosa certa:
Se·ttu lor presti, me' val a chitarli;
Che se·ttu metti pena in ra[c]quistarli,
Ciascun di lor si ferma in darti perta.

E ciascun dice ch'è religïoso
Perché vesta di sopra grossa lana,
E 'l morbido bianchetto tien nascoso;

Ma già religïone ivi non grana,
Ma grana nel cuor umile e piatoso
Che 'n trar sua vita mette pena e ana.

90

False Seeming[1]

"And so they go about praising poverty,
and they fish for riches with special nets,
and there they put all their labor,
although they cover themselves with a different cloak.

From them you can not expect anything certain:
if you lend them money, it's better just to write it off;[2]
for if you struggle to get your money back,
they are all intent on giving you a loss.

And each one says he's religious,
because he dresses in rough wool cloth,
and keeps the soft white cloth hidden underneath.

To be sure, religion does not prosper there,
but it prospers in the humble and pious heart
that assumes pain and anguish as it goes through life."

1. Cf. *Rose*, 11017–11019, 11022–11028.

2. The literal sense of the phrase is that it is better to give them, at the same time, a receipt (*quietanza* < the verb *chitare*) showing the amount loaned as paid in full.

91

Falsembiante

"Com'i' v'ò detto, in cuore umile e piano
Santa religïon grana e fiorisce:
Religïoso non si inorgoglisce;
Tuttora il truova l'uon dolce e umano.

A cotal gente i' sì do tosto mano,
Ché vita di nessun no·mm'abelisce
Se non inganna e baratta e tradisce;
Ma 'l più ch'i' posso, di lor sì mi strano,

Ché con tal gente star ben non potrei;
C[h]'a voi, gentil signor, ben dire l'oso,
Che s'i' vi stes[s]e, i' sì mi 'nfignirei.

E però il mi' volere i' sì vi chioso,
Che pender prima i' sì mi lascierei
Ched i' uscisse fuor di mi' proposo.

91

False Seeming[1]

"As I've told you, in the humble and modest heart
holy religion prospers and flourishes;
a truly religious man is not proud,
but always kind and mild.

To people such as these I yield,
for the only kind of life I like
is that of one who deceives and cheats and betrays;
and so I stay as far away from them as I can,

for I could not associate with that kind of people;
I can tell you, noble Lord,
that if I were with them, I would surely have to pretend.

Therefore, I gloss for you my desire:
I would rather let myself be hanged
before I would stray from my purpose."

1. Cf. *Rose*, 10997–11006.

92

Fa[l]sembiante

"Color con cuï sto sì ànno il mondo
Sotto da lor sì forte aviluppato,
Ched e' nonn-è nes[s]un sì gran prelato
C[h]'a lor possanza truovi riva o fondo.

Co·mmio baratto ciaschedun afondo:
Che sed e' vien alcun gra·litterato
Che voglia discovrir il mi' peccato,
Co·la forza ch'i' ò, i' sì 'l confondo.

Mastro Sighier non andò guari lieto:
A ghiado il fe' morire a gran dolore
Nella corte di Roma, ad Orbivieto.

Mastro Guiglielmo, il buon di Sant'Amore,
Fec'i' di Francia metter in divieto
E sbandir del reame a gran romore.

False Seeming[1]

"Those with whom I pass my time have so firmly
ensnared the world beneath their feet
that there is no great prelate
who can set limits to their power.[2]

With my trickery I sink each one of them,
and if an important man of letters comes along
who wants to show my sin for what it is,
I can confound him with the powers I have.

Master Siger did not meet a happy end:[3]
with a sword I made him die with great pain
in the court of Rome, at Orvieto.

As for Master William, the good man of Saint-Amour,[4]
I had the prohibition placed on him in France
and had him exiled from the realm with great outcry."

1. Cf. *Rose*, 11453–11478.

2. The literal sense of the phrase is "who can find a shore or a bottom for their power."

3. The philosopher Siger of Brabant (ca. 1240–ca. 1280/84) taught at the University of Paris where he promoted Averroist thought. His views were opposed by Bonaventure and Thomas Aquinas, and his works received two condemnations by Étienne Tempier, bishop of Paris, in 1270 and 1277. Siger was summoned to appear before Simon du Val, inquisitor of France, on October 23, 1276, but he had already fled Paris to go plead his case before the Pope. Siger was killed by his servant in Orvieto, where Pope Martin IV and the papal curia were residing.

4. The thirteenth-century theologian William of St. Amour was a secular master at the University of Paris. He was strongly opposed to the mendicant orders, which he saw as precursors of Antichrist, and his treatise on this subject, *Tractatus brevis de periculis novissimorum temporum* (1255), was countered by Albert the Great and eventually condemned. In 1256 William was relieved of his position and exiled by Pope Alexander IV.

93

Falso-Sembiante

"I' sì vo per lo mondo predicando
E dimostrando di far vita onesta;
Ogne mi' fatto sì vo' far a sesta,
E gli altrui penso andar aviluppando.

Ma chi venisse il fatto riguardando,
Ed egli avesse alquanto sale in testa,
Veder potreb[b]e in che 'l fatto si ne-sta,
Ma no'l consiglierè' andarne parlando.

Ché que' che dice cosa che mi spiaccia,
O vero a que' che seguor mi' penone,
E' convien che·ssia morto o messo in caccia,

Sanza trovar in noi mai ridenzione
Né per merzé né per cosa ch'e' faccia:
E' pur convien ch'e' vada a distruzione".

93

False Seeming[1]

"And so I go through the world preaching[2]
and giving the appearance of leading an honest life;
everything I do, I want to do perfectly,
and I try to screw up what others are doing.

But whoever would look at this matter,
if he had enough salt in his brain,
should be able to see things the way they are,
but I would not advise him to go around talking about it.

For the one who says things that displease either me
or those who follow my banner,
must either be killed or exiled,

without ever gaining our forgiveness,
either through grace or through his actions:
he must certainly go to his destruction."

1. Cf. *Rose*, 10927–10945, 11033–11052.
2. The Dominicans belong to the preaching order (*Ordo Praedicandi*).

94

Dio d'Amore e Falsembiante

Come Falso-Sembiante sì parlava,
Amor sì 'l prese allora âragionare,
E dis[s]egli, in rompendo su' parlare,
C[h]'al su' parer ver' Dio troppo fallava.

E poï il domandò se l'uon trovava
Religïone in gente seculare.
Que' disse: "Sì, nonn-è mestier dottare
'Che più che 'n altro luogo ivi fruttava;

Chéd e' sareb[b]e troppo gran dolore
Se ciaschedun su' anima perdesse
Perché vestisse drappo di colore.

Né lui né altri già ciò non credesse':
Ché 'n ogne roba porta frutto e fiore
Religïon, ma' che 'l cuor le si desse.

94

The God of Love and False Seeming[1]

As False Seeming was speaking in that way,
Love began to address him
and, interrupting his speech, said
that, in his opinion, he was sinning against God.

And then he asked him if it was possible to find
religion in lay brothers.
That one said: "Yes, there's no need to doubt
that it bore more fruit there than elsewhere;

for it would be too great a sorrow
for everyone to lose his soul,
because he wore colorful clothing.

Neither he nor others would ever believe this:
because religion produces fruit and flowers in every imaginable guise
provided that one gives one's heart wholly over to it."

1. Cf. *Rose*, 11053–11067.

95

Falsembiante

"Molti buon' santi à l'uon visti morire
E molte buone sante gloriose,
Che fuor divote e ben religiose
E robe di color' volean vestire:

Né non lasciâr perciò già di santire;
Ma elle non fur anche dispittose,
Anz'eran caritevoli e pietose
E sofferian per Dio d'esser martìre.

E s'i' volesse, i' n'andrè' assà' nomando;
Ma apressoché tutte le sante e' santi
Che·ll'uon va per lo mondo og[g]i adorando,

Ten[n]er famiglie, e sì fecer anfanti;
Vergine e caste donne gîr portando
Cotte e sorcotti di colori e manti.

95

False Seeming[1]

"Many good male Saints have been seen to die,
as well as many good and glorious female Saints
who were devout and very religious,
and wanted to wear colored clothing:

they did not for this reason stop becoming Saints.
But they were never spiteful;
rather, they were charitable and devout
and suffered to become martyrs for God.

And if I wished, I would proceed to name many of them;
but almost all the female and male Saints
that are revered in the world today

had families and produced children;
virgins and chaste women went about wearing
colorful dresses and outer-garments and cloaks."

1. Cf. *Rose*, 11068–11080.

96

Falsembiante

"L'undicimilia vergini beate
Che davanti da Dio fanno lumera,
In roba di color ciaschedun'era
Il giorno ch'elle fur martorïate:

Non ne fur per ciò da Dïo schifate.
Dunque chi dice che·ll'anima pèra
Per roba di color, già ciò non chera,
Ché già non fiar per ciò di men salvate:

Ché 'l salvamento vien del buon corag[g]io;
La roba non vi to' né non vi dona.
E questo sì dé creder ogne sag[g]io,

Che non sia intendimento di persona
Che que' che veste l'abito salvag[g]io
Si salvi, se nonn-à l'opera bona.

96

False Seeming[1]

"The eleven thousand holy virgins
who are resplendent before God,
each one was clothed in a colorful dress
on the day they were martyred:[2]

they were not for this reason rejected by God.
Thus, the one who says that the soul perishes
because of colorful clothing, should not believe it,
for they will not be any less saved because of this.

Salvation comes from a good heart;
clothing neither gives nor takes anything away from you.
And this every wise man must believe:

namely, that it should not be anyone's belief
that whoever wears unadorned clothes
is saved, if he has not performed good deeds."

1. Cf. *Rose*, 11081–11092.

2. St. Ursula and her 11,000 companions (virgins) were martyred by the Huns at Cologne in 418. See the account in Jacobus de Voragine's *Legenda aurea* (*The Golden Legend: Readings on the Saints*, trans. William Granger Ryan, 2 vols. [Princeton: Princeton University Press, 1993], 2:256–260).

97

Falsembiante

"Chi della pelle del monton fasciasse
I·lupo, e tra·lle pecore il mettesse,
Credete voi, perché monton paresse,
Che de le pecore e' non divorasse?

Già men lor sangue non desiderasse,
Ma vie più tosto inganar le potesse;
Po' che·lla pecora no'l conoscesse,
Se si fug[g]isse, impresso lui n'andasse.

Così vo io mi' abito divisando
Ched i' per lupo non sia conosciuto,
Tutto vad'io le genti divorando;

E, Dio merzé, i' son sì proveduto
Ched i' vo tutto 'l mondo og[g]i truffando,
E sì son santo e produomo tenuto.

97

False Seeming[1]

"Do you think that if someone were to dress
a wolf in the skin of a ram and then put it
among the sheep, the wolf would not
devour the sheep because it appeared to be a ram?

It would not desire their blood any less,
but rather could deceive them more rapidly,
and since the sheep would not recognize the wolf,
if it were to go away, they would follow.

Thus, I change my appearance,
so that I may not be recognized as a wolf,
even though I go about devouring people.

And, thank God, I am so wise
that I go around cheating everyone
and yet am considered a saint and a good man."

1. Cf. *Rose*, 11092–11102.

98

Falsembiante

"Sed e' ci à guari di cota' lupelli,
La Santa Chiesa sì è malbalita,
Po' che·lla sua città è asalita
Per questi apostoli, c[h]'or son, novelli:

Ch'i' son certan, po' ch'e' son suo' rubelli,
Ch'ella non potrà essere guarentita;
Presa sarà sanza darvi fedita
Né di traboc[c]hi né di manganelli.

Se Dio non vi vuol metter argomento,
La guer[r]a sì fie tosto capitata,
Sì ch'ogne cosa andrà a perdimento:

Ed a me par ch'E' l'à dimenticata,
Po' sòfera cotanto tradimento
Da color a cui guardia l'à lasciata.

98

False Seeming[1]

"If there are many of these young wolf cubs,
Holy Church is in bad shape,
since her city is attacked
by these young, newly-ordained apostles.

For I am certain, since they are her enemies,
the Church cannot be defended;
she will be taken without a single attack
launched by catapults or war machines.

If God does not wish to offer a remedy for this,
the war will soon be over,
and everything will go to ruin:

but it seems to me that God has forgotten her,
since He tolerates such betrayal
by those in whose care He's left her."

1. Cf. *Rose*, 11103–11128.

99

Falsembiante

"Sed e' vi piace, i' sì m'andrò posando
Sanza di questi fatti più parlare;
Ma tuttor sì vi vo' convenenzare
Che tutti i vostri amici andrò avanzando,

Ma' che comeco ciascun vada usando;
Sì son e' morti se no'l voglion fare;
E la mia amica convien onorare,
O 'l fatto loro andrà pur peg[g]iorando.

Egli è ben ver ched i' son traditore,
E per ladron m'à Dio pezz'à giug[g]iato,
Perch'i' ò messo il mondo in tanto er[r]ore.

Per molte volte mi son pergiurato;
Ma i' fo il fatto mio sanza romore,
Sì che nessun se n'è ancora adato.

99

False Seeming[1]

"If you like, I will refrain
from saying any more about these matters;
but still I want to promise you
that I will show favor to all your friends,

on condition that they be friends with me.
If they don't want to do it they'll die;
they must honor my friend,[2]
or their situation will get much worse.

It's quite true that I'm a traitor,
and for some time God has judged me to be a thief,
because I have put the world in so much error.

On many occasions I have sworn falsely,
but I do my business without fanfare,
so that no one has ever noticed it."

1. Cf. *Rose*, 11129–11144.
2. That is, Forced Abstinence.

100

Falsembiante

"I' fo sì fintamente ogne mio fatto
Che Protëus[so], che già si solea
Mutare in tutto ciò ched e' volea,
Non sep[p]e unquanche il quarto di baratto

Come fo io, che non tenni ancor patto,
E nonn-è ancor nessun che se n'adea,
Tanto non stea commeco o mangi o bea
Che nella fine no·gli faccia un tratto.

Chéd i' so mia faz[z]on sì ben cambiare
Ched i' non fui unquanche conosciuto
In luogo, tanto vi potesse usare:

Ché chi mi crede più aver veduto,
Cogli atti miei gli so gli oc[c]hi fasciare,
Sì ch'e' m'à incontanente isconosciuto.

100

False Seeming[1]

"Everything I do, I do with deception,
such that Proteus, who was used
to changing into whatever he desired to be
did not know even a fourth of the deceptions

that I know. Never did I keep a promise,
and no one is aware of this,
not even the one who passes time or eats or drinks with me;
in the end I'll pull a dirty trick on him.

For I know how to change my appearance so well
that I've never been recognized
anywhere, even though I may have been there long;

for the one who thinks he's seen me many times,
with my tricks I know how to swathe his eyes,
so that he immediately unrecognizes me."

1. Cf. *Rose*, 11149–11156.

101

Falsembiante

"I' sì so ben per cuor ogne linguag[g]io;
Le vite d'esto mondo i' ò provate:
Ch'un'or divento prete, un'altra frate,
Or prinze, or cavaliere, or fante, or pag[g]io,

Secondo ched i' veg[g]io mi' vantag[g]io;
Un'altr'or son prelato, un'altra abate;
Molto mi piaccion gente regolate,
Ché co·llor cuopr'i' meglio il mi' volpag[g]io.

Ancor mi fo romito e pellegrino,
Cherico e avocato e g[i]ustiziere
E monaco e calonaco e bighino;

E castellan mi fo e forestiere,
E giovane alcun'ora e vec[c]hio chino:
A brieve mott'i' son d'ogni mestiere.

101

False Seeming[1]

"I know every language by heart;
I have experienced the various ways of this world:
on one occasion I become a priest, on another a friar,
now a prince, now a knight, now a servant, now a page,

according to where I see my advantage.
Another time I'm a prelate, and then an abbot;
I really like those in religious orders,
because with them I can better hide my fox-like nature.[2]

In addition I become a hermit and pilgrim,
clerk and lawyer and judge,
monk and parish priest and beguine.

I become keeper of the castle and forester,
and sometimes a youth and an old man hunched over:
in short, I am a jack of all trades."

1. Cf. *Rose*, 11157–11170.

2. Certain characters traits were traditionally associated with animals in the Middle Ages (as they are still today). The usual traits of a fox are cleverness, fraudulence and cunning. The well-known Old French beast epic, the *Roman de Renart* (Italian version: *Rainaldo e Lesengrino*), has a fox as the title character. Bestiaries are a major source of our understanding of the symbolic and allegorical significance of animals in the Middle Ages. For the characteristics of the fox and their meaning, see, for example, *The Bestiary: A Book of Beasts*, trans. T. H. White (New York: G. P. Putnam's Sons, 1960), 53–54. For the relationship between False Seeming and the mendicant orders, see Giuseppe Mazzotta, *Dante's Vision and the Circle of Knowledge* (Princeton: Princeton University Press, 1993), 72–74.

102

Falsembiante

"Sì prendo poi, per seguir mia compagna,
Cioè madon[n]a Costretta-Astinenza,
Altri dighisamenti a sua vogl[i]enza,
Perch'ella mi sollaz[z]a e m'acompagna;

E metto pena perch'ella rimagna
Comeco, perch'ell'è di gran sofrenza
E s[ì] amostra a·ttal gran benvoglienza
Ch'ella vor[r]eb[b]e che fosse in Ispagna.

Ella si fa pinzochera e badessa
E monaca e rinchiusa e serviziale,
E fassi sopriora e prioressa.

Idio sa ben sed ell'è spiritale!
Altr'or si fa noviz[z]a, altr'or professa;
Ma, che che faccia, non pensa c[h]'a male.

102

False Seeming[1]

"Thus, in order to accompany my lady-friend,
whose name is Forced Abstinence,
I assume other disguises at her wish,
because she gives me pleasure and companionship.

And I make an effort for her to stay
with me, because she's very tolerant
and knows how to show great compassion
toward someone whom she would want to be in Spain.[2]

She becomes a mendicant and an abbess,
a nun—regular, cloistered and lay—
and she becomes a vice-prioress and prioress.

Only God knows if she is truly spiritual!
Sometimes she becomes a novice, sometimes a professed nun;
but, no matter what she does, she only thinks of doing evil."

1. Cf. *Rose*, 11171–11182.
2. That is, to be far away from her. The use of the place-name simply indicates a distant land.

103

Falsembiante

"Ancor sì no·mi par nulla travaglia
Gir per lo mondo inn-ogne regïone
E ricercar ogne religïone;
Ma della religion, sa·nulla faglia,

I' lascio il grano e prendone la paglia,
Ch'i' non vo' che·ll'abito a lor faz[z]one
E predicar dolze predicazione:
Con questi due argomenti il mondo abaglia.

Così vo io mutando e suono e verso
E dicendo parole umili e piane,
Ma molt'è il fatto mio a·dir diverso:

Ché tutti que' c[h]'og[g]i manùcar pane
No·mi ter[r]ian ch'i' non gisse traverso,
Ch'i' ne son ghiotto più che d'unto il cane".

103

False Seeming[1]

"Moreover, it seems to me no work at all
to go around the regions of the world
seeking out every religious order;
but in matters of religion I unfailingly

leave the fruit behind and take the straw,[2]
for I only want my habit to be like theirs
and to be able to preach sweet sermons:
with these two devices the world is blinded.

And thus I go about changing both tone and verse
and saying humble and simple words,
but my actions are quite different from my words;

for all those who today are eating bread[3]
could not keep me from wandering off the straight path,
for I am more desirous of this than a dog is of fat."

1. Cf. *Rose*, 11183–11192.

2. That is, he follows his hypocritical creed by focusing on what is on the outside—the external appearance—and ignoring what is on the inside.

3. That is, all those living today.

104

Amore e Falsembiante

Falso-Sembiante si volle sofrire
Sanza dir de' suo' fatti più in avante,
Ma 'l Die d'Amor non fece pa sembiante
Ched e' fosse anoiato dell'udire,

Anzi gli disse per lui ringioire:
"E' convien al postutto, Falsembiante,
C[h]'ogne tua tradigion tu sì·cci cante,
Sì che non vi rimanga nulla a dire,

Ché·ttu mi pari un uon di Gesocristo
E 'l portamento fai di santo ermito".
"Egli è ben vero, ma i' sono ipocristo".

"Predicar astinenza i' t'ò udito".
"Ver è, ma, per ch'i' faccia il viso tristo,
I' son di buon' morsei dentro farsito.

104

Love and False Seeming[1]

False Seeming wanted to stop
without saying any more about his activities,
but the God of Love gave no sign
that he was bored by these words.

Indeed, to make him happy, he said:
"In the end it's best for you, False Seeming,
to tell us of your treachery,
so that you'll have no more to say,

for you seem to me a man of Jesus Christ,
and you behave like a holy hermit."
"That's very true, but I am a hypocrite."[2]

"I heard you preach abstinence."
"It's true, but although I show a sad face,
inside I am stuffed with tasty morsels."

1. Cf. *Rose*, 11193–11205.
2. In Italian the term *ipocristo* suggests a combination of "hypocrite" and "Antichrist."

105

Falsembiante

"Di buon' morselli i' sì m'empio la pancia,
E, se si truova al mondo di buon vino,
E' convien ch'i' me ne empia lo bolino;
Ad agio vo' star più che 'l re di Francia:

Ché gli altrù' fatti so' tutti una ciancia
Verso de' mie', che son mastro divino
E le cose sacrete m'indovino
E tutto 'l mondo peso a mia bilancia.

Ancor vo' da le genti tal vantag[g]io,
Ch'i' vo' riprender sanz'esser ripreso:
Ed è ben dritto, ch'i' sono 'l più sag[g]io;

Sì porto tuttor, sotto, l'arco teso,
Per dar a quel cotal male e damag[g]io
Che 'n gastigarm[i] stesse punto inteso".

105

False Seeming[1]

"With tasty morsels I fill my belly,
and, if there's any good wine in this world,
I must fill my gut with it;
for I want to live in greater comfort than the King of France!

Other people's business is a joke
compared to mine, for I am a master of theology
and have foreknowledge of sacred things,
and I weigh all earthly things in my scale.

Still, I want people to recognize my privilege
to admonish without being admonished;
and it's quite right, for I'm the smartest!

Beneath my cloak I always carry a drawn bow
to do harm and injury to anyone
who might wish to give me the slightest reprimand."

1. Cf. *Rose*, 11204–11206, 11663–11670.

106

Amore e Falsembiante

"Tu sì va' predicando povertate
E lodila". "Ver è, ad uopo altrui,
Ch'i' non son già su' amico, né ma' fui,
Anzi le porto crudel nimistate:

Ch'i' amerei assà' meglio l'amistate
Del re di Francia che quella a colui
Che va caendo per l'uscial altrui
E muor sovente di necessitate.

E ben avess'egli anima di santo,
Il pover, no·mi piace sua contez[z]a,
E più ch'i' posso il metto da l'un canto;

E sed amor gli mostro, sì è fintez[z]a.
Ma convien ch'i' mi cuopra di quel manto:
Per mostrar ch'i' sia buon, lor fo carez[z]a.

106

Love and False Seeming[1]

"And thus you go about preaching poverty
and you praise her." "It's true that, to benefit others,
I am not now, nor ever was, her friend;
in fact, I bear her fierce animosity,

for I would prefer the friendship
of the King of France to that of one
who goes begging from door to door
and often dies of want.

And no matter how saintly a soul a poor man
might have, I don't like to associate with him,
and, as much as I can, I put him off in a corner;

and if I show him affection, it's all feigned.
But I must cover myself with that mantle:[2]
to show that I am good, I give them attention."

1. Cf. *Rose*, 11206–11214.
2. That is, the habit of the religious orders, which becomes the mantle of hypocrisy (see sonnet 80).

107

Falsembiante

"E quand'io veg[g]o ignudi que' truanti
Su' monti del litame star tremando,
Che fredo e fame gli va sì acorando
Ch'e' non posson pregar né Die né ' santi,

E 'l più ch'i' posso lor fug[g]o davanti,
Sanza girne nessun riconfortando,
Anzi lor dico: 'Al diavol v'acomando
Con tutti que' che non àn de' bisanti'.

Ché·lla lor compressione è freda e secca,
Sì ch'i' non so ch'i' di lor trar potesse:
Or che darà colui che 'l coltel lecca?

Di gran follia credo m'intramettesse
Voler insegnar vender frutta a trec[c]a,
O ch'i' a·letto del cane unto chiedesse.

107

False Seeming[1]

"And when I see those naked beggars,
trembling on mountains of manure,
and suffering so much from the cold and hunger
that they cannot pray either to God or the Saints,

as fast as I can, I flee from their sight,
without comforting any of them;
rather, I say to them: 'I commend you to the devil, you
and all those who have no *bisanti*.'[2]

Because their physical makeup is cold and dry,
I don't know what I could squeeze out of them:[3]
what can that one give who licks the knife?

I think it would be crazy for me
to teach a fruit vendor how to sell fruit,
or for me to look for fat in a dog's house."

1. Cf. *Rose*, 11215–11224.

2. Gold coins (see sonnet 53).

3. According to ancient treatises on medicine and physiology (e.g., Hippocratic works such as *On the Nature of Man*), which were closely followed in the Middle Ages, the state of a person's health was determined by the relationship among the four bodily humors (blood, phlegm, yellow bile and black bile), each of which was associated with particular qualities (hot, cold, dry and moist) and with a season of the year. It was thought that illness resulted from imbalances among the humors that varied from season to season. For further information, see, among others, David C. Lindberg, *The Beginnings of Western Science: The European Scientific Tradition in Philosophical, Religious, and Institutional Context, 600 B.C. to A.D. 1450* (Chicago: University of Chicago Press, 1992).

108

Falsembiante

"Ma quand'i' truovo un ben ricco usuraio
Infermo, vo'l sovente a vicitare,
Chéd i' ne credo danari aportare
Non con giomelle, anzi a colmo staio.

E quando posso, e' non riman danaio
A·ssua famiglia onde possa ingrassare;
Quand'egli è morto, il convio a sotter[r]are,
Po' torno e sto più ad agio che gen[n]aio.

E sed i' sono da nessun biasmato
Perch'io il pover lascio e 'l ric[c]o stringo,
Intender fo che 'l ricco à più peccato,

E perciò sì 'l conforto e sì 'l consiglio,
Insin ch'e' d'ogne ben s'è spodestato,
E dato â me, che 'n paradiso il pingo.

False Seeming[1]

"But when I find a very wealthy, but sick usurer,
I frequently pay him visits,
because I think I can take his money away,
and not just handfuls, but bushels and bushels.

And when I do this, not a single coin remains
for his family with which they can get fat.
When he's dead, I accompany him to his grave;
then I return and am more relaxed than in January.[2]

And if I'm blamed by anyone
because I flee the poor and cling to the rich,
I let it be known that the rich man has sinned more,

and for this reason I must give him comfort and advice,
until he has divested himself of all his goods
and given them to me, who then give him a shove into paradise."

1. Cf. *Rose*, 11225–11238.

2. Artistic and literary works depict the different activities and pastimes associated with the months of the year. Perhaps to provide a salutary contrast to the cold and generally inhospitable weather, the month of January was usually represented by pleasant scenes of people seated comfortably by a hot fire or of great, festive banquets with tables loaded down with great quantities of fine food. For a literary represention of these activities, see the sonnet cycle on the months of the year by Folgore da San Gimignano (as well as the parodic response given it by Cenne da la Chitarra) (*Poeti del Duecento*, 2:405–434).

109

Falsembiante

"Io dico che 'n sì grande dannazione
Va l'anima per grande povertade
Come per gran riccez[z]a, in veritade;
E ciaschedun dé aver questa 'ntenzione,

Ché 'n un su' libro dice Salamone:
'Guardami, Idio, per la Tua gran pietade,
Di gran ric[c]hez[z]a e di mendichitade,
E dàmi del Tu' ben sol per ragione.

Ché que' c[h]'à gran ric[c]hez[z]a, sì oblia
Que' che 'l criò, per lo su' gran riccore,
Di che l'anima mette i·mala via.

Colui cui povertà tien in dolore,
Convien che·ssia ladrone, o muor d'envia,
O serà falsonier o mentitore'.

109

False Seeming[1]

"In truth I say that, for great poverty
just as for great wealth, a soul
goes to a state of great damnation;
and everyone should hold this opinion,

for Solomon says in one of his books:[2]
'Protect me, o God, through your great mercy,
from great wealth and from penury,
and give me your grace only according to reason.

For the one who has great wealth forgets,
because of his great riches, the one who created him,
and thus he directs his soul down an evil path.

The one whom poverty keeps in sorrow,
must be a thief or an envious person,
or he'll be a crook or a liar'."

1. Cf. *Rose*, 11239–11260.

2. Proverbs 30:8–9: "Remove far from me vanity, and lying words. Give me neither beggary, nor riches: give me only the necessities of life. Lest perhaps being filled, I should be tempted to deny, and say: Who is the Lord? or being compelled by poverty, I should steal, and forswear the name of my God." It is interesting to note that this same passage was used by William of St. Amour in his attack on the mendicant orders (see sonnet 92).

110

Falsembiante

"Ancor sì non comanda la Scrittura
Che possent'uon di corpo cheg[g]ia pane,
Né ch'e' si metta a viver d'altrù' ane:
Questo non piace a Dio, né non n'à cura;

Né non vuol che·ll'uon faccia sale o mura,
De le limosine, alle genti strane;
Ma vuol c[h]'uon le diparta a genti umane
Di cui forza e santade à gran paura.

E sì difende 'l buon Giustinïano,
E questo fece scriver nella leg[g]e,
Che nes[s]un dia limosina a uon sano

Che truovi a guadagnare, e·ttu t'aveg[g]i[e]
Ch'a lavorare e' non vuol metter mano;
Ma vuol che·ttu 'l gastighi e cacci e feg[g]i[e].

110

False Seeming[1]

"Moreover, Scripture does not order
a man with a healthy body to beg for bread
nor to live off another's labor:
this does not please God, nor is He responsible for it;

neither does He want rooms and buildings to be built
for foreigners from collected alms;
rather He wants them to be divided among those people
whose strength and health give Him concern.

The good Justinian prohibited
—and he had this written in the law—
that charity be given to a healthy man

who can earn his keep and who, as you can see,
is unwilling to do any work;
but he requires that you punish and exile and beat him."[2]

1. Cf. *Rose*, 11287–11322.

2. The Emperor Justinian (482–565) undertook a major reform and recodification of Roman law that resulted in the *Corpus iuris civilis*. In one passage in this work he refers briefly to beggars in good health, and this reference is also mentioned by William of St. Amour in his treatise against the mendicant orders (see sonnets 92, 109, 112 and 119).

111

Falsembiante

"Chi di cotà' limosine è 'ngrassato,
In paradiso non dé atender pregio,
Anzi vi dé atender gran dispregio,
Almen s'e' non è privilegïato;

E s'alcun n'è, sì n'è fatto ingannato
E 'l papa che li diè il su' col[l]egio,
Ché dar non credo dovria privilegio
C[h]'uon sano e forte gisse mendicato:

Ché·lle limosine che son dovute
A' vec[c]hi o magagnati san' possanza,
A cui la morte seria gran salute,

Colui che·lle manuca i·lor gravanza,
Elle gli fieno ancor ben [car] vendute:
Di questo non bisogna aver dottanza.

111

False Seeming[1]

"Whoever has gotten fat from such alms
should not expect a reward in paradise;
rather, he should expect great punishment,
unless he has special privilege.

And if someone is in this position, both the Pope
who gave it to him and his college are fooling themselves,
for I don't think that they should give
a strong and healthy man the privilege of begging.

Indeed, alms are rightly given
to the old or the weak and disabled,
to whom death would be great blessing;

but the alms that are consumed to the detriment of those
who need them will cost the one who eats them dearly,
and of this there is no doubt!"

1. Cf. *Rose*, 11323–11344.

112

Falsembiante

"Tanto quanto Gesù andò per terra,
I suo' discepoli e' non dimandaro
Né pane né vino, anzi il guadagnaro
Co·le lor man, se·llo Scritto non erra.

Co' buon' mastri divin' ne feci guerra
Perché questo sermone predicaro
Al popolo a Parigi, e sì 'l provaro,
C[h]'uon ch'è truante col diavol s'aferra.

Ancor, po' che Gesù si tornò in cielo,
San Paolo predicava i compagnoni
Ched e' sì non vendes[s]er lo Guagnelo:

Sì che di grazia fecer lor sermoni;
Di lor lavor vivien, già no'l vi celo,
Sanza fondar castella né magioni.

112

False Seeming[1]

"As long as Christ went throughout the world,
his disciples did not ask
for bread or wine, but earned it
with their hands, if the Scripture does not lie.

I fought over this with the good masters of theology
because they preached this sermon
to the people of Paris and backed it up with proof:[2]
that the man who lives on alms is in the devil's clutches.

Moreover, after Jesus returned to heaven,
Saint Paul exhorted his companions
not to profit from the Gospel.[3]

And so, without reward, they preached their sermons;
they lived from their work, and this I don't conceal from you,
without building castles or palaces."

1. Cf. *Rose*, 11266–11272, 11285–11286, 11353–11361.

2. The reference is to William of St. Amour and his views on the mendicant orders (see sonnet 92).

3. See Paul's first letter to the Thessalonians (2:4, 8–9; 4:11), to which William of St. Amour also refers in his treatise.

113

Falsembiante

"Ver è ch'e' ci à persone ispeziali
Che van cherendo lor vita per Dio,
Per ch'i' vi dico ben c[h]'al parer mio
Egli è mercé far bene a que' cotali.

Di questi sono alquanti bestiali
Che non ànno iscïenza in lavorio,
Ed altri v'à che l'ànno, ma è rio
Il tempo, e' lor guadagni sì son frali.

A' 'ncor di gentil gente discacciata,
Che non son costumati a lavorare,
Ma son vi[v]uti sol di lor entrata.

A cotà' genti dé ciascun donare,
Ché lor limosina è bene impiegata,
Sì è mercé atarli governare.

113

False Seeming[1]

"It's true that there are certain people
who go begging for food in the name of God,
for which I say to you that, in my opinion,
to do good for these people is a meritorious act.

Of these some are quite ignorant
and have no concept of work,
and there are others who do have it, but times
are bad, and their earnings are very small.

Some are exiled noblemen,
who are unaccustomed to working,
living solely from their revenues.

Everyone must contribute to people such as these,
for the alms they give are well employed,
it is merciful to help them get by."

1. Cf. *Rose*, 11407–11426.

114

Falsembiante

"Ad alcun altro che·ffa lavoraggio,
Ma ben sua vita trar non ne poria,
Sì gli consente Idio ben truandia
Per quel che gli fallisce al su' managgio.

Od altro pover c[h]'avesse corag[g]io
Di volere studiar in chericia,
Gran merced'è a farli cortesia
Insin ch'e' sia de la scïenza sag[g]io.

E se 'n cavalleria alcun volesse
Intender, per la fede con sé alzare,
Non fallerïa già sed e' chiedesse

Infin ch'e' sé potesse ben montare,
E avere spezierïa ch'e' potesse
Condursi nella terra d'oltremare".

114

False Seeming[1]

"Some people work at odd jobs
but could not survive from these alone;
thus God allows them to beg
for that missing portion of their household needs.

Another poor man would like
to study for the priesthood,
and it is a meritorious act to be generous towards him
until he is done with his studies.

And if someone would desire to learn chivalric skills
in order to elevate himself and promote the faith,
he would not be wrong to beg,

until he could amass a goodly sum
and have the necessary capital with which
to travel to the land beyond the sea."[2]

1. Cf. *Rose*, 11427–11452.

2. The language of the text focuses on the man's wealth as deriving from the spice trade (*spezieria*), with the suggestion being that his travel abroad might be undertaken for business purposes (e.g., the opening of new markets) and not for the goals envisioned in a Christian crusade.

115

Dio d'Amore e Falsembiante

"Dì, Falsembiante: in che maniera puote
Seguire Idio chi à tutto venduto,
Ed àllo tutto a' pover' dispenduto,
E le sue borse son rimase vote,

Ed è forte e possente e à grosse gote?
Gli sarebbe per dritto conceduto
C[h]'a trar sua vita domandasse aiuto,
Come quest'altri che·ttu or mi note?".

"Dico di no: che se Dio fe' comando
C[h]'on desse tutto a' poveri, e po' 'L sieva,
La Sua 'ntenzion non fu in truandando,

E questo intendimento ti ne lieva,
Ma con buon'opre tuttor lavorando,
C[h]'uon forte in truandar l'anima grieva.

115

The God of Love and False Seeming[1]

"Tell me, False Seeming: in what way can a man
follow God, who has sold everything
and given it to the poor,
and whose purse remains empty,

and who is strong and vigorous and has fleshy cheeks?
Would it be right to allow him
to beg in order to survive,
just like the others whom you've listed for me now?"

"The answer is no; because when God ordered
that one should give everything to the poor, and then follow Him,
His intention was not concerned with begging for alms

—and get this opinion out of your head—
but rather with working always toward good ends,
for a strong man who begs weighs down his soul."

1. Cf. *Rose*, 11345–11351, 11377–11383.

116

Falsembiante

"Ancor una crudel costuma ab[b]iamo:
Contra cui no' prendiamo a nimistate,
Quanti no' siamo, in buona veritate,
In difamarlo noi ci asottigliamo;

E se per aventura noi sap[p]iamo
Com'e' possa venire a dignitate,
Nascosamente noi facciàn tagliate,
Sì che di quella via noi 'l ne gittiamo.

E ciò facciamo noi sì tracelato
Ch'e' non saprà per cui l'avrà perduto
Infin ch'e' non ne fia di fuor gittato.

Che s'e' l'aves[s]e da prima saputo,
Per aventura e' si saria scusato,
Sì ch'i' ne saria menzonier tenuto".

116

False Seeming[1]

"We still have a cruel custom:
in truth, all of us act
against the person we hate
by contriving to ruin his reputation;

and if, by chance, we learn
how he may come to an exalted post,
in secret we plan to cut him off
and cast him off the road.

And this we do so secretly
that he'll not know who made him lose it
until he has been cast out.

For if he had known it from the start,
perhaps he would have found a way to protect himself,
and thus I would be considered a liar."

1. Cf. *Rose*, 11607–11630.

117

Amore e Falsembiante

"Cotesta mi par gran dislealtate",
Rispose Amore, "Or non credi tu 'n Cristo?".
"I' non, chéd e' sarà pover e tristo
Colù' che viverà di lealtate:

Sì ch'io non vo' per me quelle ghignate,
Ma, come ched i' possa, i' pur a[c]quisto,
Ché da nessun nonn-è volontier visto
Colui che man terrà di povertate,

Anzi l'alunga ciascuno ed incaccia;
Già no·lli fia sì amico né parente
Ch[ed] egli il veg[g]a volontieri in faccia:

Sì ch'i' vogl[i]'anzi c[h]'on mi sia ubidente,
Come ch[ed] io a Cristo ne dispiaccia,
Ched es[s]er in servag[g]io della gente.

117

Love and False Seeming[1]

"This seems to me to be a great treachery,"
answered Love. "Do you not believe in Christ?"
"Not I, for the one who lives for loyalty
will be poor and sad.

I certainly don't want that mockery for myself;
but I continue to accumulate wealth in any way possible,
because no one thinks well
of the person who's faithful to poverty;

rather, everyone keeps him far away and chases him off.
He has no friend or relative
who would look him gladly in the face.

Even though I may not please Christ on this account,
I prefer that people be obedient to me
and not be servants to others."

1. Cf. *Rose*, 11495–11506.

118

Falsembiante

"Vedete che danari ànno usorieri,
Siniscalchi e provosti e maggiori,
Che tutti quanti son gran piatitori
E sì son argogliosi molto e fieri.

Ancor borghesi sopra i cavalieri
Son og[g]i tutti quanti venditori
Di lor derrate e aterminatori,
Sì ch'ogne gentil uon farà panieri.

E' conviene ch'e' vendan casa o terra
Infinché i borghesi siar pagati,
Che giorno e notte gli tegnono in serra.

Ma io, che porto panni devisati,
Fo creder lor che ciascheun sì erra,
E 'nganno ingannatori e ingannati.

118

False Seeming[1]

"See how much money the usurers,
seneschals, provosts and mayors have!
All of them are big swindlers,
and they are very proud and fierce.

Moreover, all of the bourgeoisie, to the detriment of the knights,
now sell their own goods
at inflated prices and on credit,[2]
so that every nobleman will be robbed.

They must sell their house and land
so that the bourgeoisie can be paid,
they who day and night keep the nobles in tight straits.

But I, who clothe myself in various garbs,
make each of them believe the other's wrong,
and I deceive both the deceivers and the deceived."

1. Cf. *Rose*, 11507–11522.

2. The members of the bourgeoisie are both the vendors (*venditori*) and the creditors (*aterminatori*) of these wares, whose sale price and rate of interest are greatly inflated, such that once the nobility has acquired an item, and cannot keep up payments, that item will be repossessed.

119

Falsembiante

"Chi se 'n vuol adirar, sì se n'adiri,
Chéd i' vi pur conterò ogne mio fatto,
S'i' dovess'es[s]er istrutto intrafatto,
O morto a torto com' furo i martìri,

O discacciato come fu 'l buon siri
Guiglielmo che di Santo Amor fu stratto:
Così 'l conciò la mogl[i]e di Baratto,
Però ch'e' mi rompea tutti mie' giri.

Chéd e' sì fu per lei sì discacciato,
E sol per verità ch'e' sostenea,
Ched e' fu del reame isbandeg[g]iato.

De mia vita fe' libro, e sì leg[g]ea
Ch'e' non volea ch'i' gisse mendicato:
Verso mia madre troppo misprendea!

119

False Seeming[1]

"Whoever wishes to get mad, let him get mad,
because I'll tell you about all my deeds,
even if I should be immediately destroyed
or unjustly killed just as the martyrs were,

or persecuted just like the good lord
William who was a native of St. Amour.[2]
In this way the wife of Deceit[3] fixed his hash,
because he was ruining all my deceptive plans.

For William was so persecuted by her,
and only for the truth that he maintained,
that he was banished from the realm.

Of my life he wrote a book,[4] and he taught
that he did not want me to go begging alms:
towards my mother he committed a grievous error!"

1. Cf. *Rose*, 11469–11487.

2. William of St. Amour, for whom see sonnet 92.

3. The wife of Deceit (*Baratto*) is Hypocrisy (*Ipocresia*), and she is the mother of False Seeming (see sonnet 80).

4. In the *Tractatus brevis de periculis novissimorum temporum* William presented his case against the mendicant orders (see sonnet 92).

120

Falsembiante

"Questo buonuon volea ch'i' rinegasse
Mendichità e gisse lavorando,
S'i' non avea che mia vita passando
Potesse, sanza c[h]'altro domandasse.

A quel consiglio mai no·m'acordasse:
Tropp'è gran noia l'andar travagliando.
Megli' amo star davante adorando
Ched i' a lavorar m'afaticasse.

Ché 'l lavorar sì no·mi può piacere,
Néd a·cciò consentir no·mi poria,
Ché molte volte fallarei in dolere.

Più amo il manto di papalardia
Portar, perciò ch'egl[i] è mag[g]ior savere,
Ché di lui cuopr'io mia gran rinaldia.

120

False Seeming[1]

"This good man[2] wanted me to renounce
begging and to go to work,
if I did not have the means to support myself
without asking for more.

I would never agree to that advice:
working is too much of an annoyance!
I prefer to keep on begging
than to tire myself out by working.

For I cannot enjoy working,
nor could I agree to do this,
for I would often faint from pain.

I prefer to wear hypocrisy's mantle,
because it's the wiser thing to do,
for with it I'm able to cover up my fox-like manner."[3]

1. Cf. *Rose*, 11485–11494.
2. William of St. Amour.
3. Cf. sonnet 101, v. 8.

121

Falsembiante

"I' sì nonn-ò più cura d'ermitag[g]i,
Né di star in diserti né 'n foresta,
Ch'e' vi cade sovente la tempesta:
Sì chito a·ssan Giovanni que' boscag[g]i!

In cittadi e 'n castella fo mie' stag[g]i
Mostrando ched i' faccia vita agresta;
Ma s'alla villa buon morsel s'aresta,
E' pur convien per forza ch'i' n'asag[g]i.

E vo dicendo ch'i' vo fuor del mondo,
Per ch'i' mi giuochi in sale e in palagi;
Ma chi vuol dire vero, i' mi v'afondo.

S'i' posso trovar via d'aver grand'agi,
Or siate certo ch'i' no·mi nascondo
[................................ -agi].

121

False Seeming[1]

"I no longer care for hermitages,
or to live in deserts and in forests,
where storms often occur:
thus, I leave these wild places to Saint John! [2]

I make my humble home in cities and in castles,
making it appear that I lead a harsh life;
but if some tasty morsel is found in the town,
then I must taste it for sure.

And I say how far removed I am from worldly things,
although I amuse myself in elegant rooms and palaces;
indeed, to tell the truth, I am completely immersed in the world.

If I can find a way to have great comforts,
now you can be sure that I'll not hide
[. . .][3]

1. Cf. *Rose*, 11671–11682.
2. St. John the Baptist spent many years in the wilderness.
3. The line is missing in the manuscript.

Falsembiante

"Ancor sì m'intrametto in far mogliaz[z]o,
Altr'or fo paci, altr'or sì son sensale;
Manovaldo mi fo, ma quel cotale
Che mi vi mette, l'ab[b]iate per paz[z]o,

Ché de' suo' beni i' fo torre e palaz[z]o,
O ver be' dormitori o belle sale,
Sì che, s'egli à figl[i]uol, poco gli vale
I ben' del padre, sì 'l te ne rispaz[z]o.

E se voi aveste nulla cosa a fare
Intorno di colui con ch'i' riparo,
Diràllami, faròlla capitare;

Ma non convien mostrar ch'e' vi si' amaro
A largamente sapermi donare,
Ché 'l mi' servigio i' 'l vendo molto caro.

122

False Seeming[1]

"Moreover, I engage myself in arranging marriages,
sometimes I am a peacemaker, other times an agent;
I become an administrator,[2] but whoever
has me do that, you should consider him crazy,

for from his properties I gain towers and palaces,
or beautiful bedrooms and lovely halls,
so that, if he has a son, little good his father's properties
will do him, because I sweep them all away.

And if you were to cook up a business deal
with one of my associates,
he'll tell me, and I'll make it happen;

but you don't have to show your displeasure
over having to pay me generously,
for I sell my service at a very high price."

1. Cf. *Rose*, 11649–11662.

2. A person in this capacity—*manovaldo*—would look after the financial interests and properties of women.

123

Falsembiante

"I' sì son de' valletti d'Antecristo,
Di quel' ladron' che dice la Scrittura
Che fanno molto santa portatura,
E ciaschedun di loro è ipocristo.

Agnol pietoso par quand'uon l'à visto,
Di fora sì fa dolze portatura;
Ma egli è dentro lupo per natura,
Che divora la gente Gesocristo.

Così ab[b]iamo impreso mare e terra,
E sì facciàn per tutto ordinamento:
Chi no·l'oserva, di[ci]àn c[h]'a fede erra.

Tanto facciàn co·nostro tradimento
Che tutto 'l mondo à preso co·noi guerra;
Ma tutti gli mettiamo a perdimento.

123

False Seeming[1]

"I'm one of the servants of Antichrist,
one of those thieves who, according to the Bible,[2]
have a very saintly appearance,
and each one of them is a hypocrite.

To those who see him, he seems a pious lamb,
so mild is his external appearance;
but inside he is a wolf by nature,
who devours the people of Jesus Christ.

In this way we have conquered land and sea,
and thus we give orders throughout the world:
those who do not follow our rules, we say they stray from the faith.[3]

With our treachery we do so much
that everyone has declared war on us;
but we are able to defeat them all."

1. Cf. *Rose*, 11683–11692.

2. See Matthew 7:15: "Beware of false prophets, who come to you in the clothing of sheep, but inwardly they are ravening wolves."

3. I.e., they are heretics.

124

Falsembiante

"Sed i' truovo in cittade o in castello,
Colà ove paterin sia riparato,
Crede[n]te ched e' sia o consolato,
Od altr'uon, ma' ch'e' sïa mio ribello,

O prete ched e' sia o chericello
Che tenga amica, o giolivo parlato,
E' convien che per me sia gastigato,
Ché ciaschedun mi dotta, sì son fello.

Ancor gastigo altressì usurai
E que' che sopravendono a credenza,
Roffïane e sorziere e bordelai;

E 'n ciasc[hed]uno i' ò malivogl[i]enza;
Ma, che che duol tu senti, no'l dirai,
Sì fortemente dotti mia sentenza.

124

False Seeming[1]

"If I find a city or castle,
in which a Paterin[2] may have taken refuge,
whether he be a *credente* or a *consolato*,[3]
or any one else, provided he is my enemy,

whether he be a priest or a young cleric
who has a lover, or a pleasure-seeking prelate,
I must punish them all,
because everyone fears me, so wicked am I.

Moreover, I punish usurers,
and those who sell on credit with inflated prices,
ruffians and spell-binders and pimps.

For each of them I feel great hatred;
but however much pain you feel, you will not complain,
so strongly do you fear my judgment."

1. Cf. *Rose*, 11693–11708.

2. The term *paterin* refers to the heretical sect known as the Cathars that was active in Italy and Southern France in the twelfth and thirteenth century. In the *Romance of the Rose* Milan is indicated as a center of this heresy.

3. These are terms designating persons of different levels in the Paterine sect. A *credente* is a regular member, but a *consolato* is one who has received the baptism of the Holy Spirit (the *consolamentum*).

125

Falsembiante

"Que' che vorrà campar del mi' furore,
Ec[c]o qui preste le mie difensioni:
Grosse lamprede, o ver di gran salmoni
Aporti, [o] lucci, sanza far sentore.

La buona anguilla nonn-è già peg[g]iore;
Alose o tinche o buoni storïoni,
Torte battute o tartere o fiadoni:
Queste son cose d'âquistar mi' amore,

O s'e' mi manda ancor grossi cavretti
O gran cappon' di muda be·nodriti
O paperi novelli o coniglietti.

Da ch'e' ci avrà di ta' morse' serviti,
No·gli bisogna di far gran disdetti:
Dica che g[i]uoco, e giuoc'a tutti 'nviti.

125

False Seeming[1]

"If someone wishes to escape my fury,
here are the weapons to defend himself from me:
let him bring huge lampreys or enormous salmons
or pike, without letting it be known.

A good eel is hardly bad,
shad or tench or some good sturgeon,
cakes or stuffed pastries or sweet breads:
these are things that will gain my love.

Or let him send me large kids,
or large, well-nourished capons who've moulted,
or young goslings and rabbits.

After he's served us such morsels,
he'll need not make any big excuses:
let him tell me what game to play, and I'll play it."

1. Cf. *Rose*, 11709–11721.

126

Falsembiante

"Que' che non pensa d'aver l'armadure
Ch'i' v'ò contate, o ver preziosi vini,
O ver di be' sac[c]hetti di fiorini,
Le mie sentenze lor fier troppo dure.

Né non si fidi già in escritture,
Ché saccian che co' mie' mastri divini
I' proverò ched e' son paterini
E farò lor sentir le gran calure.

Od i' farò almen ch'e' fien murati,
O darò lor sì dure penitenze
Che me' lor fôra ch'e' non fosser nati.

A Prato ed a Arez[z]o e a Firenze
N'ò io distrutti molti e iscacciati:
Dolente è que' che cade a mie sentenze".

126

False Seeming[1]

"Those who do not provide the defensive weapons
I've mentioned to you—not to mention fine wines
or lovely pouches full of florins—
will find my judgments on them very harsh.

They should not rely on the Scriptures,
for they should know that my theologians
and I will prove that they are Paterines,
and I will make them feel the hot fires.[2]

Or at least I'll have them imprisoned,
or give them such harsh penances
that it would be better if they'd not been born.

In Prato and in Arezzo and in Florence
I destroyed and exiled a great many of them:[3]
sorrowful is he who falls under my judgment!"

1. Cf. *Rose*, 11722–11730.

2. That is, the pyres prepared for their execution as heretics.

3. The persecution of the Paterines in Tuscany occurred in 1244–1245, and there are Florentine inquisitorial records from 1283 and 1287 that refer to other such actions.

127

Lo Dio d'Amor e Falsembiante

"Dì, Falsembiante, per gran cortesia,
Po' ch'i' t'ò ritenuto di mia gente,
E òtti fatto don sì bel[l]'e gente
Che·ttu se' re della baratteria,

Afideròm[m]i in te, o è follia?
Fa che·ttu me ne facci conoscente:
Chéd i' sarei doman troppo dolente,
Se·ttu pensassi a farmi villania".

"Per Dio merzé, messer, non vi dottate,
Chéd i' vi do la fé, tal com'i' porto,
Ched i' vi terrò pura lealtate".

"Allor", sì disse Amor, "ogno[n] si' acorto
D'armarsi con su' arme devisate,
E vadasi al castel che·ssì m'à morto".

127

The God of Love and False Seeming[1]

"False Seeming, tell me out of courtesy,
since I have accepted you among my barony
and have given such a truly noble gift to you
who are the king of fraud,

should I put my trust in you, or is it folly?
Be sure to let me know,
because I would be very sad tomorrow,
if you were planning to betray me."

"For God's mercy, my lord, don't be afraid,
for I give you my word, which is just as reliable as I am,
that I will maintain true loyalty to you."

"Then," said Love, "let each of you be quick
to arm himself with his particular weapons
and go to the castle that has ruined me."

1. Cf. *Rose*, 11951–11987.

128

L'armata de' baroni

A' l'armadure ciaschedun si prese,
E sì s'armâr con molto gran valore
Per dar a Gelosia pene e dolore,
Se contra lor [i]stesse alle difese;

Ed alcun prese scudo, altro pavese,
Ispade e lancie, a molto gran romore,
Dicendo ciaschedun al Die d'Amore
Che quelle guardie saran morte e prese.

Or sì vi conterò la contenenza
Che Falsembiante fece in quella andata
Colla su' amica Costretta-Astinenza.

E' no·mmenâr co·llor già gente armata,
Ma come gente di gran penitenza
Si mosser per fornir ben lor giornata.

128

The Army of Barons[1]

They all took their weapons
and armed themselves with great strength,
in order to give Jealousy pain and anguish,
if she were to resist them.

And some took a shield, others a pavis,
swords and spears, all with a great shout;
each one telling the God of Love
that those guards will be dead and captured.

Now I'll tell you how False Seeming
behaved in that expedition
with his friend Forced Abstinence.

They did not take any armed warriors with them,
but as people with a penitent look,
they went forth to accomplish their day's task.

1. Cf. *Rose*, 11988–12013.

129

Com'Astinenza andò a Mala-Boc[c]a

Astinenza-Costretta la primera
Sì si vestì di roba di renduta,
Velata che non fosse conosciuta;
Con un saltero i·man facea preghera.

La ciera sua non parea molto fera,
Anz'era umile e piana divenuta;
Al saltero una filza avea penduta
Di paternostri, e 'l laccio di fil iera.

Ed i·mano un bordon di ladorneccio
Portava, il qual le donò ser Baratto:
Già non era di melo né di leccio;

Il suocer le l'avea tagliato e fatto.
La scarsella avea piena di forneccio.
Ver' Mala-Bocca andò per darli matto.

129

How Abstinence Went to Bad Mouth[1]

First of all, Forced Abstinence
put on a nun's habit,
complete with veil that she might not be recognized;
she held a psalter in her hands and prayed.

Her face did not seem very fierce;
indeed, it had become humble and modest;
she had attached a rosary to her psalter,
and it was tied with thread.

And in her hand she carried
a thief's staff, which Ser Deceit had given her:
it was not made of apple wood or of oak;

her father-in-law had cut and fashioned it for her.
Her purse was full of stolen goods.[2]
She went towards Bad Mouth to checkmate him.

1. Cf. *Rose*, 12014–12050.

2. Her clothing and other items are those of the medieval pilgrim, but with some ironic variations (i.e., the staff [*bordone*] of a thief and the purse [*scarsella*] full of stolen goods).

130

Come Falsembiante andò a Mala-Bocca

Falso-Sembiante, sì com'on di coro
Religioso e di santa vita,
S'aparec[c]hiò, e sì avea vestita
La roba frate Alberto d'Agimoro.

Il su' bordon non fu di secomoro,
Ma di gran falsità ben ripulita;
La sua scarsella avea pien'e fornita
Di tradigion, più che d'argento o d'oro;

Ed una bib[b]ia al collo tutta sola
Portava: in seno avea rasoio tagl[i]ente,
Ch'el fece fab[b]ricare a Tagliagola,

Di che quel Mala-Bocca maldicente
Fu poi strangolato, che tal gola
Avëa de dir male d'ogne gente.

130

How False Seeming Went to Bad Mouth[1]

Just like a member of a religious order
or a man of holy life,
False Seeming got ready and had donned for this occasion
the habit of Albert of Agimore.[2]

His staff was not made of sycamore
but of great and highly polished falsity;
his purse was full and stocked
with treason, more than with gold or silver;

and over his shoulder he carried a volume, all by itself:
inside his shirt he had a sharp razor—
he'd had it made in Tagliagola[3]

and later used it to cut the slanderous
Bad Mouth's throat, the one who took great pleasure
in saying evil things about everyone.

1. Cf. *Rose*, 12051–12066.

2. That is, a Dominican habit like that of Albert the Great.

3. Note the play on the name of this imaginary city: *Tagliagola*, literally "Cut Throat." The phrase "ch' el fece fabbricare a Tagliagola" could also be construed to mean "which he had Tagliagola make," thus describing the name of the craftsman who fashioned the razor.

131

Mala-Boc[c]a, Falsembiante e Costretta-Astinenza

Così n'andaro in lor pellegrinag[g]io
La buona pellegrina e 'l pellegrino;
Ver' Mala-Bocca ten[n]er lor camino,
Che troppo ben guardava su' passag[g]io.

E Falsembiante malizioso e sag[g]io
Il salutò col capo molto chino,
E sì gli diss': "I' son mastro divino,
Sì siàn venuti a voi per ostellag[g]io".

Mala-Bocca conob[b]e ben Sembiante,
Ma non che·ffosse Falso; sì rispuose
C[h]'ostel dareb[b]e lor: "Venite avante".

Ad Astinenza molto mente puose,
Ché veduta l'avea per volte mante;
Ma per Costretta già mai no·lla spuose.

131

Bad Mouth, False Seeming, and Forced Abstinence[1]

And so the good pilgrims, female and male,
went on their pilgrimage;
they headed straight for Bad Mouth,
who very carefully guarded his gate.

Malicious and wise False Seeming
greeted him with his head bent low,
saying: "I am a master of theology,
and we have come to you to obtain hospitality."

Bad Mouth clearly recognized Seeming,
but not that he was False; thus, he replied
that he would give them shelter: "Come in."

He observed Abstinence very closely,
for he had seen her many times;
but he did not recognize her as Forced.

1. Cf. *Rose*, 12067–12121.

132

Mala-Bocca, Falsembiante e Costretta-Astinenza

Mala-Bocca sì 'nchiede i pellegrini
Di loro stato e di lor condizione,
E dimandò qual era la cagione
Ch'egli andavan sì matti e sì tapini.

Que' disser: "No' sì siàn mastri divini,
E sì cerchiamo in ogne regione
De l'anime che vanno a perdizione,
Per rimenargli a lor dritti camini.

Or par che·ssia piaciuto al Salvatore
D'averci qui condotti per vo' dire
E gastigar del vostro grande errore,

S'e' vi piace d'intender e d'udire".
"[.............................. -ore]
O fatto, i' sì son presto d'ubidire".

132

Bad Mouth, False Seeming, and Forced Abstinence[1]

Bad Mouth asks the pilgrims
of their status and condition,
and asked them why
they looked so discouraged and wretched.

They said: "We are masters of theology,
and so in every region we look for
souls who seem destined for hell,
in order to bring them back to the proper path.

Now it seems that it has pleased the Savior
to have brought us here to remind you
of your great sin and to chastise you for it,

if you wish to learn about it and to listen."
"[. . .][2]
or done, I am ready to obey."

1. Cf. *Rose*, 12122–12146.
2. The line is missing in the manuscript.

133

Astinenza

Astinenza sì cominciò a parlare,
E disse: "La vertude più sovrana
Che possa aver la criatura umana,
Sì è della sua lingua rifrenare.

Sovr'ogn'altra persona a noi sì pare
Ch'esto peccato in voi fiorisce e grana;
Se no'l lasciate, egli è cosa certana
Che nello 'nferno vi conviene andare:

Ché pez[z]'à c[h]'una truffola levaste
Sopra 'l valetto che vo' ben sapete:
Con gran[de] torto voi il difamaste,

Ch'e' non pensava a·cciò che vo' credete.
Bellacoglienza tanto ne gravaste
Ch'ella fu messa là ove vo' vedete".

133

Abstinence[1]

Abstinence then began to speak,
saying: "The highest virtue
that the human creature can have
is to restrain his tongue.

It seems to us that this sin
flowers and prospers in you more than in any other;
if you don't let go of it, it's certain
that you will go to hell.

For some time ago you began a vicious rumor
about the young man,[2] you know this well:
you slandered him wrongly,

for he was not planning to do what you think he was.
You made such heavy accusations against Fair Welcome
that she was placed there where you can see her."

1. Cf. *Rose*, 12147–12170.
2. The "young man" is the Lover (*Amante*).

134

Mala-Bocca

Udendo Mala-Bocca c[h]'Astinenza
Sì forte il biasimava e riprendea,
Sì·ssi crucciò, e disse ch'e' volea
C[h]'andasser fuor della su'apartenenza:

"Vo' credete coprir Bellacoglienza
Di ciò che quel valetto far credea.
Be·llo dissi e dirò, che la volea
Donargli il fior, e quest'era sua 'ntenza.

Quel [n]onn-errò del bascio, quest'è certo:
Per ch'i' vi dico, a voi divinatori,
Che questo fatto non fia già coverto.

Vo' mi parete due inganatori:
Andate fuor di casa, ché 'n aperto
Vi dico ch'i' non vo' tapinatori".

134

Bad Mouth[1]

Upon hearing the strong reproach
and criticism that Abstinence gave him,
Bad Mouth got very mad and said he wanted
them to leave his territory:

"You think you can clear Fair Welcome
of that which the young lad was thinking of doing.
I said it once and I'll say it again, that she wanted
to give him the Flower, and this was her intention.

That one did not kiss her by mistake, that's for sure:
for which I tell you, you fancy talkers,
that this deed will not be hidden.

You seem to me to be two deceivers:
get out of my house, for I'll plainly
tell you that I don't want swindlers here."

1. Cf. *Rose*, 12220–12245.

135

Falsembiante

Falso-Sembiante disse: "Per merzede
Vi priego, Mala-Bocca, c[h]'ascoltiate;
Ché, quand'uon conta pura ver[i]tate,
Molt'è folle colù' che no·lla crede.

Vo' sete ben certan che·ll'uon non vede
Che 'l valletto vi porti nimistate;
Sed egli amasse tanto l'amistate
Del fior quanto vo' dite, a buona fede,

Egli à gran pezza ch'e' v'avria morto,
Avendogli voi fatto tal oltraggio;
Ma non vi pensa e non si n'è acorto,

E·ttuttor sì vi mostra buon corag[g]io,
E servireb[b]evi a dritto e a torto
Come que' ch'è cortese e prode e saggio".

135

False Seeming[1]

False Seeming said: "For mercy's sake,
I beg you, Bad Mouth, listen to me;
for when one tells the honest truth,
he who does not believe it is very foolish.

You may be quite sure there's no evidence
that the young lad bears you hatred:
if he were to love the friendship
of the Flower as much as you say, and loyally,

he would have killed you a long time ago,
since you did him such a wrong.
But he doesn't see things that way, nor he is prepared to,

and he always shows you kindness
and would serve you in good and in bad
as someone who is courteous and valorous and wise."

1. Cf. *Rose*, 12246–12296.

136

La ripentenza Mala-Bocca

Ser Mala-Bocca si fu ripentuto
Di ciò ch'egli avea detto o pur pensato,
Ched e' credette ben aver fallato;
Sì disse a Falsembiante: "Il vostro aiuto

Convien ch'i' ag[g]ia, ch'i' non sia perduto";
E 'mantenente si fu inginoc[c]hiato,
E disse: "I' sì vogli'esser confessato
D'ogne peccato che m'è avenuto".

Astinenza-Costretta il prese allora,
Che·ss'era molto ben sobarcolata,
E Falsembiante col rasoio lavora:

A Mala-Bocca la gola à tagliata.
E po' ru[p]per la porta san' dimora:
Larghez[z]a e Cortesia l'àn[n]o passata.

136

The Repentance of Bad Mouth[1]

Ser Bad Mouth had repented
of what he'd said or even thought,
for he knew he'd made a mistake.
Thus, he said to False Seeming: "It's best that

I have your help, so that my soul may not be lost."
And immediately he kneeled down
and said: "I want to confess
every sin that I have committed."

Forced Abstinence grabbed him then,
for she had loosened her clothes a bit,
and False Seeming goes to work with his razor:

he cut Bad Mouth's throat.
And then they broke down the gate without delay:
Generosity and Lady Courtesy passed through it.

1. Cf. *Rose*, 12297–12342.

137

Cortesia e Larghezza e la Vec[c]hia

Tutti quat[t]ro passarono il portale,
E sì trovaron dentro a la porpresa
La Vec[c]hia, che del castro era [di]scesa;
Quando gli vide, le ne parve male,

Ma tuttavia non ne fece segnale.
Larghez[z]a e Cortesia sì l'àn[n]o atesa,
E disserle: "Madonna, san' difesa
Potete prender quanto il nostro vale:

Chéd egli è vostro, sanza farne parte,
E sì ve ne doniàn già la sagina
E sopra tutto vi vogliàn far carte".

La Vec[c]hia, che sapea ben la dottrina,
Ché molte volte avea studiato l'arte,
Gline marzïa molto e gline 'nchina.

137

Lady Courtesy and Generosity and the Old Woman[1]

All four of them went through the portal;
inside the walls they found the Old Woman,[2]
who had come down from the tower.
When she saw them, things looked bad to her,

but nevertheless she gave no sign of it.
Generosity and Lady Courtesy waited for her
and said: "My Lady, without any opposition
you can take all of our valuables,

for they are yours, completely,
and so we offer you this opportunity,
and, most of all, we wish to draft the proper papers."

The Old Woman who knew the theory well,
since she had practiced this art many times,[3]
gave them thanks and bows to them.

1. Cf. *Rose*, 12351–12378.

2. The figure of the old woman is common in medieval literature. She functions in several capacities: as a go-between for young lovers, as a *confidante* and / or custodian for a young woman, and as a gossip and cantankerous person.

3. The old woman is well-versed in the theory and practice of corruption.

138

Falsembiante

Falsembiante a la Vec[c]hia sì à detto:
"Per Dio, gentil madonna prezïosa
Che sempre foste e siete pïetosa,
Che vo' ag[g]iate merzé del buon valletto!

Ch'e' vi piaccia portarle un gioeletto
Da la sua parte a quella grazïosa
Bellacoglienza, che gli fu nascosa,
De ch'egli à avuto il cuor molto distretto!

Vedete qui fermagli ch'e' le manda,
E queste anella e questi intrecciatoi,
Ancora questa nobil[e] ghirlanda.

Il fatto suo si tien tratutto a voi;
Ciascun di noi per sé lui racomanda:
Del fatto vostro penserén ben noi".

138

False Seeming[1]

False Seeming said to the Old Woman:
"In God's name, noble and refined lady,
you who were and always are merciful,
may you take pity on the young lad!

May it please you to take a jewel
on his behalf to that gracious
Fair Welcome, who was hidden from him,
on account of which his heart has been terribly distressed!

See here the combs that he sends to her,
and these rings and these silk ribbons;
and this noble garland, too.

His fate is completely entrusted to you.
Each one of us gives him our blessing:
as for your situation we will take care of that."

1. Cf. *Rose*, 12379–12414.

139

La Vec[c]hia e Falsembiante

La Vec[c]hia sì rispuose san' tardare,
Ché 'l male e 'l ben sapea quantunque n'era:
"Vo' mi fate [co]sì dolze preghera
Ch'i' no lo vi saprei giamai vietare.

Questi gioelli i' sì vo' ben portare
E dargli nella più bella maniera
Che io potrò; ma una lingua fiera,
Che quaentr'è, mi fa molto dottare,

E·cciò è Mala-Bocca maldicente,
Che [con]truova ogne dì nuovi misfatti,
Né non riguarda amico né parente".

"No'l ridottate più giamai a fatti,
Ché noi sì l'ab[b]iàn morto, quel dolente,
Sanza che 'n noi trovasse trieva o patti.

139

The Old Woman and False Seeming[1]

The Old Woman answered without delay,
because she was an expert in good and evil:
"You make me such a sweet request
that I could never refuse you.

I am pleased to take and give
these jewels in the best way
that I can; but a wicked tongue
that dwells within these walls makes me very fearful,

namely Bad Mouth, the slanderer,
who every day thinks up new crimes,
and cares not for friends or relatives."

"Do not fear his deeds anymore,
for we have killed that wretch
without giving him any truce or conditions."

1. Cf. *Rose*, 12415–12433.

140

La Vec[c]hia e Falsembiante

"Certanamente noi gli ab[b]iàn segata
La gola, e giace morto nel fossato:
E' nonn-à guar' che noi l'ab[b]iàn gittato,
E 'l diavol sì n'à l'anima portata".

La Vec[c]hia sì rispuose: "Or è amendata
Nostra bisogna, po' ch'egli è sì andato.
Colui cu' vo' m'avete acomandato,
I' metterò in servirlo mia pensata.

Dit'al valetto ch'i' ne parleròe:
Quando vedrò che 'l fatto sia ben giunto,
I' tutta sola a chieder sì·ll'andròe".

Allor si parte, ed ivi fece punto,
E tutti quanti a Dio gli acomandòe.
Molto mi parve che 'l fatto sie 'n punto.

140

The Old Woman and False Seeming[1]

"For sure we sawed right through
his throat, and he lies dead in the moat.
Not long ago we pitched him there,
and the devil took his soul away."

To this the Old Woman made reply: "Now our situation
is improved, since he's no longer with us.
I will put my every thought to serving
that one whom you have recommended to me.

Tell the young lad I'll speak on his behalf:
when I see that the time is ripe,
I'll go all alone to get him."

Then she leaves, and put an end to her words,
and commended all of them to God.
It seemed to me that things were going very well.

1. Cf. *Rose*, 12434–12449.

141

La Vec[c]hia e Bellacoglienza

Dritta a la camera a la donna mia
N'andò la Vec[c]hia, quanto può trot[t]ando,
E quella la trovò molto pensando,
Come se fosse d'una voglia ria.

Crucciosa so ch'era, che non ridia:
Sì tosto al[l]or la va riconfortando,
E disse: "Figl[i]uola mia, io ti comando
Che·ttu nonn-entri già i·mmalinconia;

E vê·cciò che tu' amico ti presenta".
Allor le mostra quelle gioielette,
Pregandola c[h]'a prenderl'aconsenta:

"Reguarda com'elle son belle e nette".
E quell'a domandar non fu già lenta
Chi era colui che gliele tramette.

141

The Old Woman and Fair Welcome[1]

The Old Woman went straight to my lady's chamber,
trotting along as fast as she could,
and she found her in a very anxious state,
as though she were in a foul mood.

I know she was worried, for she did not smile:
the Old Woman quickly began to comfort her,
saying: "My child, I suggest
that you not fall prey to melancholy;

see what your friend has given you."
At that point she shows her those lovely jewels
and asks her to accept them:

"Look at how beautiful and nice they are."
And the young woman was not slow to ask
who it was who sends them to her.

1. Cf. *Rose*, 12511–12582.

142

La Vec[c]hia

"Il bel valetto di cu' biasmo avesti
Giadisse, sì [è] colui che·lle ti manda,
E 'l rimanente c[h]'à è a tua comanda:
Unquanche uon più cortese non vedesti.

E priegati, se mai ben gli volesti,
Che per l'amor di lui questa ghirlanda
Deg[g]ie portare, e sì sé racomanda
Del tutto a te: gran peccato faresti

Se 'l su' presente tu gli rifusassi;
Ch'i' son certana ch'e' si disper[r]ebbe
Se·ttu così del tutto lo sfidassi;

Ché, quanto ch'e' potesse, e' sì fareb[b]e
Per te, e sofferria che·llo 'ngaggiassi,
E, se 'l vendessi, sì gli piacereb[b]e".

142

The Old Woman[1]

"The handsome lad for whom you were once punished,
he is the one who sends them to you,
and the others that he has are at your command:
never have you seen a more refined man.

And he begs you, if you ever loved him,
that for love of him you must wear
this garland, and thus he puts himself
completely in your power. You would commit a great sin,

if you were to refuse his gift.
For I'm certain that he would despair,
if you were in this way to discourage him completely;

for he would do as much as he could for you,
and he would not object, even if you were to pawn it,
and, if you were to sell it, he would similarly be pleased."

1. Cf. *Rose*, 12585–12647.

143

Bellacoglienza e la Vec[c]hia

"Madonna, i' dotto tanto Gelosia
Ch'esto presente prender non osasse;
Che·sse domane ella mi domandasse:
'Chi 'l ti donò?', io come le diria?".

"Risposta buona i' non ti celeria:
Che s'ogn'altra risposta ti fal[l]asse,
Sì dì almen ched i' la ti donasse,
Ed i' le dirò ben che così sia".

Allor la Vec[c]hia la ghirlanda prese,
E 'n su le treccie bionde a la pulcella
La puose, e quella guar' non si contese;

E po' prese lo spec[c]hio, e sì·ll'apella,
E disse: "Vien' qua, figl[i]uola cortese.
Riguàrdati se·ttu se' punto bella".

143

Fair Welcome and the Old Woman[1]

"My Lady, I fear Jealousy so much
that I would not dare to take this gift;
for if tomorrow she would ask me:
'Who gave it to you?' what would I tell her?"

"I would not conceal a good answer from you:
if any other answer would fail you,
you can say at least that I gave it to you,
and I'll tell her that this is the case."

Then the Old Woman took the garland
and put it on the young woman's golden braids,
and she did not resist too much.

And then she took the mirror and calls her,
saying: "Come here, gentle daughter.
Look at yourself, and see how beautiful you are!"

1. Cf. *Rose*, 12663–12699.

144

Bellacoglienza e la Vec[c]hia

Al[l]or Bellacoglienza più non tarda:
Immantenente lo spec[c]hi' eb[b]e i·mmano,
Sì vide il viso suo umile e piano;
Per molte volte nello spec[c]hio guarda.

La Vec[c]hia, che·ll'avea presa en sua guarda,
Le giura e dice: "Per lo Dio sovrano,
Ch'unquanche Isotta, l'amica Tristano,
[...............................-arda]

Come tu·sse', figl[i]uola mia gentile.
Or convien che·ttu ab[b]ie il mi' consiglio,
Che cader non potessi in luogo vile.

Se non sai guari, no·mmi maraviglio,
Ché giovan uon non puot'esser sottile,
Chéd i', quanto più vivo, più asottiglio.

Fair Welcome and the Old Woman[1]

Thus Fair Welcome does not delay.
As soon as she took the mirror in hand,
she saw her humble and honest face:
she looks at herself many times in the mirror.

The Old Woman, who had taken her under her wing,
swears to her saying: "In the name of God the sovereign,
never did Isolt, Tristan's friend,[2]
[. . .][3]

as you are, my noble daughter.
It's best that you have my advice,
so that you might not fall into a bad situation.

I'm not surprised if you don't know a lot,
for a young person cannot be wise,
because the longer I live the wiser I become."

1. Cf. *Rose*, 12700–12711.

2. The adventures of Tristan and his love for Isolt were the subjects of numerous prose romances in the Middle Ages (e.g., the Old French *Roman de Tristan*, the Italian *Tavola ritonda* and *Tristano Riccardiano*, and others). Tristan's prowess in arms, Isolt's beauty and the intensity of their love became standards against which writers measured their own chivalric abilities, passion or other elements of their amorous experience. The reference here, unfortunately incomplete, would seem to follow this sort of practice.

3. The line is missing in the manuscript.

145

La Vec[c]hia

"Figl[i]uola mia cortese ed insegnata,
La tua gran gioia sì è ancor a venire.
Or me convien me pianger e languire,
Ché·lla mia sì se n'è tutta passata

Né non fie mai per me più ritrovata,
Chéd ella mi giurò di non reddire.
Or vo' consigliar te, che dé' sentire
il caldo del brandon, che sie avisata

Che non facessi sì come fec'io:
De ch'i' son trista quand'e' me'n rimembra,
Ch'i' non posso tornare a·lavorio.

Per ch'i' te dico ben ched e' mi sembra:
Se·ttu creder vor[r]à' 'l consiglio mio,
Tu sì non perderai aver né membra.

145

The Old Woman[1]

"My dear noble and well-bred daughter,
your great joy is yet to come.
Now it's my time to cry and languish,
because my joy is completely over,

and I will not find it ever again,
for it swore to me that it would not return.
Now I want to advise you, who must feel
the heat of Love's flame: you must be careful

not to do as I did;
for which I'm sad when I remember
that I cannot return to love's labor.[2]

Therefore, I'll tell you how things seem to me:
if you will follow my advice,
you'll not lose men's riches or their bodies."

1. Cf. *Rose*, 12712–12730.
2. That is, sexual intercourse (see sonnets 39–40).

146

La Vec[c]hia

"Se del giuoco d'amor i' fosse essuta
Ben sag[g]ia quand'i' era giovanella,
I' sare' ric[c]a più che damigella
O donna che·ttu ag[g]ie og[g]i veduta:

Ch'i' fu' sì trapiacente in mia venuta
Che per tutto cor[r]ëa la novella
Com'i' era cortese e gente e bella;
Ma·cciò mi pesa, ch'i' non fu' saputa.

Or sì mi doglio quand'i' mi rimiro
Dentro a lo spec[c]hio, ed i' veg[g]o invec[c]hiarmi:
Molto nel mï[o] cuore me n'adiro.

Ver è ched i' di ciò non posso atarmi,
Sì che per molte volte ne sospiro
Quand'i' veg[g]io biltate abandonarmi.

146

The Old Woman[1]

"If I had been a true expert
in the game of love when I was young,
I would be richer than any young noble woman
or lady, whom you can see today.

I was so greatly pleasing in my youth
that the news spread everywhere
of how gracious and noble and beautiful I was;
but what troubles me is that I was not wise.

So now I grieve, when I look at myself
in the mirror and see myself grown old:
I get very angry in my heart.

To be sure, I cannot help myself in this,
and so I frequently sigh,
when I see my beauty abandoning me."

1. Cf. *Rose*, 12731–12744.

147

La Vec[c]hia

"Per tutto 'l mondo i' era ricordata,
Com'io t'ò detto, de la mia bieltate,
E molte zuffe ne fur cominciate,
E molta gente alcun'ora piagata;

Ché que' che mi crede' aver più legata,
Assà' mostrav' i' più di duritate:
Le mie promesse gli venian fallate,
C[h]'altre persone m'avieno inarrata.

Per molte volte m'era l'uscio rotto
E tentennato, quand'io mi dormia;
Ma già per ciò io non facea lor motto,

Perciò ched i' avea altra compagnia,
A cui intender facea che 'l su' disdotto
Mi piacea più che null'altro che·ssia.

147

The Old Woman[1]

"As I told you, I was celebrated
throughout the world for my beauty,
and many fights were begun because of this,
and many people were often wounded.

To the one who thought he had me all to himself
I showed more harshness;
my promises to him were not kept,
because other men had engaged me with their pledges.

Many times my door was broken down[2]
and battered, when I was sleeping;
but despite this I said nothing to them,

since I had the company of another man;
I made him believe that his sexual pleasure
pleased me more than any other thing in the world."

1. Cf. *Rose*, 12742–12751.
2. The door to her house also represents metaphorically the "entrance-way" to her body.

148

La Vec[c]hia

"I' era bella e giovane e folletta,
Ma non era a la scuola de l'amore
Istata; ma i' so or ben per cuore
La pratica la qual ti fie qui detta.

Usanza me n'à fatta sì savietta
Ched i' non dotterei nessun lettore
Che di ciò mi facesse desinore,
Ma' ched i' fosse bella e giovanetta:

Chéd egli è tanto ched i' non finai
Che·lla scïenza i' ò nel mi' coraggio;
Sed e' ti piace, tu l'ascolterai,

Ma i' no l'eb[b]i sanza gran damag[g]io:
Molta pen'e travaglio vi durai;
Ma pur almen sen[n]'è [re]mas'e usag[g]io.

148

The Old Woman[1]

"I was beautiful and young and without cares,
but to the school of love I'd not yet
been; but now I know by heart
the techniques that will be related to you here.

Experience has made me so wise
that I would not fear any teacher
who might make me lose face in this subject,
if only I were beautiful and young.

I have been studying this subject for so long
that I have full knowledge of it in my heart.
If you like, you will hear it,

but I did not obtain it without great hardship:
much anguish and suffering I endured;
but at least wisdom and experience have remained."

1. Cf. *Rose*, 12771–12796.

149

La Vec[c]hia

"Molti buon'uomini i' ò già 'ngannati,
Quand'i' gli tenni ne' mie' lacci presi:
Ma prima fu' 'ngannata tanti mesi
Che' più de' mie' sollaz[z]i eran passati.

Centomilia cotanti barattati
N'avrei, s'i' a buon'or gli avesse tesi,
E conti e cavalieri e gran borgesi,
Che molti fiorin' d'oro m'avrian dati.

Ma quand'i' me n'avidi, egli era tardi,
Chéd i' era già fuor di giovanez[z]a,
Ed eranmi falliti i dolzi isguardi,

Perché 'n sua bàlia mi tenea vec[c]hiez[z]a.
Or convien, figlia mia, che tu ti guardi
Che·ttu non ti conduchi a tale strez[z]a.

149

The Old Woman[1]

"Many valorous men I once deceived,
when I had them caught in my amorous snares:
but I myself was deceived for many months
before most of my pleasure-giving features had faded.

I would have tricked a hundred thousand men
and more, if I had set my snares in time,
and counts and knights and rich merchants
would have given me lots of gold florins.

But when I realized this, it was late,
for I was already past my youth,
and my sweet looks were already gone,

since old age had me in her power.
Now, my daughter, you must take care,
so that you will not come to the same harsh pass."

1. Cf. *Rose*, 12797–12802.

150

La Vec[c]hia

"Molto mi dolea il cuor quand'i' vedea
Che·ll'uscio mïo stava in tal sog[g]iorno,
Che vi solea aver tal pressa 'ntorno
Che tutta la contrada ne dolea.

Ma, quanto a me, e' no·me ne calea,
Ché troppo più piacea loro quel torno,
Ch'i' era allora di sì grande attorno
Che tutto quanto il mondo mi' parea.

Or convenia che di dolor morisse
Quand'i' vedea que' giovani passare,
E ciaschedun parea che mi schernisse.

Vec[c]hia increspata mi facean chiamare
A colù' solamente che giadisse
Più carnalmente mi solea amare.

150

The Old Woman[1]

"My heart was truly grieved when I saw
that my door was in such a quiet state,
for there used to be such a crowd around it
that the whole neighborhood would complain.

But as for me, I didn't care,
because they liked to come around;
and I was then so wondrously beautiful
that the entire world seemed mine.

Now, it was inevitable that I should die of sorrow
when I would see those young men pass by:
each of them it seemed was mocking me.

A wrinkled old woman, they had me called
by the one who only a short while ago
had loved me with great carnal desire."

1. Cf. *Rose*, 12807–12926.

151

La Vec[c]hia

"Ancora d'altra parte cuore umano
Non pensereb[b]e il gran dolor ch'i' sento
Tratutte l'ore ch'i' ò pensamento
De' be' basciar' che m'ànno dato mano.

Ogni sollaz[z]o m'è og[g]i lontano,
Ma non ira e dolori e gran tormento:
Costor sì ànno fatto saramento
Ch'i' non uscirò lor mai di tra mano.

Or puo' veder com'i' son arivata,
Né al mi' mal nonn-à altra cagione
Se non ched i' fu' troppo tosto nata.

Ma sap[p]ie ched io ò ferma intenzione
Ch'i' sarò ancor[a] per te vendicata,
Se·ttu ben riterrai la mia lezione.

151

The Old Woman[1]

"Yet, on the other hand, a human heart
could not imagine the great pain I feel
all those many hours when I remember
the wonderful kisses that have bid me farewell.

Every joy is far from me today,
but not anger and pain and great suffering:
these have made a vow
that I will never leave their clutches.

Now you can see to what point I've come,
and for my pain there is no other cause
except that I was born too soon.

But you should know that I have a firm belief
that I will be avenged by you,
if you will learn my lesson well."

1. Cf. *Rose*, 12827–12854.

152

La Vec[c]hia

"Non ne pos[s]'altrementi far vengianza
Se non per insegnarti mia dottrina,
Perciò che·llo me' cor sì m'indovina
Che·ttu darai lor ancor gran micianza,

A que' ribaldi che tanta viltanza
Me diceano da sera e da mattina:
Tutti gli met[t]erai anche a la china,
Se·ttu sa' ben tener la tua bilanza.

Ché sie certana, s'i' fosse dell'ag[g]io,
Figl[i]uola mia, che tu·sse' or presente,
Ch'i' gli pagherè' ben di lor oltrag[g]io,

Sì che ciascuno farè' star dolente:
Già tanto non sareb[b]e pro' né sag[g]io
Ched i' non ne facesse pan-chiedente.

152

The Old Woman[1]

"I cannot avenge myself in any other way
except through teaching you my doctrine;
for my heart foresees
that you will do great harm

to those scoundrels who insulted me
both night and day.
You will bring all of them to ruin,
if you can keep them off balance.

My daughter, if I were the age
that you are now, you may be sure that
I would really pay them back for their offence

and make each one of them suffer:
indeed, no man would be so valiant or wise
that I would not turn him into a beggar."

1. Cf. *Rose*, 12863–12876.

153

La Vec[c]hia

"In gran povertà tutti gli met[t]esse,
Sì come t'ò di sopra sermonato,
E sì sareb[b]e il primo dispogliato
Colui che più cara mi tenesse.

Di nessun mai pietà no·mi'n prendesse,
Ché ciaschedun vorrè' aver disertato:
Ché sie certana ch'e' nonn-è peccato
Punir la lor malatia, chi potesse.

Ma e' non dottan guari mia minac[c]ia
Né non fan forza di cosa ch'i' dica,
Perciò ch'ò troppo crespa la mia fac[c]ia.

Figliuola mia, se Dio ti benedica,
I' non so chi vendetta me ne faccia
Se non tu, ch'i' per me son troppo antica.

153

The Old Woman[1]

"I would reduce them all to poverty,
just as I have preached to you earlier,
and the first to be stripped of wealth
would be the one who held me most dear.

Pity would never seize me for anyone,
for I would like to ruin each and every one of them;
now be assured that it is not a sin
for one to punish their vice, if one could.

But they do not fear my threats very much,
nor do they worry over what I say,
since I have so many wrinkles in my face.

My daughter, may God bless you,
I don't know who could avenge me
except for you, for I'm too old to do it myself."

1. Cf. *Rose*, 12877–12898.

154

La Vec[c]hia

“Molte volte mi disse quel ribaldo
Per cu' i' eb[b]i tanta pena e male,
Ched e' ver[r]eb[b]e ancor tal temporale
Ched i' avreï spesso fredo e caldo.

Ben disse ver, quel conto ò i' ben saldo;
Ma, per l'agio ch'i' eb[b]i, tanto e tale
Che tutto quanto il cuor mi ne trasale,
Quand'i' rimembro, sì ritorna baldo.

Giovane donna nonn-è mai oziosa,
Sed ella ben al fatto si ripensa
Per ch'ella sti' a menar vita gioiosa:

Ma' ch'ella pensi a chieder sua dispensa,
Sì ch'ella non si truovi sofrattosa
Quando vec[c]hiez[z]a vien poi che·ll'ade[n]sa.

154

The Old Woman[1]

"Many times that scoundrel said to me,
the one for whom I had so much pain and ill,
that such a time would arrive
when I would feel both cold and heat.

He certainly told the truth; that debt I've truly paid;
but, so much and so intense was the pleasure I enjoyed,
that my heart leaps up in me
when I remember, and then becomes happy once again.

A young woman is never idle,
if she considers carefully the matter
of how she may lead a joyful life,

except that she should think to fill her larder,
so that she may never find herself in need,
when old age comes and attacks her."

1. Cf. *Rose*, 12899–12914.

155

La Vec[c]hia

"Or ti dirò, figl[i]uola mia cortese,
Po' che parlar possiamo per ligire
E più arditamente, ver vo' dire,
Che·nnoi non solavàn (quest'è palese):

Tu sì sa' ben ch'i' son di stran paese,
E sì son messa qui per te nodrire;
Sì ti priego, figl[i]uola, che·tt'atire
In saper guadagnar ben tüe spese.

Non ch'i' te dica ch'i' voglia pensare
Che·ttu d'amor per me sie 'nviluppata;
Ma tuttor sì te voglio ricontare

La via ond'io dovrè' esser andata,
E 'n che maniera mi dovea menare
Anzi che mia bieltà fosse passata.

155

The Old Woman[1]

"Now I'll tell you, my noble daughter,
since we can speak freely
and more boldly, I must admit,
than we were accustomed to do (this is evident).

You know well that I'm from a foreign country,
and that I'm here to educate you:
thus, my daughter, I beg you to prepare yourself
to learn how to earn your board and keep.

Let me say that I don't intend
for you to become entangled in love's snares because of me;
but I want to tell you all the same

about the road I should have taken,
and how I should have behaved
before my beauty had faded away."

1. Cf. *Rose*, 12919–12946.

156

La Vec[c]hia

"Figl[i]uola mia, chi vuol gioir d'Amore,
Convien ch'e' sap[p]ia i suo' comandamenti.
Ver è ched e' ve n'à due dispiacenti:
Chi se ne 'mbriga, sì fa gran follore.

L'un dice che 'n un sol luogo il tu' cuore
Tu metta, sanza farne partimenti;
L'altro vuol che·ssie largo in far presenti:
Chi di ciò 'l crede, falleria ancore.

I·nulla guisa, figlia, vo' sia larga,
Né che 'l tu' cuor tu metti in un sol loco;
Ma, se mi credi, in più luoghi lo larga.

Se dài presenti, fa che vaglian poco:
Che s'e' ti dona Lucca, dàgli Barga;
Così sarai tuttor donna del g[i]uoco.

156

The Old Woman[1]

"My daughter, whoever wants to take delight in Love
must know his commandments.
In truth, two of these are unpleasant:
whoever gets tripped up by these commits great foolishness.

One commandment says that you should give your heart
to only one person and not share it with others;
the second requires generosity in giving gifts:
whoever believes Love in this would make a grave mistake.

In no way, daughter, do I want you to be generous,
nor to put your heart in only one place;
but, if you believe me, spread it out in many places.

And if you give gifts, make sure they're worth little;
if he gives you Lucca, give him Barga.[2]
In this manner you will always control the game."

1. Cf. *Rose*, 12981–13019.

2. That is, in return for an expensive present (the city of Lucca) the woman should give a very cheap one (Barga, a small community in the area of Tuscany known as the Garfagnana).

157

La Vec[c]hia

"Donar di femina si è gran follia,
Sed e' non s'è un poco a genti atrare
Là dov'ella si creda su' pro fare,
E che 'l su' don radoppiato le sia.

Quella non tengh'i' già per villania:
Ben ti consento quel cotal donare,
Ché·ttu non vi puo' se non guadagnare;
Gran senn'è a far tal mercatantia.

Agl[i] uomini lasciàn far la larghez[z]a,
Ché Natura la ci à, pez[z]'è, vietata:
Dunque a femina farla si è sempiez[z]a;

Avegna che ciascun'è sì afetata
Che volontier di lei fanno stranez[z]a,
Sed e' non s'è alcuna disperata.

157

The Old Woman[1]

"The giving of gifts by a woman is great foolishness,
unless they are small gifts used to lure men
there where she thinks she can have an advantage,
and where her gift can bring her a twofold return.

I don't believe this activity is ignoble:
indeed, I encourage you in this kind of giving,
because you can only gain from it;
it's very wise to make this sort of business deal.

We let men perform these generous acts,
since Nature has forbidden them to us for some time;
thus, for a women to do this is great foolishness.

To be sure, every woman is of such nature
that she refrains from this sort of generosity,
unless she is desperate."

1. Cf. *Rose*, 13020–13030.

158

La Vec[c]hia

"I' lodo ben, se·ttu vuo' far amico,
Che 'l bel valletto, che tant'è piacente,
Che de le gioie ti fece presente
E àtti amata di gran tempo antico,

Che·ttu sì·ll'ami; ma tuttor ti dico
Che·ttu no·ll'ami troppo fermamente,
Ma fa che degli altr'ami sag[g]iamente,
Ché 'l cuor che·nn'ama un sol, non val un fico.

Ed io te ne chiedrò degl[i] altri assai,
Sì che d'aver sarai tuttor guernita,
Ed e' n'andranno con pene e con guai.

Se·ttu mi credi, e Cristo ti dà vita,
Tu·tti fodraï d'ermine e di vai,
E la tua borsa fia tuttor fornita.

158

The Old Woman[1]

"If you want to have a lover, I certainly approve
of that handsome lad, who is so pleasing,
who gave you the jewels as a gift
and who has loved you for a very long time,

and I approve of your love for him. Nevertheless, I say to you
that you should not love him too loyally,
but make sure that you love others wisely,
for the heart that loves only one person is not worth a fig.

I will seek out lots of other lovers for you,
so that you'll always be well supplied with this sort of wealth,
and they will go around with pain and laments.

If you believe me, and if Christ gives you life,
you will be dressed in ermine and squirrel,
and your purse will always be full."

1. Cf. *Rose*, 13063–13074.

159

La Vec[c]hia

"Buon acontar fa uon c[h]'ab[b]ia danari,
Ma' ched e' sia chi ben pelar li saccia:
Con quel cotal fa buon intrar in caccia,
Ma' ched e' no·gli tenga troppo cari.

L'acontanza a color che·sson avari
Sì par c[h]'a Dio e al mondo dispiaccia:
Non dar mangiar a que' cotali in taccia,
Ché ' pagamenti lor son troppo amari.

Ma fa pur ch'e' ti paghi inanzi mano:
Ché, quand'e' sarà ben volonteroso,
Per la fé ched i' dô a san Germano,

E' non potrà tener nulla nascoso,
Già tanto non fia sag[g]io né certano,
Sed e' sarà di quel disideroso.

159

The Old Woman[1]

"It's good to know a man who has money,
provided that someone knows how to skin him;
and it's a good idea to go hunting with this 'someone'
unless he values money too highly.[2]

It appears that associating with avaricious people
is displeasing both to God and to the world:
don't feed such people at a set price,
for payments make them very sad.

But make sure they pay you in advance;
for when he'll be overwhelmed with desire for you,
by the faith I put in Saint Germain,[3]

he'll not be able to keep anything hidden,
no matter how wise and astute he may be,
so desirous will he be for sex."

1. Cf. *Rose*, 13075–13077.
2. I.e., unless he is a miser.
3. The bishop of Paris who died in 576 (see sonnet 203).

160

La Vec[c]hia

"E quando sol'a sol con lui sarai,
Sì fa che·ttu gli facci saramenti
Che·ttu per suo danar non ti consenti,
Ma sol per grande amor che·ttu in lui ài.

Se fosser mille, a ciascun lo dirai,
E sì 'l te crederanno, que' dolenti;
E saccie far sì che ciascuno adenti
Insin c[h]'a povertà gli metterai.

Che·ttu·sse' tutta loro, dé' giurare;
Se·tti spergiuri, non vi metter piato,
Ché Dio non se ne fa se non ghignare:

Ché sie certana ch'e' non è peccato,
Chi si spergiura per voler pelare
Colui che fie di te così ingannato.

160

The Old Woman[1]

"And when you'll be alone with him,
make sure you swear to him
that you're not giving yourself to him because of his money,
but only for the great love you have for him.

And if there were thousands, to each one you'll say it,
and they'll believe you for sure, those wretched ones;
and do it in such a way that you put the bite on all of them,
until you have reduced them to poverty.

You must swear that you're all theirs;
if you commit perjury, don't worry about it,
for God won't do anything but laugh.

You may be sure that it's no sin
to commit perjury in order to skin
that one who'll be deceived by you."

1. Cf. *Rose*, 13078–13096.

161

La Vec[c]hia

"A gran pena può femina venire
A buon capo di questa gente rea.
Dido non potte ritenere Enea
Ched e' non si volesse pur fug[g]ire,

Che mise tanta pena in lui servire.
Or che fece Gesono de Medea,
Che, per gl'incantamenti che sapea,
El[l]a 'l sep[p]e di morte guarentire,

E po' sì la lasciò, quel disleale?
Und'è c[he] ' figl[i]uoli ched ella avea
Di lui, gli mise a morte, e fece male;

Ma era tanto il ben ch'ella volea,
Ch'ella lasciò tutta pietà carnale
Per crucciar que' che tanto le piacea.

161

The Old Woman[1]

"With much effort a woman can get
ahead of these faithless people.
Dido could not keep Aeneas
from running away from her,

and she had put so much effort into serving him.[2]
And what did Jason do with Medea?
Through all the enchantments she knew
she was able to protect him from death,

and then he left her, that unfaithful one.[3]
For which reason, she killed the children
she had with him, and did other evil things;

but so great was her love
that she abandoned all of her maternal compassion
to make that one suffer who had pleased her so much."

1. Cf. *Rose*, 13143–13232.

2. Virgil recounts the story of the tragic love of Dido for Aeneas in the fourth book of the *Aeneid*. There Aeneas abandons Dido in order to pursue his divinely ordained mission to found the city of Rome, whereupon Dido commits suicide.

3. Ovid tells the story of Medea's love for Jason and her revenge (the slaying of their children) for his abandonment in the *Metamorphoses* (7.1–424) and in the *Heroides* (12). Ovid is the principal source for this story in the Middle Ages.

162

La Vec[c]hia

"Molti d'assempri dartene saprei,
Ma troppo saria lungo parlamento:
Ciascuna dé aver fermo intendimento
Di scorticargli, sì son falsi e rei.

S'i' fosse giovane, io ben lo farei;
Ma io so' fuor di quel proponimento,
Ché troppo fu tosto il mi' nascimento,
Sì ch'i' vendetta far non ne potrei.

Ma·ttu, figl[i]uola mia, che·sse' fornita
D'ogn'armadura per farne vengianza,
Sì fa che 'nverso lor sie ben sentita,

E presta di dar lor pen'e micianza:
Se·ttu 'l fai, d'ogni mal m'avrà' guerita
E alleg[g]iata d'ogne mia pesanza.

162

The Old Woman[1]

"I could give you many examples,
but my speech would be too long.
Each woman must be constant in her desire
to skin men, so false and evil are they.

If I were young, I would certainly do it;
but I no longer think this way,
for I was born too early,
and thus could not take revenge.

But you, my daughter, who are endowed
with every weapon with which to wreak revenge,
do it so that you are quite judicious in their regard

and quick to give them pain and misfortune.
If you do this, you will have healed me of every ill
and relieved me of all my sorrow."

1. Cf. *Rose*, 13233–13234.

163

La Vec[c]hia

"Tutti quanti le vann'og[g]i blasmando,
E ciaschedun sì le 'ntende a 'ngannare:
Così ciascuna di noi dé pensare
A far che·lla ric[c]hez[z]a i metta bando.

E non dob[b]iamo andar il cuor fic[c]ando
In un sol luogo, ma dob[b]iàn pensare
In che maniera gli possiàn pigliare,
E girgli tutti quanti dispogliando.

La femina dé aver amici molti,
E di ciascun sì dé prender su' agio,
E far sì c[h]'uon gli tenga per istolti;

E far lor vender la tor[r]e e 'l palagio,
O casa o casolari o vero i colti,
Sì che ciascun ci viva a gran misagio.

163

The Old Woman[1]

"Nowadays all men go around cursing women,
and each one plots to deceive them:
and thus each one of us must devise ways
to have Wealth banish them from her realm.

And we must not put our heart
only in one place, but think
of ways to ensnare them
and take away all their wealth.

A woman must have many lovers,
and from each of them she must get what's coming to her
and do it in such a way that they're taken for fools;

she must make them sell their tower and palace,
or home or farm or even their cultivated lands,
so that they all live in great discomfort."

1. Cf. *Rose*, 13235–13242.

164

La Vec[c]hia

"Ne·libro mio so ben che studierai,
Figlia, quando sarai da me partita:
Certana son, se Dio ti dona vita,
Che·ttu ter[r]aï scuola e leg[g]erai.

Di leg[g]erne da me congìo tu n'ài;
Ma guàrdati che·ttu sie ben fornita
Di ritener la lezion c[h]'ài udita,
E saviamente la ripeterai.

In casa non istar punto rinch[i]usa:
A chiesa o vero a ballo o vero a piaz[z]a,
In queste cota' luogora sì usa;

E fa che·ttu gli die ben de la maz[z]a,
A que' che per vederti sta a la musa
E che d'averti giorno e notte impaz[z]a.

164

The Old Woman[1]

"I know that you will study my book,
my daughter, when you have left me:
if God gives you life, I'm certain
you'll have a school in which you'll teach.

You have my permission to lecture from it;
but make sure that you're well equipped
to retain the lesson that you've heard,
and you'll repeat it wisely.

Never stay closed up in your house:
go to church, or better to a dance or to the square,
these are the places you should frequent.

And make sure you give a good beating
to that one who stops to moon over you
and who day and night yearns to have you."

1. Cf. *Rose*, 13243–13246, 13469–13498.

165

La Vec[c]hia

"Or sì·tti vo' parlar del guernimento,
Come ciascuna dé andar parata,
Che per sua falta non fosse lasciata
Sì ch'ella fosse sanza adornamento.

In ben lisciarsi sia su' 'ntendimento;
Ma, prima che si mostri a la brigata,
Convien ch'ella si sia ben ispec[c]hiata,
Che sopra lei non ag[g]ia fallimento.

E s'ella va da·ssera o da mattina
Fuor di sua casa, vada contamente:
Non vada troppo ritta né tro' china,

Sì ch'ella piaccia a chi·lla terrà mente;
E se·lla roba troppo le traina,
Levila un poco, e fiene più piacente.

165

The Old Woman[1]

"Now I want to speak with you about your wardrobe,
about how each woman must be well dressed
and how through no fault of her own
she should not be left without proper adornment.

Let her goal be to make herself beautiful;
but, before she shows herself to her friends,
she must look closely in the mirror
to be sure she has no blemish.

And when she leaves her house
by night or day she should go elegantly:
she should not walk too erectly or too bent over,

so that she may please those who gaze at her;
and if her dress touches the ground,
she should lift it a bit, and will be thus more pleasing."

1. Cf. *Rose*, 13499–13524.

166

La Vec[c]hia

"E s'ella nonn-è bella di visag[g]io,
Cortesemente lor torni la testa,
E sì lor mostri, sanza far aresta,
Le belle bionde treccie d'avantag[g]io.

Se non son bionde, tingale in erbag[g]io
E a l'uovo, e po' vada a noz[z]e e a festa;
E, quando va, si muova sì a sesta
C[h]'al su' muover nonn-ab[b]ia punt'oltrag[g]io.

E gentamente vada balestrando
Intorno a·ssé cogli oc[c]hi a chi la guarda,
E 'l più che puote ne vad'acrocando.

Faccia sembianti che molto le tarda
Ched ella fosse tutta al su' comando;
Ma d'amar nullo non fosse musarda.

166

The Old Woman[1]

"And if she does not have a beautiful face,
let her turn her head toward them in a noble fashion,
thus showing them without delay
her very beautiful golden braids.

If her hair is not blonde, let her dye it with herbs
and eggs, and then she may go to weddings and to parties;
and when she goes about, let her move in such a balanced way
that her motion is not exaggerated.

And with all courtesy let her make crossbows
of her eyes and take aim at all those who look at her,
and let her hook as many as she can.

Let her pretend that she can't wait
to be completely at his command,
but she should not be so foolish as to love anyone."

1. Cf. *Rose*, 13271–13274, 13529–13549.

167

La Vec[c]hia

"La lupa intendo che, per non fallire
A prender ella pecora o montone,
Quand'e' le par di mangiar [i]stagione,
Ne va, per una, un cento e più asalire.

Così si dé la femina civire
Sed ella avesse in sé nulla ragione:
Contra ciascuno riz[z]ar dé il pennone
Per fargli nella sua rete fedire;

Chéd ella non sa quale riman preso,
Insin ch'ella no·gli à tarpata l'ala,
Sì dé tener tuttor l'aiuol su' teso,

E prendergli a' gheroni e a la sala;
Ma se sapesse, o ch'ell'avesse inteso,
Ch'e' fosse pover, gittil per la scala.

167

The Old Woman[1]

"I hear that, in order not to fail
to take the sheep or ram, the she-wolf,
when she thinks it's time to eat,
attacks more than a hundred to get just one.

In this way, the woman must get prepared,
if she had any sense at all:
against them all she must raise her flag
to make them fall into her net.

Since she doesn't know who'll be caught
until she's clipped their wing,
she must always keep her net stretched out,

and capture them in the folds and hems of her dress.
But if she learned or heard
that he was poor, then let her throw him down the stairs."

1. Cf. *Rose*, 13551–13570.

168

La Vecchia

"E s'ella ne prendesse gran funata,
Di que' che ciaschedun la vuol brocciare,
Sì si dé ben la femina avisare
D'assegnar a ciascun la sua giornata:

Chéd ella rimar[r]ia troppo 'ngannata
Se·ll'un l'altro vi potesse trovare,
C[h]'almen le conver[r]eb[b]e pur fallare
Alla gioia che ciascun l'avria recata.

Ché non si vuoi lasciar già lor nïente
Di ch'e' potesser far grande 'ngrassata,
Ch'egli è perduto tutto il rimanente.

Perciò convien che ciascuna avisata
Sia, sì che pover rimanga il dolente,
Ed ella sïa ricca e ben calzata.

168

The Old Woman[1]

"And if she should have a whole line-up
of those who want to run her through,[2]
the woman must be careful
to assign each one his particular day;

because she would be betrayed,
if one were to find the other there;
for she would at least have to give up
the jewelry that they brought her.

Because one must not leave them anything
with which they could get fat,[3]
for all the rest is lost.

Therefore, every woman must be shrewd,
so that the poor man may remain miserable,
and she may be wealthy and well dressed."

1. Cf. *Rose*, 13571–13586.
2. Note the combination of martial and sexual imagery.
3. I.e., with any wealth whatsoever.

169

La Vecchia

"In poveruon no·metter già tu'amore,
Ché nonn-è cosa che poveruon vaglia:
Di lu' non puo' tu aver se non battaglia
E pena e povertate e gran dolore.

Lasciar ti farian robe di colore
E sovente dormire in su la paglia:
Non t'intrametter di cotal merda[g]lia,
Ché troppo i' 'l ti por[r]ia a gran fallore.

Né non amar già oste trapassante:
Però che mutan tante ostellerie
C[h]'aver non posson cuor fermo né stante;

Lor fatti non son che baratterie.
Ma se·tti donan, non sie rifusante;
E fa co·llui infinte druderie.

169

The Old Woman[1]

"Don't place your love in a poor man,
because a poor man is worth nothing:
from him you can have nothing but arguments
and anguish and poverty and great pain.

They would make you give up beautiful clothing
and often make you sleep on straw:
don't let yourself get trapped in that crap,
because I would say you've made a big mistake.

And never love a foreigner passing through:
because they change their inns so many times,
they cannot have a faithful or constant heart;

their actions are nothing but tricks.
But if they give you gifts, do not refuse them,
and make false shows of affection for them."

1. Cf. *Rose*, 13587–13600.

170

La Vec[c]hia

"Né non amar già uon che 'n sua bel[l]ez[z]a
Si fidi, né ch'egli a lisciarsi 'ntenda:
In quel cotal non vo' che·ttu t'intenda,
Ma 'l più che puo', da·llu' fa ïstranez[z]a.

L'uon che si piace, fa gran scipidez[z]a
E grand'orgoglio, e l'ira di Dio atenda;
E Tolemeo sì 'l dice in sua leg[g]enda,
C[h]'aver non p[u]ote amore né franchez[z]a;

Né non puote aver cuor di ben amare:
Ché tutto ciò ch'egli avrà detto a l'una,
Sì tosto il va a l'altra ricontare;

E così pensa a far di ciascheduna,
Né non intende c[h]'a·llor barattare:
Udita n'ò la pianta di più d'una.

170

The Old Woman[1]

"Never love a man who's taken
with his own beauty, nor one who likes to preen:
I don't want you to fall in love with such a man,
but stay as far away from him as you can.

The man who likes himself is very foolish
and proud: may he receive God's fury;
and Ptolemy says in his work[2]
that such a man cannot have love and spiritual freedom.

Nor can he have a heart that loves nobly,
because all that he has said to one woman,
he will just as quickly repeat to another;

and in this way he plans to deal with every woman
and intends only to deceive them:
I have heard the lament of more than one."

1. Cf. *Rose*, 13601–13616.

2. The second-century A.D. Egyptian astronomer/geographer devised the system of the universe as it was generally accepted in the Middle Ages and up to the time of Copernicus. In the *Dicta et gesta philosophorum antiquorum* we find the sentence: "Qui sui plurimum est contentus, dignus est ira Dei."

171

La Vec[c]hia

"E s'e' viene alcuno che·tti prometta,
E per promessa vuol c[h]'a·llui t'attacci,
I' non vo' già perciò che·ttu lo scacci,
Ma digli c[h]'altro termine ti metta,

Perciò c[h]'avrai allor troppo gran fretta;
E sì vo' ben che 'l basci e che·ll'abracci,
Ma guarda che co·llui più non t'impacci,
S'e' non iscioglie prima la maletta.

O s'alcun ti mandasse alcuno scritto,
Sì guarda ben la sua intenzïone,
Ched e' non ab[b]ia fintamente scritto;

E poi sì gl[i]ene fa risponsïone,
Ma non sì tosto: atendi un petitto,
Sì ch'egli un poco stea in sospez[z]one.

171

The Old Woman[1]

"And if someone comes along who makes you promises
and wants you to attach yourself to him with promises,
I don't want you to send him away for this reason,
but tell him to give you another deadline,

since you will then be in too great a rush.
And so I want you to kiss and embrace him,
but be careful not to get too involved with him
unless he unties his purse strings first.

And if someone were to send you a written note,
make sure that you know his intention
and that he has not written with deception in mind;

and then give him an answer,
but not too quickly: wait a little bit,
so that he may be in suspense for a little while."

1. Cf. *Rose*, 13617–13630.

172

La Vec[c]hia

"E quando tu udirai la sua domanda,
Già troppo tosto non sie d'acordanza,
Né non fare di lui gran rifusanza:
Nostr'arte sì no'l vuol né no'l comanda.

Cortesemente da·tte sì 'l ne manda,
E stea il su' fatto tuttora in bilanza,
Sì ch'egli ab[b]ia paura ed isperanza
Insin ch'e' sia del tutto a tua comanda.

E quand'e' ti farà più pregheria,
Tu gli dirai tuttor che·ttu sie presta
A fargli tutta quanta cortesia,

E dì che 'l su'amor forte ti molesta;
E così caccia la paura via.
Po' dimora con lui e fagli festa.

172

The Old Woman[1]

"And when you hear his amorous request,
don't give yourself to him too quickly,
but don't give him a great refusal either:
our amorous art neither wants nor requires this.

Send him away from you politely,
and may his state always be uncertain,
so that he may have both fear and hope
until he is completely at your command.

And when he will beg you even more,
you'll always tell him that you're ready
to grant him all manner of courtesy,

and tell him that his love makes you suffer terribly;
by so doing you chase away his fear.
Then stay with him and give him warm welcome."

1. Cf. *Rose*, 13633–13647.

173

La Vec[c]hia

"Gran festa gli farai e grand'onore,
E dì come gli ti se' tutta data,
Ma non per cosa ch'e' t'ag[g]ia donata,
Se non per fino e per leal amore;

Che·ttu à' rifiutato gran signore,
Che riccamente t'avreb[b]e dotata:
'Ma credo che m'avete incantata,
Per ched i' son entrata in quest'errore'.

Allor sì 'l bascierai istrettamente,
Pregando'l che·lla cosa sia sagreta,
Sì che no'l senta mai nessuna gente.

A·cciò ch'e' vorrà fare, istarà' cheta;
Ma guarda che non fosse aconsentente
A nessun, se non se per la moneta.

173

The Old Woman[1]

"You'll welcome him most warmly and with great honor
and say that you've given yourself completely to him,
but not for anything that he may have given you,
but only through noble and faithful love.

Say that you have refused an eminent lord,
who would have given you much wealth:
'But I believe that you've bewitched me,
for which reason I'm caught up in this passionate error.'

Then you'll kiss him long and hard,
begging him to keep your love a secret,
so that no one will ever know about it.

To anything he'll want to do, you'll agree silently,
but be careful not to consent
to any one, except for money."

1. Cf. *Rose*, 13648–13666.

174

La Vec[c]hia

"Chi 'l su' amico non cessa di pelare
Infin ch'egli ag[g]ia penna in ala o in dosso
E che d'ogn'altro bene e' sia sì scosso
Ched e' non si ne possa mai volare,

Quella cotal dovria l'uon maneg[g]iare:
Ché, quanto ch'ella costa più di grosso,
Più fia tenuta cara, dirlo posso,
E più la vorrà que' tuttor amare.

Ché·ttu non pregi nulla cosa mai
Se nonn-è quel che·ttu n'avrà' pagato:
Se poco costa, poco il pregerai;

E quel che·tti sarà as[s]ai costato,
A l'avenante caro il ti terrai,
Con tutto n'ag[g]ie tu ben mal mercato.

174

The Old Woman[1]

"Whoever has no difficulty in skinning her friend,
as long as he has feathers left on his wing or back
or until he is deprived of every other good
so that he can no longer fly,

in this way she should handle the man:
for I can say that the more she costs
the more precious she will be held,
and the more he will always want to love her.

Because you never value anything very highly
except that for which you have paid:
if it costs little, little will you value it;

and that which has cost you a lot,
in comparison you will hold it dear,
although you may be making a really bad deal."

1. Cf. *Rose*, 13667–13678.

175

La Vec[c]hia

"E al pelar convien aver maniera,
Sì che l'uomo a veder non si ne desse,
Che tutto in pruova l'uon glile facesse:
Forse ch'e' volgeria la sua bandiera.

Ma faccia sì la madre, o ciamberiera,
Od altri in cui fidar ben si potesse,
Che ciascuna di lor sì gli chiedesse
Paternostri o coreg[g]ia od amoniera.

Ancor la cameriera dica: 'Sire,
A questa donna una roba bisogna,
Ma sì vi teme che no'l v'osa dire.

Gran danno l'à già fatto [la] vergogna,
Ma vo' sì no'l dovreste sofferire;
Nonn-à dove le carni sue ripogna'.

175

The Old Woman[1]

"And in the skinning process you must have a certain style,
so that it may not be evident
that everything is being done as a kind of game:
perhaps he would change his mind.

But let her mother or the chambermaid,
or someone else whom she could trust,
let anyone of them ask him
for rosaries or a girdle or a purse.

Moreover, let the chambermaid say: 'Sir,
this lady needs a dress,
but she fears you so much that she dares not ask you for it.

Her shameful reluctance has already caused her much harm,
but you should not allow it;
she does not have anything to cover her body'."

1. Cf. *Rose*, 13679–13685, 13697–13698.

176

La Vec[c]hia

"Ancor gli dica un'altra de l'ostello:
'Se madonna volesse far fol[l]ag[g]io
Con un bel[l]issim'uon di gran parag[g]io,
Il fatto suo sareb[b]e ben e bello,

E sì sareb[b]e donna d'un castello;
Ma 'nverso voi à sì leal corag[g]io
Ch'ella non prendereb[b]e nul vantag[g]io
Di che doman vo' foste su' ribello'.

Allor la donna, come ch'e' le piaccia
Udir quelle parole, sì lor dica
E comandi che ciascuna si taccia;

E puote dir: 'Se Dio mi benedica,
Tropp'ò del su' quand'i' l'ò tra·lle braccia';
E facciagli sott'al mantel la fica.

176

The Old Woman[1]

"Moreover, let another woman of the house say to him:
'If my lady would want to commit an act of folly
with a handsome man of good lineage,
her situation would be fine and dandy,

and thus she would be the lady of a castle;
but towards you she has such a loyal heart
that she would not take any personal profit,
on account of which you would be her enemy tomorrow.'

Then let the lady, although she may like
to hear those words, say to them
and command each of them to be silent;

she can say: 'May God bless me,
I already have so much of him when I have him in my arms';
and let her give him the finger under her cape."[2]

1. Cf. *Rose*, 13699–13710.

2. The Italian text refers to the obscene gesture of the "fig," that is, the placing of the thumb between the index and middle finger of the hand to indicate sexual intercourse. It is this gesture that the Pistoian thief Vanni Fucci gives to God in *Inf.* 25.2–3.

177

La Vec[c]hia

"E se·lla donna punto s'avedesse
Che quel dolente fosse ravisato
Che troppo largamente l'à donato,
E ch'e' di sua follia si ripentesse,

Allora in presto domandar dovesse
E dir di renderglile a dì nomato;
Ma egli è ben in mia lezion vietato
Ched ella mai nessun non ne rendesse.

E quando un altro vien, gli faccia segno
Ched ella sia crudelmente cruc[c]iata,
E dica che·lla roba sua sia 'n pegno:

'Molto mi duol c[h]'uon crede ch'i' si'agiata'.
E que' procaccierà danari o pegno,
Sì che la roba sua fie dispegnata.

177

The Old Woman[1]

"And if the lady were aware at all
that that sad jerk had understood
that he had given her much too generously
and that he might repent of his foolishness,

then she should ask him to lend her money
and say she'll pay him back on a specific day;
but in my teachings this is forbidden,
because she should never return anything to anyone.

And when another man comes to her, let her give him a sign
that she is cruelly tormented,
and let her say that her dress is in hock:

'It grieves me much that people think I am so wealthy.'
And that one will get her the money or the pawn,
so that her dress may be returned to her."

1. Cf. *Rose*, 13711–13738.

La Vec[c]hia

"E se 'l diavol l'avesse fatto sag[g]io,
E che·lla donna veg[g]ia ch'à dottanza
Di non volerle far questa prestanza,
Imantenente sì gli mandi un gaggio:

La roba ch'ell'avrà più d'avantaggio;
E dica che·lla tenga in rimembranza
De' suo' danari, e non faccia mostranza
Ched e' le paia noia né oltrag[g]io.

E poi atenderà alcuna festa,
Pasqua o Kalendi Mag[g]io o Pentecosta,
E sia intorno a·llui sanza far resta,

Dicendo che giamai a la sua costa
Non dormirà, se que' no gl[i]ele presta:
La roba, in questa guisa, sì gl[i]el'osta.

178

The Old Woman

"And if, by chance, the devil had made him wise,
and if the lady sees that he is afraid
to make her this loan,
immediately let her send him a pledge:

the best dress that she has.
She should tell him to keep it as a pledge
for his money, and she should not let it be known
that this act seems to bother or offend her.

And then she'll wait for some holiday,
Easter or the calends of May[1] or Pentecost,
and let her be around him all the time,

saying that she will never sleep
at his side, if he does not lend her the money.
In this way, she'll surely take the dress away from him."

1. I.e., May 1.

179

La Vec[c]hia

"E s'alcun altro nonn-à che donare,
Ma vorràssi passar per saramenta,
E dirà che·lla 'ndoman più di trenta
O livre o soldi le dovrà recare,

Le saramenta lor non dé pregiare,
Chéd e' non è nes[s]un che non ti menta;
E dice l'un a l'altro: 'La giomenta
Che·ttu ti sai, mi credette ingannare;

Ingannar mi credette, i' l'ò 'ngannata'.
Per che già femina non dee servire
Insin ch'ella non è prima pagata:

Ché, quando à fatto, e' si pensa fug[g]ire,
Ed ella si riman ivi scornata.
Per molte volte fui a quel martire.

179

The Old Woman[1]

"And if there's someone who has nothing to give,
but will want to get away with only a pledge,
he'll say that the next day
he'll bring her more than thirty *livre* or *soldi*.[2]

She must not value their pledges,
for there's no one who doesn't lie to you;
one says to another: 'The prostitute,
whom you know, thought she could deceive me;

she thought she could deceive me, but I deceived her!'
For this reason no woman must give herself to anyone
unless she is paid first;

for when he's done it, he plans to run away,
but she remains there scorned.
Many times I found myself in that awful state."

1. Cf. *Rose*, 13751–13760.

2. This appears to be ironic, since a *lira* was divided into twelve *denari* and these into twenty *soldi*.

180

La Vec[c]hia

"Sì dé la donna, s'ell'è ben sentita,
Quando ricever dovrà quell'amante,
Mostralli di paura gran sembiante,
E ch'ella dotta troppo es[s]er udita,

E che si mette a rischio de la vita.
Allor dé esser tutta tremolante,
Dir ch'ivi non puot'es[s]er dimorante:
Poi stea, che·llor gioia sia compita.

Ancor convien ched ella si' acorta
Di far ch'e' v'entri per qualche spiraglio,
Ben potess'egli entrarvi per la porta:

Ché tutte cose c[h]'uom'à con travaglio,
Par c[h]'uon le pregi più, e fed' i' porta;
Quel che non costa, l'uon non pregia un aglio.

180

The Old Woman[1]

"And if she's wise, the lady,
when she receives that lover,
must show him that she's afraid
and that she greatly fears being heard,

and that she's putting her life in danger.
Then she must tremble all over
and say that he cannot stay in that place:
then let him stay until their joy is complete.

Moreover, she must be careful
to have her lover enter through a secret passage,
even though he could enter through the door;

for all the things obtained through hard work
seem to be more highly valued and inspire trust.
What costs nothing is not worth anything."[2]

1. Cf. *Rose*, 13671–13675, 13765–13785.
2. I.e., people do not place any value (not even a garlic!) on something that costs nothing.

181

La Vec[c]hia

"E quand'ella serà rasicurata,
Tantosto sì gli dé cor[r]ere indosso,
E dir: 'Lassa tapina, be·mi posso
Chìamar dolente, s'i' son arivata

Ched i' sì amo, e sì non son amata!
Molt'ò lo 'ntendimento rud'e grosso,
Quando il me' core s'è sì forte ismosso
D'esser di voi così inamorata'.

E po' sì gli rimuova quistïone,
E dica: 'La lontana dimoranza
C[h]'avete fatta, nonn·è san' cagione.

Ben so che voi avete un'altr'amanza,
La qual tenete in camera o 'n pregione';
Sì moster[r]à d'averne gran pesanza.

181

The Old Woman[1]

"And as soon as she has been reassured,
she must immediately run up to him
and say: 'Wretched me, I can certainly
call myself unfortunate, if I have arrived at the point

where I love, but am not loved in return!
My reasoning becomes very rough and dull,
when my heart is so powerfully moved
by my great love for you.'

Then she should start her complaint once again,
saying: 'Your long stay away from me
is not without reason.

I well know that you have another lover,
whom you keep in your bedroom or in some secret place.'
And so, she will show her great sorrow over it."

1. Cf. *Rose*, 13793–13804.

182

La Vec[c]hia

"Quando 'l cattivo ch'è·ssarà 'ncacato,
La cui pensëa non serà verace,
Sì crederà che 'l fatto su' ti piace
Tanto, c[h]'ogn'altro n'ài abandonato,

E che 'l tu' cuor gli s'è tretutto dato;
Né non si guarderà de la fallacie
In che la volpe si riposa e giace,
Insin ch'e' non serà ben corredato.

Ché molt'è folle que' che cred'avere
Nessuna femina che·ssia sua propia,
Per don ched e' facesse di su'avere.

Que' che·lla vuol, la cheg[g]ia 'nn-Atïopia,
Ché qua no·lla pott'io ancor vedere,
E s'ella ci è, sì porta l'aritropia.

182

The Old Woman[1]

"When this wretched man has been besmirched,[2]
he won't be thinking right;
he'll think you like everything about him
so much that you have rejected every other man

and that your heart has been given completely to him;
and he will not guard against the deceitful ways
of the fox who rests and lies in wait,[3]
until he's been properly mistreated.

For very foolish is the man who thinks he can have
any woman to be his, and his alone,
because of the gifts he's given her with his wealth.

Whoever wants such a woman, let him seek her in Ethiopia,
because I've not yet seen one here,
and if she's here, then she must be carrying the heliotrope."[4]

1. Cf. *Rose*, 13805–13822.

2. Literally, the term *incacare* means "to be befouled with excrement." This unseemly, but highly realistic expression accords well with the comic inspiration that lies behind the Old Woman's discourse.

3. Again, we note the reference to the shrewd, fox-like nature of some of the characters, such as False Seeming (see sonnets 101 and 120).

4. According to medieval lapidaries, the stone known as the heliotrope had the power to make its bearer invisible. See, for example, Boccaccio's tale of Calandrino (*Decameron* 8.3) and Dante's reference to the properties of this stone in *Inf.* 24.89.

183

La Vec[c]hia

"Da l'altra parte elle son franche nate:
La leg[g]e sì·lle trâ di lor franchez[z]a,
Dove Natura per sua nobilez[z]a
Le mise quando prima fur criate.

Or l'à la leg[g]e sì condizionate
Ed àlle messe a sì gran distrezza,
Che ciascheduna volontier s'adrez[z]a
Come tornar potesse a franchitate.

Vedi l'uccel del bosco quand'è 'n gab[b]ia:
E' canterà di cuor, ciò vi fi'aviso,
Ma no·gli piace vivanda ch'egli ab[b]ia;

Ché Natur'a franchez[z]a l'à sì miso
Che giorno e notte de l'uscirne arrab[b]ia,
Nonn-avrà tanto miglio o grano o riso.

183

The Old Woman[1]

"On the other hand, women are born free:
the law takes away from them their free state,[2]
where Nature through her generosity
put them as soon as they were created.

Now the law has so bound them
and put them in such distress
that they all willingly strive
to return to this state of freedom.

You see how the wild bird, when it's in a cage,
will sing with all its heart—this will be clear to you—
but it does not like the food it has;

for Nature has instilled such freedom in it
that day and night it seeks feverishly to escape,
although it has enough millet or wheat or rice."

1. Cf. *Rose*, 13845–13848, 13911–13936.
2. The "law" of matrimony.

184

La Vec[c]hia

"E se quell'uon desdir non si degnasse,
Anzi dirà, per farla più crucciosa,
Che·nn'à un'altra, ch'è·ssì amorosa
Di lui che per null'altro no'l cambiasse,

Guardisi quella che non si crucciasse.
Con tutto ciò se ne mostri dogliosa
Di fuor, ma dentr'al cuor ne sia gioiosa:
Ancora più s'egli s'a[re]negasse;

E dicagli che già quella vendetta
Non sarà fatta se non sol per lei,
Sì ch'ella il pagherà di quella detta.

Allor da·llui sì mi dipartirei;
Di far amico moster[r]è' gran fretta,
Sì ch'io in quella angoscia il lascierei.

184

The Old Woman[1]

"And if that man would not deign to deny the fact,
and instead will say, to make her angrier,
that he has another woman who's so in love
with him that she would not exchange him for any other,

then that woman should guard against getting angry.
In spite of this, she should feign sadness
on the outside, but in her heart she should rejoice;
she should rejoice even more if he were to deny it;

and she should tell him that, indeed, revenge
will be taken only by her,
such that she will repay him for that debt.

Then, I would go away from him;
I would be quick to find myself another lover,
so that I would leave him in that sorrowful state."

1. Cf. *Rose*, 14173–14196.

185

La Vec[c]hia

"S'avessi messo termine a un'ora
A due, c[h]'avresti fatto gran follia,
E l'un conteco in camera sia,
E l'altro viene apresso san' dimora,

Al di dietro dirai ch'egl[i] è ancora
El signor tuo lassù; ch'e' non poria
Far dimoranza, ma tost'una fia:
'Il fante o voi, tornate a poca d'ora'.

E poi sì 'l butti fuori e torni suso,
E trag[g]a l'altro fuor della burella,
Che molto gli è anoiato star rinchiuso;

[E] posi la guarnac[c]a e la gonella,
Dicendo ch'ell'è tanto stata giuso
Per lo marito ch'era nella cella.

185

The Old Woman[1]

"If you've made appointments for the same hour
with two men—and in this you've been very foolish—
suppose that one of them is with you in the bedroom,
and the other one arrives immediately afterwards,

to this second one you will say that
your husband is still upstairs, and that he should not
be there too much longer, but one of the following will occur:
'Either you or your servant, come back shortly.'

And then she should kick him out and go back upstairs,[2]
and bring the other one out of the hiding place,
where he has not appreciated being locked up;

and then she should take off her robe and dress,
saying that she had to be downstairs so long
because of her husband, who was in the cellar."

1. Cf. *Rose*, 14211–14239.

2. Note the changeover in subject from the second person singular (you) to the third person (she).

186

La Vec[c]hia

"Ne·letto su' si metta in braccio in braccio
Co·llui insiem'e faccian lor diporto;
Ma dica tuttor: 'Lassa, crudel torto
È questo che 'nverso il mi' sire faccio'.

E nella gioia c[h]'à, gli metta impaccio,
Sì ch'egli ab[b]ia paura e disconforto:
Dicer li dëe ch'e' sarebbe morto,
Sanz'averne rispetto, molt'avaccio,

Se·ll'uon sapesse ch'e' fosse co·llei:
'Ed i' lassa dolente, malaurata,
So che vitiperata ne sarei

E ch'i' per man de' mie' sarè' ismembrata'.
E in questa paura i' 'l metterei,
Che da lui ne sareb[b]e più amata.

186

The Old Woman[1]

"In her bed she should embrace him,
and together have their pleasure;
but she should say over and over: 'O wretched me!
This is a terrible wrong I'm doing to my husband.'

And in the midst of his joy, she should introduce this difficulty,
so that he may be afraid and uneasy:
she must say to him that he would be killed
without any consideration and quickly,

if it were known that he was with her:
'And poor wretched me, unlucky one,
I know that I would be maligned,

and torn apart at the hands of my relatives.'
I would put him in this state of fear,
so that she would be loved by him even more."

1. Cf. *Rose*, 14237–14250.

187

La Vec[c]hia

"Quand'a quel lavorio messi saranno,
Ben sag[g]iamente deg[g]ian operare,
E l'un atender e l'altro studiare,
Secondo ch'egli al[l]or si sentiranno;

Né sì non dé parer lor già affanno
Di voler ben a modo mantacare,
C[h]'amendue insieme deg[g]ian afinare
Lor dilettanza; e dimorasse un anno!

E se·lla donna non v'à dilettanza,
Sì 'nfinga in tutte guise che vi sia,
Sì gline mostri molto gran sembianza:

Istringa 'l forte e basci 'l tuttavia;
Quando l'uom'avrà süa dilettanza,
Sì paia ch'ella tramortita sia.

187

The Old Woman[1]

"When they'll be engaged in that work,[2]
they should work together wisely;
one should slow down and the other quicken the pace,
according to what their senses tell them.

Their desire to move and pant like bellows
should hardly seem painful to them,
for both of them together should refine
their pleasure; and would that it would last a year!

And if the lady does not have the supreme delight,[3]
she should pretend in every possible way that she is about to,
and show in her appearance that this is so:

let her squeeze him tightly and kiss him constantly;
when the man has had his pleasure,
she should pretend to faint."

1. Cf. *Rose*, 14263–14280.
2. The usual term for sexual intercourse.
3. I.e., orgasm.

188

La Vec[c]hia

"Se l'uon può tanto far ched ella vada
Al su'albergo la notte a dormire,
Sì dé alla femina ben sovenire
Ched ella il faccia star un poco a bada.

E que', che guarderà tuttor la strada,
Certana sie ch'e' li parrà morire
Insin ched e' no·lla vedrà venire:
Ché·ll'amor c[h]'uom'atarda, vie più agrada.

E quand'ella sarà a l'ostel venuta,
Sì dica a que', che·nn'è sì amoroso,
Ched ella per su'amor tropp'è arguta;

Ché 'l su' marito n'è troppo geloso,
Sì che dubita molto esser battuta:
Così gli faccia forte il päuroso.

188

The Old Woman[1]

"If the man arranges for her to go
to his house to sleep overnight,
the woman must remember
to make him wait a bit.

You may be sure that the man, who'll be
constantly watching the street, will think he'll die
before he sees her coming;
for love delayed is much more satisfying.

And when she has arrived at his house,
she should say to that one who's so in love with her
that for love of him she's become very bold;

her husband is so jealous of her,
that she fears she'll be beaten:
thus, let she play well the role of the fearful one for him."

1. Cf. *Rose*, 14281–14306.

189

La Vec[c]hia

"Se quel geloso la tien sì fermata
Ch'ella non poss'andar là ov'ella vuole,
Sì gli faccia intendente che·ssi duole
D'una sua gotta, che d'averl'è usata:

Per ch'e' convien ch'ella sïa stufata,
Ché colla stufa guerir se ne suole;
Po' bullirà ramerin e vïuole
E camamilla e salvia, e fie bagnata.

E 'l geloso dirà: 'Va arditamente,
E mena teco buona compagnia';
Ma molto ne fia nel su' cuor dolente,

Ma vede ch'e' desdir no·gliel poria.
Quella mena conseco alcuna gente,
La qual sapranno ben sua malatia.

189

The Old Woman[1]

"If that jealous one keeps her so locked up
that she cannot go wherever she wants,
she should make him believe that she is suffering
from a case of gout, which she's had for some time;

for this reason she must go to the baths,
since this sickness is usually cured with hot baths.
Then she will boil rosemary and violets
and camomile and sage, and bathe in this solution.

And the jealous husband will say: 'Go freely,
and take some good companions with you';
but in his heart he will be very sad,

but he sees that he can not prevent her from going.
She takes some companions with her,
who will know her sickness well."[2]

1. Cf. *Rose*, 14307–14340.
2. Her sickness is that of love, *hereos*, and not gout.

190

La Vec[c]hia

"Ancor non dé aver femina credenza
Che nessun uon malia farle potesse,
Néd ella ancor altrui, s'ella volesse
C[h]'altri l'amasse contra sua voglienza.

Medea, in cui fu tanta sapïenza,
Non potte far che Gesono tenesse
Per arte nulla ch'ella gli facesse,
Sì che 'nver' lei tornasse la sua 'ntenza.

Sì non dea nessun don, che guari vaglia,
A null'amante, tanto l'apregiasse:
Doni borsa, guanciale o tovaglia,

O cinturetta che poco costasse,
Covricef[f]o o aguglier di bella taglia,
O gumitol di fil, s'egli 'l degnasse.

190

The Old Woman[1]

"Moreover, a woman must not believe
that any man can cast a spell on her,
nor that she could do the same with men, if she would wish
them to love her against their will.

Medea, who was so knowledgeable in these matters,
could not keep her hold on Jason,
despite the magic spells she tried on him
to make him direct his love towards her.[2]

A woman should not give expensive gifts,
to any lover, no matter how much she might prize him:
let her give a purse, a pillow or a tablecloth,

or a very inexpensive belt,
a cap or a nicely crafted pin case,
or a skein of yarn if he would deem it worthy."

1. Cf. *Rose*, 14365–14388.
2. For Medea, see sonnet 161, note 3.

191

La Vec[c]hia

"Ma ciascun uon c[h]'avesse in sé ragione
O che del mondo ben savio sareb[b]e,
Ma' don' di femina non prendereb[b]e,
Ché non son che·llacci di tradigione:

Ché quella che facesse donagione,
Contra la sua natura pec[c]hereb[b]e,
E 'n gran follia ciascun gliele por[r]eb[b]e,
Sed ella no'l facesse a falligione.

Perciò ciascuna pensi, quando dona,
Che doni nella guisa c[h]'ò parlato:
Sì che, quand'ella avrà passata nona,

Il guardacuor suo sïa sì fodrato
Ch'ella non cag[g]ia a merzé di persona;
E ciò tien tutto al ben aver guardato.

191

The Old Woman[1]

"But any man who was astute
or wise in worldly ways
would never take gifts from a woman,
for they are nothing but the snares of treachery.

For the woman who would give gifts
would sin against her nature,
and everyone would think her quite foolish,
if she were not doing it to deceive.

Therefore, when giving a gift, let every woman plan
to give in the manner that I've described,
so that, when she has passed the ninth hour,[2]

her overcoat may be so well-lined
that she does not have to count on the charity of anyone:
and this depends on her having set wealth aside."

1. Cf. *Rose*, 14399–14404, 14411–14426.

2. That is, when she is on in years. In the Middle Ages, the day was divided into four parts, the third of which is nones [*nona*] or 3:00 P.M.

192

La Vec[c]hia

"Al ben guardar fallì', lassa dolente,
Ché·cciò c[h]'all'un togliea, a l'altro donava:
Come 'l danaio venia, così n'andava;
Non facea forza d'aver rimanente.

I' era di ciascun molto prendente,
E tutto quanto a un ribaldo il dava,
Che puttana comune mi chiamava
E mi battea la schiena ben sovente.

Questi era que' che più mi piacea,
E gli altri 'amici dolci' i' apellava,
Ma solamente a costui ben volea,

Che mol[to] tosto s'apacificava
Comeco, sì battuta no·m'avea,
Ché troppo dolzemente mi scuf[f]iava.

192

The Old Woman[1]

"I failed to set wealth aside, oh wretched, sorry me,
for what I took from one, I gave to another;
as money came in, so it went out;
I made no effort to save any of it.

I was used to taking gifts from every man,
and all of these I gave to a scoundrel,
who called me a common whore
and would frequently beat me.

He was the one I loved the most,
and I would call the others 'sweet friends,'
but he was the only one I loved,

and he would quickly make up
with me, although he'd beaten me up,
for he screwed me most sweetly."

1. Cf. *Rose*, 14427–14480.

193

La Vec[c]hia

"S'i' fosse stata, per l'anima mia,
Ben savia in giovanez[z]a e conos[c]ente,
Ch'i' era allor sì bella e sì piacente
Che 'n ogne parte novelle ne gia,

I' sarè' troppo ric[c]a, in fede mia;
Ma i' sì 'l dava tutto a quel dolente,
C[h]'a ben far non fu anche intendente,
Ma tutto dispendea in ribalderia.

Né no·gli pia[c]que nulla risparmiare,
Ch'e' tutto no'l beves[s]e e no'l giucasse,
Tant'era temperato a pur mal fare:

Sì c[h]'a la fin conven[n]e ch'i' lasciasse,
Quand'i' non eb[b]i più che gli donare;
E me e sé di gran ric[c]hez[z]a trasse".

193

The Old Woman[1]

"If I had been, for my sake,
very wise and intelligent in my youth,
when I was still so beautiful and pleasing
that news of me went everywhere,

I would be very rich, believe me;
but I gave everything to that wretch,
who was not smart enough to do wise things,
and he spent it all in debauchery.

He didn't like to save anything,
but drank and gambled it all away,
so singularly predisposed was he to vice;

so in the end I had to leave him,
when I no longer had anything to give him;
he took wealth away from me and from himself."

1. Cf. *Rose*, 14441–14448, 14489–14506.

194

La Vec[c]hia

Così à quella vec[c]hia sermonato.
Bellacoglienza molto queta è stata
E molto volontier l'à ascoltata,
E molto e' n'è 'l su' cuor rasicurato:

Sì ch'e' seria leg[g]ier a far mercato,
Se Gelosia non vi fosse trovata
E' tre portier', che fanno gran veg[g]hiata,
Ché ciascun dotta d'es[s]er barattato.

Di Mala-Bocca, che già era morto,
Nessun di lor non facea lada ciera,
Ché chi l'amasse sì faria gran torto:

Ché non finava di dìe né da sera
Di dar a Gelosia nuovo sconforto,
Né non dicea giamai parola vera.

194

The Old Woman[1]

In this way that old woman preached.
Fair Welcome was very quiet
and listened to her most willingly,
and her heart is greatly reassured by it.

Thus, it would be easy to close the deal,
if Jealousy had not been there
and the three gatekeepers[2] who are so vigilant,
for each one is afraid of being deceived.

None of them was very concerned
about Bad Mouth, who was already dead,
for whoever would love him would make a big mistake;

for day and night he never stopped
giving Jealousy new trouble,
and never did he utter a true word.

1. Cf. *Rose*, 14517–14535, 14540–14556.
2. Resistance, Modesty and Fear.

195

Bellacoglienza

Bellacoglienza la parola prese
E sì rispuose, come ben parlante:
"Gentil madonna, i' vi fo grazie mante
Che di vostr'arte mi siete cortese;

Ma 'l fatto de l'amor no·m'è palese,
Se non se in parole trapassante.
Ched i' sia di danar ben procacciante?
I' n'ò assai per farne belle spese.

D'avere in me maniera bella e gente,
A·cciò vogl'i' ben metter mia balia,
In tal maniera che·ssia sofficiente.

Se voi mi parlate di malia,
Ch'ella non può tornar già cuor di gente:
Creda 'l chi vuol, ch'i' la teng'a·ffollia.

195

Fair Welcome[1]

Fair Welcome began to speak
and answered with well-chosen words:
"My noble Lady, I thank you very much
for having been generous to me with your art;

but the facts of love are not clear to me,
because I know them only through fleeting words.
Why should I be an avid procurer of money?
I have enough to make some nice purchases.

It's toward acquiring noble and charming ways for myself
that I wish to apply my powers,
so that I may be well-supplied.

When you say to me that magic powers
cannot change the hearts of people,
let anyone believe it who so desires, but I consider it to be folly!"

1. Cf. *Rose*, 14575–14592.

196

Bellacoglienza

"Del bel valetto che vo' mi parlate,
In cui tanta vertute è riposata,
Sed e' la s'à, per me gli sia chitata:
S'i' l'amo, i' l'amerò come mi' frate.

Ma, per le gioie ch'e' m'à presentate,
La mia veduta no·gli fia vietata;
Ma venga il più che puote a la celata,
E sed e' piace a voi, sì 'l ci menate.

Ma' che sia fatto tosto san' dimora,
Perciò che Gelosia non può sofrire
Ched ella stea sanza vedermi un'ora:

Ché molte volte si parte per gire,
E 'l diavol, che di notte in lei lavora,
Sì·lla fa·mantenente rivenire".

196

Fair Welcome[1]

"You've spoken to me about the handsome lad,
the one in whom so much virtue is found;
if he has this virtue, let him keep it for my sake:
if I love him, I will love him like a brother.

But, because of the jewels he gave me,
he should not be prevented from seeing me;
but let him come as often as he can in secret,
and if you like, then bring him here.

But this should be done quickly and without delay,
since Jealousy cannot allow
an hour to pass without checking on me;

for many times she starts to go away,
and the devil, who works in her by night,
makes her come back immediately."

1. Cf. *Rose*, 14593–14626.

197

La Vec[c]hia e Bellacoglienza

La Vec[c]hia sì la va rasicurando,
E dice: "Sopra me lascia la cura
Di questo fatto; non aver paura,
Chéd io il saprò ben andar celando.

E gisse Gelosia tuttor cercando
Qua entro, sì seria grande sciagura
S'ella 'l trovasse, ma i' son sicura
Che poco le varria su' gir sognando".

"Dunque potete voi farlo venire,
Ma' ched e' si contegna come sag[g]io,
Ch'e' non pensasse a·ffar nes[s]un ardire".

"Figl[i]uola mia, e' non fece anche oltrag[g]io
I·nessun luogo, ch'i' udisse dire,
Ma troppo il loda l'uon di gran vantag[g]io".

197

The Old Woman and Fair Welcome[1]

The Old Woman thus goes about reassuring her
and says: "Let me take care
of this matter; don't be afraid,
for I'll know how to keep it hidden.

And should Jealousy continue to snoop around
inside here, it would be a great disaster
if she were to find him, but I am sure
that her fantastications will do her little good."

"Therefore, you can have him come,
on condition that he behave wisely
and that he not think to do any bold deed."

"My darling daughter, he never went beyond good measure
anywhere, at least that I heard about;
in fact, people greatly praise him for his excellence."

1. Cf. *Rose*, 14633–14648.

198

L'Amante e la Vec[c]hia

Al[l]or sì fecer fine al parlamento.
La Vec[c]hia se ne venne al mi' ostello,
E disse: "Avrò io sorcotto e mantello
Sed i' t'aporto alcun buon argomento

Che ti trarrà di questo tuo tormento?".
I' dissi: "Sì, d'un verde fino e bello;
Ma, sì sacciate, non fia san' pennello
Di grigio, con ogn'altro guernimento".

D'Amico mi sovenne, che mi disse
Ched i' facesse larga promessione,
Ma 'l più ch'i' posso, il pagar soferisse:

Avegna ch'i' avea ferma 'ntenzione
De dar ben a coste', s'ella m'aprisse,
Che quell'uscisse fuor della pregione.

198

Lover and the Old Woman[1]

At that point they ended their conversation.
The Old Woman came to my house
and said: "Will I have coat and mantle,
if I bring you some good remedy

that will take away your sorrow?"
"Yes," I said, "and they will be in a noble and beautiful green;
but, you should know, they'll have a gray
lining and every other sort of ornament."[2]

I remembered that Friend told me
that I should make a generous promise,
but that I should delay payment as long as I can;

although I had good intentions to compensate her well,
if for me she would unlock the door
to release that lady from confinement.[3]

1. Cf. *Rose*, 14649–14688.
2. The gray lining refers to the squirrel fur used in clothing of the time (see sonnet 158).
3. "That lady" is Fair Welcome.

199

La Vec[c]hia

La Vec[c]hia disse allor: "Amico mio,
Queste son le novelle ch'i' t'aporto:
Bellacoglienza salute e conforto
Te manda, se m'aiuti l'alto Dio;

Sì ch'i' ti dico ben ched i' cred'io
Che·lla tua nave ariverà a tal porto
Che·ttu sì coglierai il fior dell'orto".
(Questo motto fu quel che mi guerìo).

"Or te dirò, amico, che farai:
All'uscio c[h]'apre verso del giardino,
Ben chetamente tu te ne ver[r]ai;

Ed i' sì me ne vo 'l dritto camino,
E sì farò c[h]'aperto il troverai,
Sì che·ttu avrai il fior in tuo dimino".

199

The Old Woman

The Old Woman then said: "My friend,
this is the news I bring you:
Fair Welcome sends you greetings
and encouragement, so help me Almighty God.

Thus, I say to you that I believe
your ship will arrive in such a port
that you will pluck the Flower in the garden."[1]
These are the words that healed me.

"Now I'll tell you, my friend, what you'll do:
you will come very quietly
to the gate that opens to the garden;

and I will go along the straight road
and make sure you'll find the gate open,
so that you will have the Flower in your possession."

1. For the nautical imagery see sonnet 33.

200

L'Amante

La Vec[c]hia atanto da me si diparte,
E 'l camin eb[b]e tosto passeg[g]iato;
E quand'i fui un poco dimorato,
Verso 'l giardin n'andai da l'altra parte,

Pregando Idio che mi conduca 'n parte
Ch'i' de mia malatia fosse sanato.
Aperto l'uscio sì eb[b]i trovato;
Ver è ch'era soc[c]hiuso tutto ad arte.

Con molto gran paura dentro entrai;
Ma, quand'i' vidi Mala-Bocca morto,
Vie men del fatto mio sì mi dottai.

Amor trovai, che mi diè gran conforto
Co·l'oste sua, e molto m'allegrai
Che ciascun v'era 'n aiutarm'acorto.

200

Lover[1]

Meanwhile the Old Woman leaves me,
and had quickly passed along the path;
and after I had waited a bit,
I went toward the garden by the other way,

praying that God may guide me to that place
where I would be cured of my sickness.
I found the gate open;
in truth, it was half-closed on purpose.

With much trepidation I went inside;
but, when I saw Bad Mouth dead,
I was much less fearful about my situation.

I found Love who gave me much encouragement
with his army, and I rejoiced
that everyone there was ready to help me.

1. Cf. *Rose*, 14689–14704.

201

L'Amante e Bellacoglienza

Com'i' v'ò detto, a tutto lor podere
Lo Dio d'Amor e la sua baronia
Presti eran tutti a far senn'e follia
Per acompiérmi tutto 'l mio volere.

Allor pensai s'i' potesse vedere
Dolze-Riguardo per cosa che sia:
Inmantenente Amor a me lo 'nvia,
Di che mi fece molto gran piacere.

E que' sì mi mostrò Bellacoglienza,
Che 'nmantenente venne a salutarmi,
E sì mi fece grande proferenza;

E po' sì cominciò a merzïarmi
Delle mie gioie: di ch'ell'avea vogl[i]enza
Di quel presente ancor guiderdonarmi.

201

Lover and Fair Welcome[1]

As I told you, the God of Love and his army
of nobles, with all their might,
were ready to do whatever it took,
both wise and foolish, to satisfy my desire.

At that point I thought I would like to see
Sweet Glance above all else:
immediately Love sends him to me,
and this gave me great pleasure.

And that one showed me Fair Welcome,
who immediately came to greet me
and welcomed me warmly;

and then she began to thank me
for my jewels, since she wanted
to compensate me for that gift.

1. Cf. *Rose*, 14723–14743.

202

L'Amante e Bellacoglienza

I' le dissi: "Madonna, grazie rendo
A voï, quando prender le degnaste,
Che tanto forte me ne consolaste
Ch'a pena maï mag[g]ior gioia atendo;

E s'i' l'ò mai, da voi aver la '[n]tendo;
Sì c[h]'a me piace se ciò che pigliaste
O la persona mia ancora ingag[g]iaste
O la vendeste: mai non vi contendo".

Quella mi disse: "Molto gran merzede.
Di me vi dico fate 'l somigliante,
C[h]'a bene e a onore i' v'amo, a·ffede".

Delle sue cose i' non fu' rifusante;
Ma spesso falla ciò che 'l folle crede:
Così avenne al buon di ser Durante.

202

Lover and Fair Welcome[1]

I said to her: "My Lady, I give thanks to you
when you deigned to accept them;
you comforted me so much
that I can hardly expect to have greater joy;

and if I ever have it, I know I have it thanks to you.
Thus, I am content, even if you were to pawn or sell
either the gift you received from me
or my very person; I will never dispute with you."

She said to me: "Many thanks.
And I tell you to do the same with me,
for I love you properly, honorably and faithfully."

I did not refuse her things;
but often what fools believe does not come to pass:
thus it happened to the good Ser Durante.[2]

1. Cf. *Rose*, 14744–14770.
2. This is the second time that the narrator's name appears in the text (see sonnet 82).

203

L'Amante e lo Schifo

Quand'i' udì' l'oferta che facea,
Del fatto mi' credett'es[s]er certano:
Allor sì volli al fior porre la mano,
Che molto ringrossato mi parea.

Lo Schifo sopra me forte correa
Dicendo: "Trât'adietro, mal villano;
Che·sse m'aiuti Idio e san Germano,
I' non son or quel ch'i' esser solea.

El diavol sì ti ci à or [r]amenato:
Se mi trovasti a l'altra volta lento,
Or sie certan ch'i' ti parrò cambiato.

Me' ti varria che fossi a Benivento".
Allor al capez[z]al m'eb[b]e pigliato,
E domandò chi era mi' guarento.

203

Lover and Resistance[1]

When I heard the offer she was making,
I thought for sure the deal was done:
thus, I decided to touch the Flower,
which seemed to me quite ripe to pick.[2]

Resistance ran up to me quickly
saying: "Get back, you disloyal rogue,
for so help me God and St. Germain,[3]
I am not now the one I used to be.[4]

The devil has brought you here again;
if the time before you found me slow,
you can now be sure that I have changed.

It would be better for you to be in Benevento."[5]
Then he took me by the collar
and asked who was my guarantor.

1. Cf. *Rose*, 14771–14805.

2. The bud has increased in size (*ringrossato*), suggesting that it is about to bloom and providing a thinly-veiled sexual allusion.

3. For St. Germain, see sonnet 159.

4. In sonnets 12–16 Resistance helped Lover.

5. Here, as elsewhere in the poem (e.g., Spain, in sonnet 102) the place-name serves to indicate a distant place.

204

Vergogna e Paura

Po' sentì 'l fatto Vergogna e Paura,
Quand'ell'udiron quel villan gridare,
Ciascuna sì vi corse a·llui aitare,
E quello Schifo molto s'assicura.

Idio e tutti i santi ciascun giura
Ched el[l]e 'l mi faranno comperare:
Allor ciascun mi cominciò a buttare;
Molto mi fecer dispett'e ladura;

E disson ch'i' avea troppo fallato,
Po' che Bellacoglienza per su' onore
E lei e 'l suo m'avea abandonato,

Ched i' pensava d'imbolarle il fiore.
Dritt'era ch'i' ne fosse gastigato,
Sì ch'i' ne stesse ma' sempre in dolore.

204

Modesty and Fear[1]

After hearing that uncourtly one shout,
Modesty and Fear understood the situation
and ran to help him,
and Resistance is very glad.

Each one swears to God and all the Saints
that they will make me pay;
then they began to chase me off
and gave me scorn and much abuse.

And they said I had committed a great sin,
since Fair Welcome had honorably
given me herself and her possessions,

because I was planning to steal the Flower from her.
It was right for me to be punished,
so that I would be in pain forever.

1. Cf. *Rose*, 14806–14902.

205

L'Amante

Allor Bellacoglienza fu fermata
Da questi tre portier' sotto tre porte,
E con una catena molto forte
Quella gentil eb[b]ero 'ncatenata.

Po' corser sopra me, quella brigata,
E disson: "Sopra te cadran le sorte".
Allor credetti ben ricever morte,
Tanto facean di me gran malmenata:

Sì ch'i' misericordia domandai
A Paura, a Vergogna e a quel crudele;
Ma i·nessuna guisa la trovai.

Ciascun sì mi era più amar che fele;
Per molte volte merzé lor gridai:
Que' mi dicëan: "Per nïente bele".

205

Lover[1]

Then Fair Welcome was enclosed
by these three gatekeepers behind three gates,
and with a very strong chain
they chained that noble one.

Then that group ran toward me
and said: "Upon you the burden will fall."
Then I thought for sure I'd die,
for they were giving me a great beating.

I begged for mercy from
Fear, Modesty, and that cruel one;[2]
but I received none at all.

Each one was more bitter than gall towards me;
many times I shouted to them for mercy:
they said to me: "You're bleating in vain."

1. Cf. *Rose*, 14903–15037.
2. I.e., Resistance.

206

L'Amante

Come costor m'andavar tormentando,
E l'oste al Die d'Amor si fu sentita,
E sì cognob[b]or ch'i' avea infralita
La boce: inmantenente miser bando

Che ciasc[hed]un si vada apparec[c]hiando
A me socor[r]ere a campar la vita,
Ch'ella sareb[b]e in poca d'or fallita
Sed e' no·mi venis[s]er confortando.

Quando i portir' sentiron quel baratto,
Inmantenente tra lor si giuraro
Di non renderla a forza né a patto;

E que' di fuor ancor sì si legaro
Di non partirsi se non fosse fatto,
E di questo tra·llor si fidanzaro.

206

Lover[1]

The army of the God of Love became aware
of how these three were tormenting me,
and recognized how weak my voice had become:
immediately they gave orders

that each one of them prepare
to help me save my life,
which would be over in a short while,
if they did not come to help me.

When the gatekeepers heard that commotion,
immediately they vowed among themselves
not to give her up, either by force or by negotiations.

And those outside[2] similarly vowed
not to leave until the battle was over,
and they made this oath among themselves.

1. Cf. *Rose*, 15038–15104.
2. That is, the army of the God of Love.

207

La battaglia

Franchez[z]a sì venne primieramente
Contra lo Schifo, ch'è molto oltrag[g]ioso
E per sembianti fiero e corag[g]ioso;
Ma quella venne molto umilemente.

Lo Schifo sì ponea trop[p]o ben mente,
Ché 'n ben guardar era molto invïoso,
Che quella non potesse di nascoso
Entrar dentr'a la porta con sua gente.

Franchez[z]a mise mano ad una lancia,
Sì s'aperse per dare a quel cagnone,
E crudelmente contra lui la lancia.

Lo Schifo sì avea in mano un gran bastone,
E co·lo scudo il colpo sì·llo schiancia,
E fiede a·llei e falla gir boccone.

207

The Battle[1]

First Sincerity moved
against Resistance, who is so haughty
and fierce and bold in his demeanor;
but the former came very humbly.

Resistance considered the matter well,
for he was very careful in making sure
that Sincerity could not secretly enter
through the gate with her companions.

Sincerity took a spear in hand;
she dropped her guard to attack that ugly watch-dog
and cruelly hurls her lance at him.

In his hand, Resistance held a huge club,
and with his shield parries the blow,
and hits her and makes her fall face down.

1. Cf. *Rose*, 15273–15337.

208

Lo Schifo e Franchez[z]a

La lancia a pez[z]i a pez[z]i à dispez[z]ata,
E po' avisa un colpo ismisurato,
Sì che tutto lo scudo à squartellato:
Franchez[z]a sì è in terra rovesciata.

E que' de' colpi fa gran dimenata,
E la bella merzé gli à domandato,
Sì c[h]'a Pietà ne prese gran peccato:
Verso il villan sì·ss'è adiriz[z]ata;

E con uno spunton lo gì pungendo,
E di lagrime tuttora il bagnava,
Sì che 'l vlllan si venïa rendendo,

C[h]'aviso gli era ched egli afogava.
Allor Vergogna vi venne cor[r]endo
Perché lo Schifo "Socorso!" gridava.

208

Resistance and Sincerity[1]

Resistance smashed the spear to smithereens,
and then he deals a tremendous blow,
such that the entire shield is shattered:
Sincerity is sent crashing to the ground.

Then he strikes her many times,
and the beautiful one so begged for mercy
that Mercy felt great compassion for her:
she advances towards the evil one,

and with a pointed spear she wounded him,
and she bathed him with incessant tears,
such that the uncourtly one surrendered,

since he thought he was drowning.
Then, Modesty came running up,
because Resistance was crying "Help!"

1. Cf. *Rose*, 15337–15423.

209

[...]

Vergogna sì venne contra Pietate,
E molto fortemente la minaccia;
E quella, che dottava sua minaccia,
Sì s'aparec[c]hia a mostrar sua bontate,

Ché ben conosce sua diversitate.
Vergogna a una spada la man caccia,
Sì disse: "I' vo' ben che ciaschedun saccia
Ched i' te pagherò di tue der[r]ate".

Allora alza la spada a·llei fedire;
Ma Diletto sì venne a·llei atare,
E di suo scudo la sep[p]e coprire;

E poi si torna per lei vendicare:
Ma Vergogna sapea sì lo schermire
Che que' no·lla potëa magagnare.

209[1]

Then Modesty moved against Mercy
and threatens her very harshly;
and that one who feared her threat
prepares to show her goodness,

for she knows how cruel Modesty can be.
Modesty takes her sword in hand
and said: "I want everyone to know
that I will pay you back in kind."

Then she raises her sword to strike her,
but Delight moved to help Mercy
and with his shield was able to cover her;

and then he turns to avenge her,
but Modesty knew how to duel so well
that he was unable to wound her.

1. Cf. *Rose*, 15424–15449. At this point the manuscript no longer has the descriptive rubrics indicating the nature of the action and/or the characters.

210

[...]

Vergogna mise allor man a la spada
E sì se ne vien dritta ver' Diletto.
Inmantenente lo scudo eb[b]e al petto,
E disse: "Come vuole andar, sì vada,

Ched i' te pur farò votar la strada,
O tu farai di piana terra letto".
Allor lo fie' co·molto gran dispetto,
Come colei ch'a uc[c]iderlo bada;

Sì che lo mise giù tutto stenduto,
E sì l'avreb[b]e fesso insino a' denti;
Ma, quando Ben-Celar l'eb[b]e veduto,

Perciò ch'egli eran distretti parenti,
Inmantenente sì gli fece aiuto.
Vergogna disse: "I' vi farò dolenti".

210[1]

Modesty then took her sword in hand
and advances toward Delight.
Immediately she held the shield close to her breast
and said: "May it go as it must go,

for either I'll make you leave the field,
or you'll make your bed on the ground."
Then she strikes him with great anger,
as one intent on killing him;

she sent him sprawling on the ground
and would have split him to his teeth;
but when Well-Hidden had seen this,

since they were close relatives,
he immediately went to his aid.
Modesty said: "I'll make both of you sorry."

1. Cf. *Rose*, 15450–15456.

211

[...]

Molt'era buon guer[r]ier quel Ben-Celare:
Alzò la spada, e sì fiede Vergogna
Sì gran colpo ched ella tutta ingrogna,
E poco ne fallì d'a terra andare.

E poi la cominciò a predicare,
E disse: "Tu non devi aver vergogna
Di me, chéd e' nonn-à di qui a Bologna
Nessun c[h]'un fatto saccia me' celare

Che saprò io, e perciò porto il nome".
Vergogna sì non sep[p]e allor che dire.
Paura la sgridò: "Cugina, come?

À' tu perduto tutto tuo ardire?
Or veg[g]h'i' ben che viltà troppo dome,
Quando tu ài paura di morire".

211[1]

Well-Hidden was a very good warrior:
he raised his sword and strikes Modesty
with such great force that she's completely stunned
and almost fell to the ground.

And then he began to lecture her,
saying: "You must not be modest
because of me; because there's no one from here to Bologna[2]
who knows how to hide something better

than I, and for this I have my name."[3]
Modesty did not then know what to say.
Fear shouted to her: "Cousin, what's the matter?

Have you completely lost your boldness?
Now I see how you overcome your cowardice,
when you are afraid to die."

1. Cf. *Rose*, 15459–15484.
2. Again, the use of the name of a city to indicate a distant place (see sonnet 203).
3. We can see here the play on the names of the characters: Modesty who should not feel "modesty" because of what *Ben-Celare* (Well-Hidden) has been able to do in terms of "hiding well" his prowess and striking her when she was least expecting it.

212

[...]

A la sua spada mise man Paura
Per soccor[r]er Vergogna sua cugina:
A Ben-Celar diè per sì grande aina
Ched e' fu de la vita inn-aventura.

Contra leï battaglia poco dura:
Ardimento s'occorse a la miccina
Con una spada molto chiara e fina,
E sì·lle fece molto gran paura.

Ma tuttavia Paura si conforta
E prese cuore in far sua difensione
E disse c[h]'ameria me' d'esser morta

C[h]'Ardimento le tolga sua ragione:
Allora in testa gli diè tal iscorta
Ched ella 'l mise giù in terra boccone.

212[1]

Fear took her sword in hand
to help Modesty, her cousin:
she struck Well-Hidden with such hatred
that his life was in danger.

Battles do not last long against her:
Boldness fought against the young woman
with a very sharp and shiny sword,
and so he scared her very much.

But Fear rallies all the same
and became courageous in her defense,
and said she'd prefer to be dead

than for Boldness to take away what's hers.
Then she gave him such compensation on his head
that she sent him face down on the ground.

1. Cf. *Rose*, 15485–15521.

213

[...]

Quando Sicurtà vide c[h]'Ardimento
Contra Paura avea tutto perduto,
Sì corse là per dargli il su' aiuto
E cominciò il su' tornïamento.

Ma contra lei non eb[b]e duramento:
Paura quello stormo eb[b]e vincuto,
E anche un altro, s'e' vi fosse essuto.
Ma Sicurtà sì eb[b]e acorgimento:

Ispada e scudo gittò tosto in terra,
E·mantenente con ambo le mani
A le tempie a Paura sì s'aferra.

E gli altri, ch'eran tutti lassi e vani,
Ciascun si levò suso, e sì s'aserra
A quella zuffa, com'e' fosser cani.

213[1]

When Safety saw that Boldness
had lost everything against Fear,
she hurried there to give him help
and began her own combat.

But against her she could not last long:
Fear had won that skirmish,
and even another, if there had been one.
But Safety was very shrewd:

she threw her sword and shield to the ground
and immediately, with both hands,
grabs Fear around the head.

And the others, who were all weary and without strength,
got up and throw themselves
into that scuffle, as though they were dogs.

1. Cf. *Rose*, 15526–15584.

214

[...]

Molto durò tra·llor quella battaglia,
Che ciascun roba e carni vi si straccia.
L'un l'altro abatte per forza di braccia.
Non fu veduta mai tal trapresaglia,

Che que' d'entro facien troppo gran taglia
Di que' di fuor; Amor allor procaccia
Che tra lor una trieva sì si faccia
Di venti dì, o di più, che me' vaglia:

Ch'e' vede ben che mai quella fortez[z]a,
Se·lla madre non v'è, non prendereb[b]e.
Allor la manda a chieder per Franchez[z]a.

Contra colei sa ben non si ter[r]eb[b]e:
Che s'ella il su' brandon ver' lor adrez[z]a,
Imantenente tutti gli ardereb[b]e.

214[1]

That battle between them went on and on,
and their clothing and bodies were torn to shreds.
They knock each other down with brute strength.
Such a fight had never been seen:

those inside the castle were slaughtering
those outside. Then Love proposes a truce
of twenty days, or more,
whichever may be better.

For he clearly sees that he would never
take that fortress, if his mother does not take part.[2]
Then he sends Sincerity to summon her.

He knows that she would not say no to her;
if Venus turns her torch against them,
she would immediately set them all on fire.

1. Cf. *Rose*, 15585–15608.
2. Love's mother is Venus.

215

[...]

Franchez[z]a sì s'è de l'oste partita,
E Amor sì·ll'à ben incaricato
Che·lli dica a la madre ogne su' stato,
Com'egli è a gran rischio de la vita,

E che sua forza è molto infiebolita:
Ch'ella faccia che per lei si' aiutato.
Allor Franchez[z]a sì à cavalcato,
E dritto a Ceceron sì se n'è ita,

Credendo che vi fosse la dïessa:
Ma el[l]'er'ita in bosco per cacciare,
Sì che Franchez[z]a n'andò dritt'a essa.

Sott'una quercia la trovò ombreare:
Quella sì tosto in ginoc[c]hie s'è messa,
E dolzemente l'eb[b]e a salutare.

215[1]

Sincerity left the army of the barons,
and Love gave her instructions
to tell his mother all about his current state—
how his life is in great danger,

and how his strength is greatly diminished—
and to do what she can to help him.
Then Sincerity rode off
and went straight to Mount Cecerone,[2]

believing that the goddess would be there;
but she had gone into the woods to hunt;
and so Sincerity went directly to her.

She found her resting in the shade of an oak tree.
Sincerity quickly kneeled before her
and greeted her courteously.

1. Cf. *Rose*, 15629–15656.

2. The Greek mountain Citerone (or Cicerone: sonnets 217–218) was considered in the Middle Ages to be the home of Venus. In classical antiquity her cult was located on the island of Citerea.

216

[...]

"Molte salute, madonna, v'aporto
Dal vostro figlio: e' priegavi per Dio
Che 'l socor[r]iate, od egli è in punto rio,
Ché Gelosia gli fa troppo gran torto;

Ch' e' nonn-à guar ched e' fu quasi morto
'N una battaglia, nella qual fu' io.
Ancor si par ben nel visag[g]io mio,
Che molto mi vi fu strett'ed atorto".

Allor Venusso fu molto crucciata,
E disse ben che·lla fortez[z]a fia
Molto tosto per lei tutta 'mbraciata;

Ed a malgrado ancor di Gelosia
Ella serà per terra rovesciata:
No·lle varrà già guardia che vi sia.

216[1]

"My Lady, I bring you many greetings
from your son, who begs you, in the name of God,
that you help him, or else he is in serious trouble,
because Jealousy is giving him many problems.

A short while ago he was almost killed
in a battle, in which I too took part.
My face still clearly shows
that I was in the thick of battle."

Then Venus became enraged
and said that very soon
she will set the fortress on fire;

and despite the efforts of Jealousy,
the fortress will be destroyed:
no guard whatsoever will be able to save it.

1. Cf. *Rose*, 15738–15748.

217

[...]

Venusso sì montò sus'un ronzino
Corsiere, ch'era buon da cacciagione,
E con sua gente n'andò a Cicerone:
Sì comanda che sia prest'al matino

Il carro süo, ch'era d'oro fino.
Imantenente fu messo i·limone
E presto tutto, sì ben per ragione
Che, quando vuol, puote entrar in camino.

Ma non volle caval per limoniere
Né per tirare il car[r]o, anzi fe' trare
Cinque colombi d'un su' colombiere:

A corde di fil d'or gli fe' legare.
Non bisognava avervi carettiere,
Ché·lla dea gli sapëa ben guidare.

217[1]

Venus mounted her swift
steed, which was good for hunting,
and with her company she went to Mount Cicerone:
she orders that her war chariot of pure gold

be ready in the morning.
The pole was quickly attached to the chariot,
and all was readied so that
they can begin the journey whenever they want.

But she refused to have a guide horse
pull the chariot; rather, she took
five doves from one of her dovecotes

and had them tied to it with golden threads.
A coachman was not needed,
for the goddess was an expert driver.

1. Cf. *Rose*, 15749–15756.

218

[...]

Di gran vantag[g]io fu 'l carro prestato.
Venusso ben matin v'è su salita,
E sì sacciate ch'ell'era guernita
E d'arco e di brandon ben impennato;

E seco porta fuoco temperato.
Così da Ciceron sì s'è partita,
E dritta all'oste del figl[i]uol n'è ita
Con suo' colombi che 'l car[r]'àn tirato.

Lo Dio d'Amor sì avea rotte le trieve
Prima che Veno vi fosse arivata,
Ché troppo gli parea l'atender grieve.

Venus[so] dritta a lui sì se n'è andata,
Sì disse: "Figl[i]uol, non dottar, ché 'n brieve
Questa fortez[z]a no' avremo ater[r]ata.

218[1]

The chariot was readied in excellent fashion.
Early in the morning Venus climbed aboard,
and you should know that she was well equipped
with a bow and a well-feathered torch,

and with her she brought a well-tempered fire.
In this way she left Mount Cicerone
and went straight to her son's army
with her doves that pulled the chariot.

The God of Love had broken the truce,
before Venus had arrived,
for the wait seemed to him intolerable.

Venus went straight to him
and said: "My son, do not fear, for in no time
we'll have brought this fortress down."

1. Cf. *Rose*, 15757–15770.

219

[...]

"Figl[i]uol mi', tu farai un saramento,
E io d'altra parte sì 'l faròe,
Che castitate i' ma' non lascieròe
In femina che ag[g]ia intendimento,

Né tu in uon che·tti si' a piacimento.
Ed i' te dico ben ch'i' lavorròe
Col mi' brandone: sì gli scalderòe
Che ciaschedun verrà a comandamento".

Per far le saramenta sì aportaro,
En luogo di relique e di messale,
Brandoni e archi e saette; sì giuraro

Di suso, e dis[s]er c[h]'altrettanto vale.
Color de l'oste ancor vi s'acordaro,
Ché ciaschedun sapea le Dicretale.

219[1]

"My son, you will make a pledge,
and I will make one too:
namely, that I will never let chastity remain
in any woman who has common sense,[2]

and you should do the same with any man you like.
And I say to you that I will go to work
with my torch, and I'll heat them up
so much that each one will obey our command."

In order to make these vows, they brought—
in the place of relics and a missal—
torches and bows and arrows; and so they swore

on these objects, declaring them to be equally valid.[3]
All those in the army of Love were in agreement,
for each one of them knew the Decretals.[4]

1. Cf. *Rose*, 15800–15807, 15847–15860.
2. Or, any woman who has a lover, i.e., someone who loves her.
3. See sonnet 5, for the "religion" of Love.
4. For the Decretals, see sonnet 37.

220

[...]

Venus[so], che d'assalire era presta,
Sì comanda a ciascun ched e' s'arenda
O che la mercé ciascheduno atenda,
Ch'ella la guarda lor tratutta presta.

E sì lor à giurato, per sua testa,
Ched e' non fia nessun che si difenda,
Ch'ella de la persona no·gli afenda:
E così ciaschedun sì amonesta.

Vergogna sì respuose: "I' non vi dotto.
Se nel castel non fosse se non io,
Non crederei che fosse per voi rotto.

Quando vi piace intrare a·lavorio,
Già per minaccie no·mi 'ntrate sotto,
Né vo' né que' che d'amor si fa dio".

220[1]

Venus, who was ready to attack,
orders everyone either to surrender
or to wait for their reward,
which she has good and ready for them.

And so she swore to them on her own head
that no one will be able to defend himself
from the bodily wounds that she'll inflict;
and thus, she gives each and every one fair warning.

Modesty answered: "I'm not afraid of you.
Even if I were the only one in the castle,
I would not believe that it could be destroyed by you.

Whenever you want, you can begin your efforts;
you'll not take the castle with threats alone,
not you nor that one who calls himself the God of Love."

1. Cf. *Rose*, 20681–20688.

221

[...]

Quando Venùs intese che Vergogna
Parlò sì arditamente contr'a·llei,
Sì gl[i] à giurato per tutti gli dèi
Ch'ella le farà ancor gran vergogna;

E poi villanamente la rampogna,
Dicendo: "Garza, poco pregerei
Il mi' brandon, sed i' te non potrei
Farti ricoverare in una fogna.

Già tanto non se' figlia di Ragione,
Che sempre co' figl[i]uoi m'à guer[r]eg[g]iato,
Ch'i' non ti metta fuoco nel groppone".

Ed a Paura ancor da l'altro lato:
"Ben poco varrà vostra difensione,
Quand'i' v'avrò il fornel ben riscaldato".

221[1]

When Venus heard Modesty
speak so boldly against her,
she quickly swore on all the gods
that she will bring her great disgrace.

And then rudely she rebukes her,
saying: "You slut, little would I value
my torch, if I could not make
you take refuge in a sewer.

You aren't so much the daughter of Reason,
who has always battled me with her children,
that I won't set your ass on fire."

And to Fear who's still on the other side:
"Your defense won't be worth too much to you,
once I've stoked up your hot little oven."[2]

1. Cf. *Rose*, 20689–20701.
2. For the sexual allusion to the "oven" see sonnet 32.

222

[...]

Molto le va Venus[so] minacciando,
Dicendo, se no·rendono il castello,
Ched ella metterà fuoco al fornello,
Sì che per forza le n'andrà cacciando.

E disse: "A mille diavol' v'acomando,
Chi amor fug[g]e, e fosse mi' fratello!
Perdio, i' le farò tener bordello,
Color che l'amor vanno sì schifando:

Chéd e' non è più gioia che ben amare.
Rendetemi il castel, o veramente
I' 'l farò imantenente giù versare;

E poi avremo il fior certanamente,
E sì 'l faremo in tal modo sfogliare
Che poi non fia vetato a nulla gente".

222[1]

Venus threatens these two a lot,[2]
saying that, if they don't surrender the castle,
then she'll set their burners on fire,
so that she will surely drive them out.

She said: "To a thousand devils I commend anyone
who flees from love, even if it were my own brother!
By God, all those who put up resistance to Love
I'll turn them into whores.

For there's no greater joy than loving well.
Surrender the castle to me, or truly
I'll have it quickly destroyed;

and then we'll certainly take the Flower,
and have it deflowered in such a way
that it will no longer be off limits to any one."

1. Cf. *Rose*, 15800–15846, 20711–20716, 20721–20724.
2. Modesty and Fear.

223

[...]

Venus[so] la sua roba à socorciata,
Crucciosa per sembianti molto e fiera;
Verso 'l castel tenne sua caminiera,
E ivi sì s'è un poco riposata;

E riposando sì eb[b]e avisata,
Come cole' ch'era sottil archiera,
Tra due pilastri una balestriera,
La qual Natura v'avea compas[s]ata.

In su' pilastri una image avea asisa;
D'argento fin sembiava, sì lucea:
Trop[p]'era ben tagl[i]ata a gran divisa.

Di sotto un santüaro sì avea:
D'un drap[p]o era coperto, sì in ta' guisa
Che 'l santüaro punto non parea.

223[1]

Venus hiked her skirt up to her waist;
she was angry in her disposition and fierce:
she began to march toward the castle,
and, once there, she rested for a bit.

And while she was resting, she noted,
since she was an expert archer,
a loophole between two pillars,[2]
which Nature had designed with care.

Atop the pillars was placed an image;
it seemed to be made of fine silver, so it shone;
it was fashioned with great skill.

Underneath there was a reliquary,
covered by a cloth in such a way
that the reliquary was not at all visible.[3]

1. Cf. *Rose*, 20755–20778.

2. The loophole is the narrow slit in the castle through which archers could shoot their arrows. The aperture here, however, also suggests that of the female sex organ, the vagina. See sonnet 229 for a less ambiguous reading.

3. The reliquary, or sanctuary, is another term for the female sex organ.

224

[...]

Troppo avea quel[l]'imagine 'l [vi]saggio
Tagliato di tranobile faz[z]one:
Molto pensai d'andarvi a processione
E di fornirvi mie pelligrinag[g]io;

E sì no·mi saria paruto oltrag[g]io
Di starvi un dì davanti ginoc[c]hione,
E poi di notte es[s]ervi su boccone,
E di donarne ancor ben gran logag[g]io.

Ched i' era certan, sed i' toccasse
L'erlique che di sotto eran riposte,
Che ogne mal ch'i' avesse mi sanasse;

E fosse mal di capo, o ver di coste,
Od altra malatia, che mi gravasse,
A tutte m'avria fatto donar soste.

224[1]

The face of that image was very well-fashioned
and had an exceedingly noble appearance;
My only thought was to go there in procession
and to complete my pilgrimage there.[2]

And it would not have seemed to me too much
to kneel before it for an entire day
and then at night to lie prostrate before it,
and to make a great offering in addition.

For I was sure that, if I were able to touch
the relics that were kept below the image,
my every ill would be healed;

and if I suffered from headaches, or back pains,
or any other grievous sickness,
these relics would give me relief from all of them.

1. Cf. *Rose*, 20779–20831.
2. For similar language used by Friend, see sonnet 65.

225

[...]

Venùs allora già più non atende,
Però ched ella sì vuol ben mostrare
A ciaschedun ciò ched ella sa fare:
Imantenente l'arco su' sì tende,

E poi prende il brandone e sì l'ac[c]ende;
Sì no·lle parve pena lo scoc[c]are,
E per la balestriera il fe' volare,
Sì che 'l castel ma' più non si difende.

Imantenente il fuoco sì s'aprese:
Per lo castello ciascun si fug[g]ìo,
Sì che nessun vi fece più difese.

Lo Schifo disse: "Qui no·sto più io";
Vergogna si fug[g]ì in istran paese,
Paura a gra·fatica si partìo.

225[1]

At this point Venus waits no longer,
since she wants to demonstrate
to everyone that she knows what to do:
immediately she bends her bow,

and then takes the torch and lights it.
She released the torch with ease
and made it fly right through the loophole,
such that the castle can no longer be defended.

Immediately the fire took hold:
everyone fled the castle;
no one defended it any more.

Resistance said: "I can't stay here any longer."
Modesty fled to a foreign land,
and Fear left with great difficulty.

1. Cf. *Rose*, 21221–21243.

226

[...]

Quando 'l castello fu così imbrasciato
E che·lle guardie fur fug[g]ite via,
Alor sì v'entrò entro Cortesia
Per la figl[i]uola trar di quello stato;

E Franchez[z]'e Pietà da l'altro lato
Sì andaron co·llei in compagnia.
Cortesia sì·lle disse: "Figlia mia,
Molt'ò avuto di te il cuor crucciato,

Ché stata se' gran tempo impregionata.
La Gelosia ag[g]i'or mala ventura,
Quando tenuta t'à tanto serrata.

Lo Schifo e Vergogna con Paura
Se son fug[g]iti, e la gol'à tagliata
Ser Mala-Bocca per sua disventura.

226[1]

When the castle was thus reduced to ashes
and the guards had run away,
Lady Courtesy went inside
to free her daughter from that state.[2]

And on each side Sincerity and Mercy
accompanied her.
Lady Courtesy said to her: "My daughter,
my heart has been in such pain for you,

for you were imprisoned such a long time.
May Jealousy now have a terrible fate,
since she kept you imprisoned for so long.

Resistance and Modesty with Fear
have fled, and Ser Bad Mouth
has his throat cut to his misfortune."

1. Cf. *Rose*, 21244–21280.
2. I.e., Fair Welcome.

227

[...]

"Figl[i]uola mia, per Dio e per merzede,
Ag[g]ie pietà di quel leal amante,
Che per te à soferte pene tante
Che dir no'l ti poria, in buona fede.

In nessun altro idio che·tte non crede,
E tuttora a·cciò è stato fermo e stante:
Figl[i]uola mia, or gli fa tal sembiante
Ch'e' sia certano di ciò c[h]'or non vede".

Bellacoglienza disse: "I' gli abandono
E me e 'l fiore e ciò ch'i' ò 'n podere,
E ched e' prenda tutto quanto in dono.

Per altre volte avea alcun volere,
Ma nonn-era sì agiata com'or sono:
Or ne può fare tutto 'l su' piacere".

227[1]

"My daughter, in the name of God and mercy,
have pity on that loyal lover,
who for you has suffered so many torments
that he could not tell you, in good faith.

He believes in no other god but you,[2]
and has been always loyal and constant in this belief.
My daughter, now give him such a look
that he may be certain of that which now he cannot see."[3]

Fair Welcome said: "I give to him
both myself and the Flower, and all that I possess:
may he accept all of this as a gift!

On other occasions, I had some desire to do this,
but then I wasn't in the position that I'm in now:
now he can do all that he wishes."

1. Cf. *Rose*, 21281–21315.
2. Note the parody of the first commandment (Exodus 20:3).
3. Cf. sonnet 5.

228

[...]

Quand'i' udì' quel buon risposto fino
Che·lla gentil rispuose, [m'inviai]
Ed a balestriera m'adriz[z]ai,
Ché quel sì era il mi' dritto camino;

E sì v'andai come buon pellegrino,
Ch'un bordon noderuto v'aportai,
E la scarsella non dimenticai,
La qual v'apiccò buon mastro divino.

Tutto mi' arnese, tal chent'i' portava,
Se di condurl'al port'ò in mia ventura,
Di toccarne l'erlique i' pur pensava.

Nel mi' bordon non avea fer[r]atura,
Ché giamai contra pietre no·ll'urtava;
La scarsella sì era san' costura.

228[1]

When I heard that kind and courtly response
which the noble lady gave, I got up
and went directly to the loophole,
for that was the straight and proper road for me.

I went there like a good pilgrim;
I brought my gnarled staff with me
and did not forget my money-bag,[2]
which the good divine craftsman had hung on me.

All my tackle, all that I had with me,
I thought only of using it to touch the relics,
if I am lucky enough to steer it into port.

My staff was not tipped with iron,
for never did I have to thrust it against stones;
the purse was not stitched.

1. Cf. *Rose*, 21316–21337, 21553–21556.

2. While the staff and the moneybag he brings with him are typical equipment for medieval pilgrims, these are thinly veiled allusions to the male genitalia.

229

[...]

Tant'andai giorno e notte caminando,
Col mi' bordon che non era ferrato,
Che 'ntra' duo be' pilastri fu' arivato:
Molto s'andò il mi' cuor riconfortando.

Dritt'a l'erlique venni apressimando,
E·mantenente mi fu' inginoc[c]hiato
Per adorar quel [bel] corpo beato;
Po' venni la coverta solevando.

E poi provai sed i' potea il bordone,
In quella balestriera ch'i' v'ò detto,
Metterlo dentro tutto di randone;

Ma i' non potti, ch'ell'era sì stretto
L'entrata, che 'l fatto andò in falligione.
La prima volta i' vi fu' ben distretto.

229[1]

All night and all day I traveled on
with my staff that was not tipped with iron,
until I arrived between the two beautiful columns:
my heart was gaining greater confidence.

Straight to the relics I came, closer and closer,
and immediately I knelt down
to worship that lovely blessed body;
then I began to lift the covering.

And then I tried to see if I could stick my staff
into that loophole I told you about,
to stick it all in with a sudden thrust;

but I could not, for the entrance
was so tight that the act ended in failure.
The first time I was truly distraught.

1. Cf. *Rose*, 21557–21579.

230

[...]

Pe·più volte fallì' a·llui ficcare,
Perciò che 'n nulla guisa vi capea;
E·lla scarsella c[h]'al bordon pendea,
Tuttor di sotto la facea urtare,

Credendo il bordon me' far entrare;
Ma già nessuna cosa mi valea.
Ma a la fine i' pur tanto scotea
Ched i' pur lo facea oltre passare:

Sì ch'io allora il fior tutto sfogl[i]ai,
E la semenza ch'i' avea portata,
Quand'eb[b]i arato, sì·lla seminai.

La semenza del fior v'era cascata:
Amendue insieme sì·lle mescolai,
Che molta di buon'erba n'è po' nata.

230[1]

Time and again I failed to stick it in,
since it wouldn't fit in there in any way;
and my moneybag that was hanging from my staff,
I continued banging it down below,

thinking thus to ease my staff inside;
but nothing worked for me.
However, in the end I shook it so much
that I finally got it to go inside:

thus I succeeded in deflowering the Flower,
and with the seed that I had carried,
after the plowing, so came the sowing.[2]

The seed of the Flower had descended;
I mixed the two of them together
such that much good fruit has issued forth.[3]

1. Cf. *Rose*, 21580–21700.
2. For the image of plowing and sowing, see sonnets 9 and 65.
3. In medieval medicine, conception of the human embryo occurred as the result of the mixing of the male seed with the female seed—understood as the mixing of the more highly purified "blood" of the man (semen) with the blood of the woman—in the uterus. In *Purgatorio* 25 Dante presents a disquisition on the subject of embryology.

231

[...]

Quand'i' mi vidi in così alto grado,
Tutti i mie' benfattori ringraziai,
E più gli amo og[g]i ch'i' non feci mai,
Che molto si penâr di far mi' grado.

Al Die d'Amor ed a la madre i' bado,
E a' baron' de l'oste chiamo assai
D'esser lor[o] fedele a sempremai
E di servirgli e non guardar ma' guado.

Al buono Amico e a Bellacoglienza
Rendé' grazïe mille e mille volte;
Ma di Ragion non eb[b]i sovenenza,

Che·lle mie gioie mi credette aver tolte.
Ma contra lei i' eb[b]i provedenza,
Sì ch'i' l'ò tutte quante avute e colte.

231[1]

When I saw myself in such an exalted state,
I gave thanks to all my benefactors,
and I love them more today than ever before,
for they worked hard to make my pleasure possible.

I follow the commands of Love and his mother,
and to the army of Love[2] I proclaim
that I will be loyal to them forever
and will serve them and always honor my pledge.[3]

To the good Friend and Fair Welcome
I gave thanks a thousand times and more,
but I never gave a thought to Reason,

who thought she had taken away my joys.
But against her I used such shrewdness
that I have enjoyed and gathered them all.

1. Cf. *Rose*, 21713–21731.

2. See sonnets 79 and 84 for a listing of the members of the army.

3. The interpretation of the phrase *guardar ma' guado* is uncertain. The phrase could also be construed as *guardarm' a guado*. In the present context it would appear to indicate the third element of Lover's declaration to the God of Love and his associates: he will be faithful to them, he will serve them, and he will never be dissuaded from these actions because of the possible risks involved therein. *Guado* can mean either the "fording place" on a river (< Latin *vadum*) or the pledge that one makes to one's liege lord (< French *gage*), and both of these meanings would fit the general sense of the phrase: *e non guardarm' a guado* = "and keep myself from failing to honor my pledge," or "not protect myself against the risks of the passageway," and *e non guardar ma' guado* = "and never be concerned with the passageway" (i.e., with the means of obtaining what he desires).

232

[...]

Malgrado di Ric[c]hez[z]a la spietata,
Ch'unquanche di pietà non seppe usare,
Che del camin c[h]'à nome Troppo-Dare
Le pia[c]que di vietarmene l'entrata!

Ancor di Gelosia, ch'è·ssì spietata
Che dagli amanti vuole il fior guardare!
Ma pure 'l mio non sep[p]'ella murare,
Ched i' non vi trovasse alcuna entrata;

Ond'io le tolsi il fior ch'ella guardava:
E sì ne stava in sì gran sospez[z]one
Che·lla sua gente tuttor inveg[g]hiava.

Bellacoglienza ne tenne in pregione,
Perch'ella punto in lei non si fidava:
E sì n'er'ella don[n]a di ragione.

232[1]

I've had all this despite heartless Wealth,
who never showed any compassion
and who delighted in denying me access
to the path whose name is Extravagance!

All this despite Jealousy, who is so heartless
that she wants to protect the Flower from lovers!
But still she was unable to imprison my Flower so well
that I could not find an entranceway.

Thus, I took from her the Flower she was guarding:
so great was her concern
that her henchmen were always keeping watch.

Jealousy kept Fair Welcome in prison,
because she placed no trust in her at all:
and yet Fair Welcome was the proper mistress of the Flower.

1. Cf. *Rose*, 21732–21742.

The Detto d'Amore

Introduction

The *Detto d'Amore:* Manuscript and Composition

The incomplete poem called the *Detto d'Amore*[1] is extant in four folios (with some *lacunae*) in the Laurentian Library of Florence under the shelf number Ashburnham 1234. The handwriting of the poem is identical to that of the *Fiore*.[2] Indeed, a century and a half ago, around 1849, Guglielmo Libri removed without authorization—i.e., stole—the four folios containing the text from the manuscript of the *Fiore* (H 438) in the Bibliothèque Universitaire in Montpellier.[3] The first editor of the *Detto* (1888), Salomone Morpurgo,[4] discovered and identified the text, which comprises 480 heptasyllabic verses (*settenari*) in rhymed couplets in sixteen columns (two columns per page) of thirty lines each.[5]

The Content of the *Detto d'Amore*

The *Detto* can be divided into two parts. The first part, consisting of vv. 1–270, presents the psychology of love; the second part, vv. 271–480, delineates the social ethics upon which a courtly society is based. The first five lines of part one form a prologue in which the author declares the objectives of the poem: "Love so decrees, and deems it proper, / that I should speak in this particular way / and compose a *detto*, / so that it may be proclaimed everywhere / how well I served him" (1–5). In vv. 6–74, the poet declares his allegiance to the God of Love, but notes that Reason is opposed: erotic love is

1. All passages from the *Detto* come from Dante Alighieri, *Il Fiore e il Detto d'Amore attribuibili a Dante Alighieri*, ed. Gianfranco Contini (Milan-Naples: Ricciardi, 1984).

2. See *Il Fiore e il Detto d'Amore attribuiti a Dante Alighieri. Testo del secolo XIII*, ed. Guido Mazzoni (Florence: Alinari, 1923).

3. Teresa De Robertis Boniforti, "Nota sul codice e la sua scrittura," in *The Fiore in Context: Dante, France, Tuscany*, ed. Zygmunt G. Barański and Patrick Boyde (Notre Dame: University of Notre Dame Press, 1997), 50.

4. Salomone Morpurgo, "Detto d'Amore, antiche rime imitate dal *Roman de la Rose*," *Il Propugnatore* n.s. 1 (1888), 16–61.

5. Luigi Vanossi, "Detto d'Amore," in *Enciclopedia dantesca*, 6 vols. (Rome: Istituto della Enciclopedia Italiana, 1984), 2:393–395.

ephemeral, whereas the love of reason should belong to the love of God which is eternal and unchanging. Reason tries to persuade the poet to abandon his love of the fleeting and ephemeral, urging him to seek higher goals: "For God's sake, get away / from that false pleasure, / and let my pleasure be yours, / for it is perfect / and gives unending joy" (106–110). In verses 125–166 the poet responds to Reason, and in verses 167–270 he praises the fine qualities of his lady. Following this defense of love and feminine beauty, the poet, in the second part of the *Detto*, describes the perfect lover, who must behave according to the rules of a courtly society.

The Authorship of the *Detto*

Scholars have argued much more vigorously about the authorship of the *Detto d'Amore*[6] than they have about that of the *Fiore*. Critics have often cited the equivocal language of the *Detto*—language which recalls that of Guittone—to justify their opposition to Dante as author.[7] Commenting on the language of the *Detto*, Vanossi argues that its versification resembles the technical language found both in Dante's early rhymes[8] and in the *rime petrose*.[9] Specifically, he sees the sonnet "Non canoscendo, amico, vostro nomo" (*Rime*, 3a [XLIV]) as incorporating a style very close to that of the *Detto*, for in this particular poem Dante constructs a discourse based on equivocal rhymes.[10]

The *Detto d'Amore:* Questions of Influence and Translation

Although the *Detto* does not have the same narrative structure as the *Fiore*, and does not have many passages corresponding to those of the *Rose*,

6. For a study that contested Dante's authorship of the *Detto*, see Ernesto Giacomo Parodi, "Prefazione," in his edition, *Il Fiore e il Detto d'Amore*, appendix to *Le opere di Dante* (Florence: Bemporad, 1922), v–xx.

7. For a history of Tuscan poetry, see Ignazio Baldelli, "La letteratura volgare in Toscana dalle origini ai primi decenni del secolo XIII," in *Letteratura italiana: Storia e geografia, l'età medievale* (Turin: Einaudi, 1987), 65–77. For the poetry of Guittone, see *Poeti del Duecento,* ed. Gianfranco Contini, 2 vols. (Milan and Naples: Ricciardi, 1960), 1:189–255. For other studies of the early lyric tradition see, among others, Teodolinda Barolini, *Dante's Poets: Textuality and Truth in the "Comedy"* (Princeton: Princeton University Press, 1984), and Christopher Kleinhenz, *The Early Italian Sonnet: The First Century (1220–1321)* (Lecce: Milella, 1986).

8. For Dante's lyric poetry (including the *petrose*), see Dante Alighieri, *Rime,* ed. Gianfranco Contini (Turin: Einaudi, 1965).

9. Recent studies on the *petrose* include Robert M. Durling and Ronald Martinez, *Time and the Crystal: Studies in Dante's "Rime Petrose"* (Berkeley: University of California Press, 1990), and Robert M. Durling, "The Audiences of the *De Vulgari Eloquentia* and the *Petrose," Dante Studies* 110 (1992), 25–35.

10. Luigi Vanossi, *La teologia poetica del Detto d'Amore dantesco* (Florence: Olschki, 1974), 2.

the poem can be identified as a *summa* of courtly love—a love which ennobles the lover as he searches for perfect and loyal service to the God of Love: "And this will be a perfect example / for every lover, / so that Amore will not / be bitter to him in the end" (10–14).[11] Furthermore, the *Detto,* like the *Fiore*, reflects a new art of translation of the *Rose*[12] or, as Harrison states of the *Fiore*, "the poem becomes provocative primarily in those features that set it off from the *Rose*," thus becoming an emblematic adaptation of the *Rose*.[13]

What are the characteristic features of the *Detto* that relate it to the *Rose* and to the author of the *Fiore*? First of all, the *Detto* recalls the courtly mythology of the section of the *Rose* composed by Guillaume de Lorris.[14] Secondly, Vanossi has identified the *Detto* as the transition between the traditional poetry of courtly love and the new poetics of the *Dolce Stil Novo*. For example, in the *Detto* (239–242), the poet recalls the *topos* of the siren, which, for example, can also be found in *Il mare amoroso*: "e 'l bel cantare m'ha conquiso e morto / a simiglianza de la serenella / che uccide 'l marinar col suo bel canto" ("and her beautiful singing has conquered me and made me die just like that of the siren that kills the sailor with her beautiful song," 111–113).[15] The verses of *Il mare amoroso* recall the traditional qualities of the wily siren who possesses destructive powers. Instead, in the *Detto* the poet overturns this particular *topos*, assigning the siren a benevolent disposition: "Her dancing and singing / are more enchanting than those / of any siren, / for they calm the atmosphere" (239–242). The lady thus becomes the object of desire which will allow the poet to create a poetry resonant of the tension that dwells in the space between desire and the fulfillment of that very desire. The lover must control his desire: "For I remember well / what pleasure he offered me, / provided that I would serve him faithfully. / To be sure there is a shorter / way, but I do not take it, / for which I have no profit, / since I could enter only one / step through that door" (274–281). This passage recalls the

11. For studies regarding the theme of courtly love see Bernard O'Donoghue, *The Courtly Love Tradition* (Manchester: Manchester University Press, 1982), and *In Pursuit of Perfection: Courtly Love in Medieval Literature*, ed. Joan M. Ferrante, George D. Economou, and Frederick Goldin (Port Washington, N.Y.: Kennikat Press, 1975). For a study of the relationship between Dante and the courtly tradition, see Christopher Kleinhenz, "Dante as Reader and Critic of Courtly Literature," in *Courtly Literature: Culture and Context*, ed. Keith Busby and Erik Kooper (Amsterdam: Benjamins, 1990), 379–393.

12. For the art of translation, see the introduction to the *Fiore*, "The *Fiore* and the *Rose*: Questions of Influence and *Translatio*."

13. Robert Pogue Harrison, "The Bare Essential: The Landscape of *Il Fiore*," in *Rethinking the "Romance of the Rose,"* ed. Kevin Brownlee and Sylvia Huot (Philadelphia: University of Pennsylvania Press, 1992), 293.

14. Vanossi, *La teologia poetica*, 2.

15. For the text of the *Mare amoroso*, see *Poeti del Duecento*, 1:483–500.

path to sexual conquest traced in Ovid's *Ars Amatoria*,[16] where the Roman poet instructs the reader in the art of seduction. In book I of the treatise, Ovid provides instruction in the art of love: "Siquis in hoc artem populo non novit amandi, / Hoc legat et lecto carmine doctus amet. / Arte citae veloque rates remoque moventur, / Arte leves currus: arte regendus amor. [. . .] Principio, quod amare velis, reperire labora, / Qui nova nunc primum miles in arma venis. / Proximus huic labor est placitam exorare puellam: / Tertius, ut longo tempore duret amor. [. . .] Non ego quaerentem vento dare vela iubebo, / Nec tibi, ut invenias, longa terenda via est" ("If anyone among this people knows not the art of loving, let him read my poem, and having read be skilled in love. By skill swift ships are sailed and rowed, by skill nimble chariots are driven: by skill must Love be guided. [. . .] First, strive, to find an object for your love, you who now for the first time come to fight in warfare new. The next task is, to win the girl that takes your fancy; the third, to make love long endure. [. . .] I will not bid you in your search set sails before the wind, nor, that you may find, need a long road be travelled," 1–4, 35–38, 51–52). The author of the *Detto* rejects Ovid's suggestion of the shorter way. In their editions, Contini, Marchiori and Rossi all refer to the "shorter way" as the road that leads to the conquest of the lady. However, these critics do not suggest that the verses "Ben ci è egli un cammino / Più corto, né 'l camino" ("To be sure there is a shorter / way, but I do not take it," 277–278) refer to the sexual act, the act that will bring immediate satisfaction. Here the lover is responding to Reason's request that he not plow a bad field: "Thus, do not follow his path, / if you want to escape from him; / otherwise you are plowing a bad field / in which good grain will not grow; / indeed, whoever sows there / will lose his seed. / For God's sake, get away from that false pleasure, / and let my pleasure be yours, / for it is perfect / and gives unending joy" (100–110). These verses recall the metaphor of the seeds found both in the *Fiore* and in the *Planctus* (see the introduction to the *Fiore*, above). However, if in the *Fiore* the author eliminates the tension that exists between sexual and grammatical perversion expressed in the *Planctus*, in the *Detto* he inverts this tension which questions the very eroticism of the *Fiore*. In other words, the binary opposition that exists between desire and *ratio* serves to deny the poet's own erotic desire and to establish the ethics of the reason of love. Thus, in rejecting this immediate satisfaction, the poet creates a tension that hovers between desire and fulfillment, a space which is relinquished by

16. All passages from the *Ars Amatoria* come from J. H. Mozley's translation (Loeb Classical Library): Ovid, *The Art of Love and Other Poems*, 2nd ed. (Cambridge, Mass.: Harvard University Press; London: Heinemann, 1985).

the lover's perfect adherence to the precepts of courtly love: "Goodbye, for I am leaving, / and will return to being a perfect lover / in order to compose another part / to describe how well proportioned she is, / both in her body and in her members, / just as I remember them" (161–166). The metaphor of the perfect lover describes a love which transcends the real and transports the poet into an ecstasy focused on the ideal. The lines that follow (167–225) describe the lady part by part, thus turning her into an object of his own creation to be contemplated: "Her noble condition / puts everyone who gazes at her / in a blissful state. / For this reason my heart gazes / on her day and night, / and thus with her I always greet the dawn, / because Love has willed it so, / nor has my heart asked / if this could come to an end, / for it would want to love endlessly" (223–232). This contemplation continues by elevating the material to the ideal in the following verses: "But Love has so precisely / painted her in my mind / that, no matter if I sleep or am awake, / I see her painted in my heart" (256–259). These lines bring to mind the verses in the poem "Meravigliosamente" of Giacomo da Lentini where the lady is painted in the poet's heart: "Meravigliosamente / un amor mi distringe / e mi tene ad ogn'ora. / Com'om che pone mente / in altro exemplo pinge la simile pintura, / così, bella, facc'eo, / che 'nfra lo core meo / porto la tua figura. / In cor par ch'eo vi porti, / pinta como parete, e non pare di fore" ("Marvelously a love destroys me and keeps me in its ropes every hour. And like a painter who, having observed the object, paints the image just as it appears, so I do the same, my beautiful one, and in my heart I carry your image. It seems I bear you in my heart painted as you appear, and, alas, this does not appear on the outside," 1–9).[17] As da Lentini, the poet attempts to create an inner, ideal image of feminine beauty, thereby opening a space within which creative tension transmutes the real into the ideal. In opening this space between desire and the fulfillment of desire, he implicitly rejects base eroticism by idealizing the feminine in terms of medieval *fin'amors* and using this *topos* to elevate corporeal reality into a disembodied ideal—an ideal which adheres to the feudal precepts of courtly society.[18]

17. For the text of this poem, see *Poeti del Duecento*, 1:55–57.

18. For a study of the genres of courtly literature, see David F. Hult, *Self-fulfilling Prophecies: Readership and Authority in the First "Roman de la Rose"* (Cambridge: Cambridge University Press, 1986), 186–262.

The Detto d'Amore

Amor sì vuole, e par-li,
Ch'i' 'n ogni guisa parli
E ched i' faccia un detto,
Che sia per tutto detto,
Ch'i' l'ag[g]ia ben servito.
Po' ch'e' m'eb[b]e 'nservito
E ch'i' gli feci omaggio,
I' l'ò tenuto o·maggio
E ter[r]ò giamà' sempre;
E questo fa asempr'è
A ciascun amoroso,
Sì c[h]'Amor amoroso
No·gli sia nella fine,
Anzi ch'e' metta a fine
Ciò ch'e' disira avere,
Che val me' c[h]'altro avere.
Ed egli è sì cortese
Che chi gli sta cortese
Od a man giunte avante,
Esso sì 'l mette avante
Di ciò ched e' disira,
E di tutto il dis-ira.
Amor non vuol logag[g]io,
Ma e' vuol ben, lo gag[g]io,
Ch'è 'l tu' cuor, si'a lu' fermo.
Allor dice: "I' t'afermo
Di ciò che·ttu domandi,
Sanza che·ttu do·mandi";
E dònati in presente,
Sanz'esservi presente
Di fino argento o d'oro,
Perch'i' a·llui m'adoro
Come leal amante.

Love so decrees, and deems it proper,
that I should speak in this particular way
and compose a *detto*,[1]
so that it may be proclaimed everywhere
how well I served him.
Since he took me in his service
and I made my pledge to him,
I have held him as my lord
and will do so forever.
And this will be a perfect example
for every lover,
so that Love will not
be bitter to him in the end,[2]
but rather that Love will let him have
the object of his desire,
which is more valuable than anything else.
And he is so courteous
that if someone appears before him humbly[3]
or in a position of supplication,[4]
he will help that one obtain
whatever he desires
and will take all his displeasure away.
Love desires no payment,
but he does require this pledge:
that your heart be faithful to him.
Then he says: "I grant you
all that you ask
without your sending any gifts."
And immediately he gives you a gift
without there being any gifts
of fine silver and gold,
for which reason I worship him
as a devout lover.

1. The "title" of the work is taken from this word, *detto* ("poem"), that derives from Old French *dit*, i.e., a narrative poem of intermediate length, often amorous or didactic and sometimes satirical.
2. The word *amoroso* would appear to be a mistake for *amaro* ("bitter"). Cf. v. 142.
3. That is, with his arms crossed across his chest.
4. Literally, with his hands clasped before him.

A·llu' fo graz[z]e, amante
Quella che d'ogne bene
E sì guernita bene
Che 'n le' non truov' uon pare;
E quand' ella m'apare,
Sì grande gioia mi dona
Che lo me' cor s'adona
A le' sempre servire,
E di le' vo' serv'ire,
Tant'à in le' piacimento.
Non so se piacimento
Le' fia ched i' la serva:
Almen può dir che serv'à,
Come ch'i' poco vaglia.
Amor nessun non vaglia,
Ma ciascun vuole ed ama,
Chi di lui ben s'inama,
E di colu' fa forza
Che ['n] compiacer fa forza
E nonn-à, i·nulla, parte.
Amor i·nulla part'è
Ch'e' non sia tutto presto
A fine amante presto.
Così sue cose livera
A chi l'amor no·llivera
E mette pene e 'ntenza
In far sua penetenza
Tal chente Amor comanda
A chi a·llu' s'acomanda;
E chi la porta in grado,
Il mette in alto grado
Di ciò ched e' disia:
Per me cotal dì sia!
Per ch'i' già non dispero,
Ma ciaschedun dì spero

To him I give thanks, for I love
that lady who is so well endowed
with every good quality
that her equal cannot be found;
and when she appears before me,
she gives me such great joy
that my heart gives itself over
to serving her constantly,
and I want to become her servant
for so much pleasure is in her.
I don't know if she wants
me to serve her:
at least she can say she has a servant,
although I am of little worth.
Love refuses no one,
but desires and loves all those
who eagerly fall in love,[5]
and esteems those
who strive to please him
and are completely subservient.
Love is always
completely willing to help
a perfect lover who's willing to serve.
Thus, he gives his bounty
to the one who does not abandon love
and puts much effort and desire
into doing such penance
as Love imposes
on the one who trusts him;
and if one bears the penance gladly,
Love puts this one in a high place
with respect to the object of his desire:
May such a day dawn for me!
For this reason I do not despair,
but every day hope

5. Literally, those who are securely hooked by him. Note the verbal play on *amo* = "I love" and *amo* = "hook."

Merzé, po' 'n su' travaglio
I' son sanza travaglio,
E sonvi sì legato
Ch'i' non vo' che legato
Giamai me ne prosciolga:
Se·nn'à d'altri pro', sciolga!
Ch'i' vo' ch'Amor m'aleghi,
Che che Ragion m'alleghi:
Di lei il me' cor sicura,
Né più di lei non cura;
Ella si fa dïessa:
Né·ffu né fia di essa.
Amor blasma ed isfama
E dice ch'e' di[s]fama,
Ma non del mi', certano:
Perch'i' per le' certan ò
Che ciaschedun s'abatte;
Me' ched Amor sa, batte.
Ed a me dice: "Folle,
Perché così t'afolle
D'aver tal signoria?
I' dico, signò·ri'à
Chi porta su' sug[g]ello.
I' per me non sug[g]ello,
Della sua 'mprenta, breve,
Ch'è troppo corta e breve
La gioia, e la noia lunga.
Or taglia ' geti, e lunga
Da lui, ch'egl[i] è di parte
Che, chi da lu' si parte,
E' fug[g]e e si va via.
Or non tener sua via,
Se vuo' da·llu' campare;
E se non, mal camp'are,

for favors, since, in his torture chamber,
I am without pain
and am bound there so securely
that I do not wish a papal legate
to ever loose my bonds:
if others may profit from it, let them be loosed!
For I wish to be bound to Love
no matter what Reason may allege;
Love protects my heart from her,
and it is no longer concerned with her;
she declares herself a goddess,
but she never was nor ever will be one.
Reason censures and disparages Love
and says that he's dishonorable,
but certainly not with me:[6]
because from her I know for sure
that anyone can be defeated;
she attacks Love as best she knows how.
And she says to me: "Foolish one,
why do you strive so foolishly
to have such a lordship?
I mean that whoever
bears his seal has a terrible lord.
For myself I do not put my seal
on any paper that bears his stamp,
for happiness is too short and fleeting,
and unpleasantness much too long.
Now cut your bonds[7] and go far away
from him, for Love's nature is such that,
he shuns the one who gets away from him,
and goes the other way.
Thus, do not follow his path,
if you want to escape from him;
otherwise you are plowing a bad field

6. The sense seems to be that Love's bad reputation carries over to his adherents.

7. The term *geti* derives from falconry and refers to the leather strips that bind the feet of the hunting birds.

Che biado non vi grana,
Anzi perde la grana
Chiunque la vi getta.
Perdio, or te ne getta
Di quel falso diletto,
E fa che si' a diletto
Del mi', ched egli è fine,
Che dà gioia sanza fine.
Lo dio dov'ài credenza
Non ti farà credenza
Se non come Fortuna.
Tu·sse' in gran fortuna,
Se non prendi buon porto
Per quel ched i' t'ò porto,
Ed a me non t'aprendi
E 'l mi' sermone aprendi.
Or mi rispondi e di',
Ch'egli è ancor gran dì
A farmi tua risposta;
Ma non mi far risposta
A ciò ch'i' ò proposato.
Dì tu se pro' posat'ò".

E, quand'i' eb[b]i intesa
Ragion, ch'è stata intesa
A trarmi de la regola
D'Amor, che 'l mondo regola,
I' le dissi: "Ragione,
I' ò salda ragione
Con Amor, e d'acordo
Siàn ben del nostro acordo,
Ed è scritto a mi' conto
Ch'i' non sia più tu' conto.
È la ragion dannata;
Perch'i' t'ò per dannata,
Ed eb[b]i, per convento,

in which good grain will not grow;
indeed, whoever sows there
will lose his seed.
For God's sake, get away
from that false pleasure,
and let my pleasure be yours,
for it is perfect
and gives unending joy.
The god in whom you put your faith
will give you no guarantees,
except those that Fortune gives.
You will be in a great storm,
if you do not find a safe harbor
according to what I've told you,
and if you don't cling to me
and learn from what I've said.
Now answer me and speak,
for there's still a lot of time
for you to give me your answer;
but don't simply reject
what I've proposed.
Tell me if I've framed the problem well."[8]

And, after I had heard
Reason, who was intent
upon leading me away from the rule
of Love, who rules the world,
I said to her: "Reason,
I have a sound arrangement
with Love, and we are very happy
with our agreement,
and it's written in my ledger
that I'm no longer indebted to you.
That account is closed;
for which reason I do—and did—consider you
to be all washed up, as these matters go,

8. There is a blank space in the manuscript at this point, as though marking a division in the text.

Po' ch'i' fu' del convento
D'Amor, cu' Dio man tenga,
E sempr'e' me mantenga.
Tu mi vuo' trar d'amare
E di' c[h]'Amor amar'è:
I' 'l truovà' dolce e fine,
E su' comincio e fine
Mi pia[c]que e piacerà,
Ché 'n sé gran piacer'à.
Or come viverêo?
Sanz'Amor vive reo
Chi si governa al mondo;
Sanz'Amor egli è mondo
D'ogne buona vertute,
Né non può far vertute;
Sanz'Amor sì è 'nuìa,
Che, con cu' regna, envia
D'andarne dritto al luogo
Là dove Envia à·lluogo.
E perciò non ti credo,
Se·ttu dicess'il Credo
E 'l Paternostro e·ll'Ave,
Sì poco in te senn'àve.
Adio, ched i' mi torno,
E fine amante torno
Per devisar partita
Com'ell'è ben partita
E di cors e di membra,
Sì come a me mi membra".

Cape' d'oro battuto
Paion, che m'àn battuto,
Quelli che porta in capo,
Per ch'i' a·llor fo capo.

ever since I made my pact
with Love, to whom may God extend a hand,
and may he always keep me safe and sound.
You want to keep me from loving
and you say that Love is bitter,
but I have found him sweet and perfect,
and I liked and will like
his beginning and end,
because in him there is great pleasure.
Now, how could I live?
Whoever lives in the world
lives badly without Love:
without Love he is bereft
of every good virtue,
and he cannot perform good deeds;
without Love there is unpleasantness
who entices the one who dwells with her[9]
to go straight to the place
where Envy has her home.
Therefore, I don't believe you,
even if you were to say the Creed
and the Our Father, and the Hail Mary,
for so little wisdom is in you.
Goodbye, for I am leaving,
and I will return to being a perfect lover
in order to compose another part[10]
to describe how well proportioned she is,
both in her body and in her members,
just as I remember them."[11]

Her fine head of hair
seems fashioned of gold,
golden strands that conquered me,
and with these I'll begin.

9. *Noia*, "unpleasantness," is personified.

10. Another part of my *Detto*.

11. There is a blank space in the manuscript at this point, as though marking a division in the text.

La sua piacente ciera
Nonn-è sembiante a cera,
Anz'è sì fresca e bella
Che lo me' cor s'abella
Di non le mai affare,
Tant'à piacente affare.
La sua fronte, e le ciglia,
Bieltà d'ogn'altr'eciglia:
Tanto son ben voltati
Che ' mie' pensier' voltati
Ànno ver' lei, che gioia
Mi dà più c[h]'altra gioia
In su' dolze riguardo.
Di n[i]u·mal à riguardo
Cu' ella guarda in viso,
Tant'à piacente aviso;
Ed à sì chiara luce
Ch'al sol to' la sua luce,
E l'oscura e l'aluna
Sì come il sol la luna.
Per ch'i' a quella spera
Ò messa la mia spera,
E s'i' ben co·llei regno,
I' non vogli'altro regno.
La bocca e 'l naso e 'l mento
À più belli, e non mento,
Ch'unque nonn-eb[b]e Alena;
Ed à più dolce alena
C[h]e n[e]ssuna pantera.
Per ch'i' ver' sua pantera
I' mi sono, 'n fed', ito,

Her lovely face
does not resemble wax;[12]
indeed, it is so radiant and beautiful
that my heart takes satisfaction
in never comparing it to others,
such a lovely thing it is.
Her forehead and her eyebrows surpass
the beauty of every other woman:[13]
they are so perfectly arched
that they have turned my thoughts
toward her, who gives me
with her sweet look
more happiness than any jewel.
No one on whom she gazes
is concerned about any sickness,[14]
so lovely is her countenance.
The pupils of her eyes are so brilliant
that they take away the sun's light
and darken and eclipse it
just as the sun does to the moon.
For this reason I've put
all my hope in that star,
and since I live so well with her,
I desire no other earthly realm.
Her mouth and nose and chin
are more beautiful—and I don't lie—
than those that Helen had;[15]
and her breath is more fragrant
than any panther.[16]
For this reason I have, in good faith,
moved toward her net

12. That is, it does not have the color of wax.

13. The woman's brows are specified as her superlative features.

14. Or, the one on whom she gazes cannot have bad thoughts about anyone. Cf. Guido Guinizzelli, "Io voglio del ver la mia donna laudare," v. 14: "null'om pò mal pensar fin che la vede" (*Poeti del Duecento*, ed. Gianfranco Contini, 2 vols. [Milan and Naples: Ricciardi, 1960], 2:472).

15. Helen of Troy, legendary paragon of beauty.

16. According to medieval bestiaries, the panther's breath was so sweet that it attracted all other animals. See Dante, *De vulgari eloquentia*, 1.16.1.

E dentro v'ò fedito;
Ed èmene sì preso
Ched i' vi son sì preso
Che mai, di mia partita,
No·mi farò partita.
La gola sua, e 'l petto,
Sì chiar'è, ch'a Dio a petto
Mi par esser la dia
Ch'i' veg[g]io quella dia.
Tant'è bianca e lattata,
Che ma' non fu alattata
Nulla di tal valuta.
A me tropp'è valuta,
Ched ella sì m'à dritto
In saper tutto 'l dritto
C[h]'Amor usa in sua corte,
Ch'e' non v'à leg[g]e corte.
Mani à lunghette e braccia,
E chi co llei s'abraccia
Giamai mal nonn-à gotta
Né di ren' né di gotta:
Il su' nobile stato
Sì mette in buono stato
Chiunque la rimira.
Per che 'l me' cor si mira
In lei e notte e giorno,
E sempre a·llei ag[g]iorno,
Ch'Amor sì·ll'à inchesto,
Néd e' non à inchesto
Se potesse aver termine,
C[h]'amar vorria san' termine.
E quando va per via,
Ciascun di lei à 'nvia
Per l'andatura gente;

and have stumbled into it;
and thus it's happened
that I've been so firmly ensnared there
that never, by my own choice,
will I leave it.
Her throat and her breast
are so resplendent that
I seem to be in God's presence
on that day in which I look upon that goddess.
So white and creamy is she
that no creature has ever been
born who is as worthy as she.
She is most precious to me,
for she guided me
to make a full study of the law
that Love follows in his court,
where there are no useless laws.
Her hands and arms are slender,
and whoever embraces her
never suffers any ill,
no kidney disease, no gout:
her noble condition
puts everyone who gazes at her
in a blissful state.
For this reason my heart gazes
on her day and night,
and with thoughts of her I always greet the dawn,
because Love has willed it so,
nor has my heart asked
if this could come to an end,
for it would want to love endlessly.
And when she goes along the street,
everyone desires her
for her noble movement;[17]

17. The scene of the woman who passes along the street is a frequent occurrence in the early Italian love lyric. Cf. Guinizzelli, "Io voglio del ver la mia donna laudare"; Guido Cavalcanti, "Chi è questa che vèn, ch'ogn'om la mira" (*Poeti del Duecento*, 2:472, 495); Dante, "Tanto gentile e tanto onesta pare" (*Vita nuova*, 26).

E quando parla a gente,
Sì umilmente parla
Che boce d'agnol par là.
Il su' danzar e 'l canto
Val vie più ad incanto
Che di nulla serena,
Ché·ll'aria fa serena:
Q[u]ando la boce lieva,
Ogne nuvol si lieva
E l'aria riman chiara.
Per che 'l me' cor sì chiar'à
Di non far giamai cambio
Di lei a nessun cambio;
Ch'ell'è di sì gran pregio
Ch'i' non troveria pregio
Nessun, che mai la vaglia.
Amor, se Dio mi vaglia,
Il terreb[b]e a·ffollore,
E ben seria foll'o re'
Quand'io il pensasse punto.
M'Amor l'à sì a punto
Nella mia mente pinta,
Ch'i' la mi veg[g]io pinta
Nel cor, s'i' dormo o veglio.
Unque asessino a·Veglio
Non fu giamai sì presto,
Né a Dio mai il Presto,
Com'io a servir [a]mante
Per le vertù ch'à mante.

and when she speaks with someone,
she speaks so sweetly
that it seems to be an angel's voice.
Her dancing and singing
are more enchanting than those
of any siren,[18]
for they calm the atmosphere.
When she begins to speak
every cloud leaves the sky,
and the air remains crystal clear.
For this reason my heart is so faithful
that it will never seek to exchange her
for another at any rate:
for she is of such worth
that I could never find any
treasure that would be equal to her.
Love, so help me God,
would consider it madness,
and I would indeed be foolish or wicked
if I were to consider this at all.
But Love has so precisely
painted her in my mind
that, no matter if I sleep or am awake,
I see her painted in my heart.[19]
Never was an assassin
so willingly disposed to the Old Man,[20]
nor Prester John to God,
as I am to serve for love
because of the many virtues she possesses.

18. For the legendary allure of the siren's song, see Boethius, *Consolation of Philosophy* (1, prose 1), and Dante, *Purg.* 19.1–33.

19. The motif of the lady painted in the lover's heart first appears in the poetry of Giacomo da Lentini, "Meravigliosamente," vv. 10–11: "In cọr par ch'eo vi porti / pinta como parete . . ." (*Poeti del Duecento*, 1:55–57).

20. The faithfulness of the "Assassin" to the "Old Man" is well known in Italy (see, among others, the last tale in the *Novellino*, the *Detto del gatto lupesco*, and Guido delle Colonne's poem, "Gioiosamente canto"). According to the legend, these bodyguards of the Old Man of the Mountain were so devout that they would willingly kill themselves by jumping from high places on command. Cf. sonnet 2 of the *Fiore*.

E s'io in lei pietanza
Truov', o d'una pietanza
Del su'amor son contento,
I' sarò più contento,
Per la sua gran valenza,
Che s'io avesse Valenza.
Se Gelosia à 'n sé gina
Di tormene segina,
Lo Dio d'Amor mi mente:
Chéd i' ò ben a mente
Ciò ched e' m'eb[b]e in grado
Sed i' 'l servisse a grado.
Ben ci à egli un camino
Più corto, né 'l camino,
Perciò ch'i' nonn-ò entrata
Ched i' per quell'entrata
Potesse entrar un passo.
Ric[c]hez[z]a guarda il passo,
Che non fa buona cara
A que' che no·ll'à cara.
E sì fu' i' sì sag[g]io
Ched i' ne feci sag[g]io
S'i' potesse oltre gire.
"Per neente t'ag[g]ire",
Mi disse, e co· mal viso:
"Tu sse' da me diviso,
Perciò il passo ti vieto;
Non perché·ttu sie vieto,
Ma·ttu no·m'acontasti
Unque, ma mi contasti;
E ïo ciascù·schifo,
Chi di me si fa schifo.
Va tua via e sì procaccia,
Ch'i' so ben, chi pro' caccia,
Convien che bestia prenda.
Se fai che Veno imprenda

And if find pity in her
or if I am granted
a little portion of her love,
I will be happier,
because of her great worth,
than if I were to possess Valencia.[21]
If Jealousy has in herself the ability
to take her away from me,
then the God of Love is lying to me.
For I remember well
what pleasure he offered me,
provided that I would serve him faithfully.
To be sure there is a shorter
way, but I do not take it,
for which I have no profit,
since I could enter only one
step through that door.
Guarding the passage is Riches,
who does not look kindly
on those who do not hold her dear.
And yet I was so wise
that I made an attempt
to see if I could go beyond.
"You are wasting your time,"
she said to me with a harsh look.
"You aren't known to me,
and for this reason I forbid your passage.
It's not because you're old,
but because you've never made my acquaintance,
and, in fact, you resist me,
and I am hostile to anyone
who avoids me.
Go on your way, and do the best you can,
for this I know well: the able hunter
will certainly catch his prey.
If you do it so that Venus declares

21. City in Spain.

La guerr'a Gelosia,
Come che 'n gelo sia,
Convien ch'ella si renda,
E ched ella ti renda
Del servir guiderdone,
Sanza che guiderdone.
Ma tutor ti ricorde:
Se ma' meco t'acorde,
Oro e argento aporta;
I' t'aprirò la porta,
Sanza che ttu facci'oste.
E sì avrai ad oste
Folle-Larghez[z]a mala,
Che scioglierà la mala
E farà gran dispensa
In sale ed in dispensa
E 'n guardarobe e 'n cella.
Povertà è su'ancella:
Quella convien t'apanni
E che tti trag[g]a ' panni
E le tue buone calze,
Che giamai no·lle calze,
E la camiscia e brache,
Se·ttu co·lle' t'imbrache.
Figlia fu a Cuor-Fallito:
Perdio, guarda 'n fall'ito
Non sia ciò ch'i' t'ò detto;
E sie conmeco adetto,
E mostra ben voglienza
D'aver mia benvoglienza;
Ché Povertat'è insom[m]a
D'ogne dolor la somma.

war on Jealousy,
the latter, even though she's cold,
will have to surrender,
and your lady will reward you[22]
for your service
without any cost to you.
But keep this in mind:
if one day you wish to deal with me
be sure to bring gold and silver;
I will open the door for you
without your waging war.
And so you will be welcomed
by the evil *Folle Larghezza*[23]
who will loosen the purse strings
and will lay in great supplies
of salt and pantry items
and clothes and wines.
Poverty is her servant:
she'll rob you
and take your clothes,
including your nice trousers
that you'll never wear again,
and your shirt and undergarments,
if you get involved with her.
She was the daughter of *Cuor Fallito*:[24]
for God's sake, be sure that
what I've told you doesn't go unheeded.
Be loyal to me,
and show your good will
to have my favor;
for Poverty is, in fact,
the epitome of every sorrow.

22. The term *guiderdone* indicates the highly prized goal of love service: the gift of love, the lady herself. For the importance of this particular term, see the canzone "Guiderdone aspetto avire," variously attributed in the manuscripts to Giacomo da Lentini and Rinaldo d'Aquino (*Le rime della scuola siciliana*, ed. Bruno Panvini [Florence: Olschki, 1962], 401–403).

23. That is, Foolish Generosity.

24. That is, Faint Heart.

Ancor non t'ò nomato
Un su' figliuol nomato:
Imbolar uon l'apella;
Chi da·llu' non s'apella,
Egli 'l mena a le forche,
Là dove nonn-à for che
E' monti per la scala,
Dov'ogne ben gli scala,
E danza a·ssuon di vento,
Sanz'avé·mai avento.
Or sì·tt'ò letto il salmo:
Ben credo, a mente sa' 'l mo',
Sì 'l t'ò mostrato ad agio.
Se mai vien' per mi' agio,
Pensa d'esser maestro
Di ciò ch'i' t'amaestro,
Che Povertà tua serva
Non sia, né mai ti serva,
Ché 'l su' servigio è malo,
E ben può dicer "mal ò"
Cu' ella spoglia o scalza:
Ché d'ogne ben lo scalza,
E mettelo in tal punto
Ch'a vederlo par punto.
E gli amici e ' parenti
No gli son aparenti:
Ciascun le ren' gli torna
E ciascun se ne torna"...

...Perch'Amor m'ag[gi]a matto,
O che mi tenga a matto
Ragion, cui poco amo,
Già, se Dio piace, ad amo
Ch'ell'ag[g]ia no m'acroc[c]o.
Amor m'à cinto il croc[c]o,

I have not yet told you
about one of her notorious sons:
they call him *Imbolare*;[25]
anyone who makes no defense against him,
that one he leads to the gallows,
there where his only choice
is to climb the stairs;
there all good things come to an end,
and he dances to the sound of the wind
without ever having rest.
Now that I've read you the psalm,
I believe you know it now by heart,
so clearly I've explained it to you.
If you ever wish to be a comfort to me,
think of becoming a teacher
of that subject I'm teaching you here:
consider that Poverty is not your servant,
nor will she ever serve you,
because her service is bad,
and the one whose clothes and shoes she removes
can well say: "I have misfortune";
for she takes from him every good thing
and reduces him to such a state
that it's painful to see him.
And his friends and relatives
do not come around him:
they all turn their backs on him
and go away. . . ."[26]

. . .for the fact that Love has enslaved me
or that Reason, whom I love little,
considers me to be foolish
I will never, God willing, nibble
at whatever hook he may present.
Love has armed me with a skewer

25. That is, Thievery.
26. There is a lacuna in the manuscript.

Con che vuol ched i' tenda
S'i' vo' gir co·llui 'n tenda.
E dice, s'i' balestro
Se non col su' balestro,
O s'i' credo a Ragione
Di nulla sua ragione
Ch'ella mi dica o punga,
O sed i' metto in punga
Ric[c]hez[z]a per guardare,
O s'i' miro in guardare,
A·llui se non, ciò ch'ò,
Di lui non faccia cò;
Ma mi getta di taglia,
E dice che 'n sua taglia
I' non prenda ma' soldo,
Per livra né per soldo
Ched i' giamà' gli doni.
Amor vuol questi doni:
Corpo e avere e anima;
E con colui s'inanima,
Chi gliel dà certamente
(E chi altr'ac[c]erta, mente),
E sol lui per tesoro
Vuol ch'uon metta 'n tesoro.
E chi di lui è preso,
Sì vuol ch'e' sia apreso
D'ogne bell'ordinanza
Che 'l su' bellor dinanza.
Chi 'l cheta com'e' dee,
S'achita ciò ch'e' dee.
D'orgoglio vuol sie vòto,
Chéd egli à fatto voto
D[i] non amarti guar' dì
Se d'orgoglio no'l guardi:
Ché fortemente pec[c]a
Que' che d'orgoglio à pec[c]a.

which he requires me to wield
if I wish to go in his company.
And he says that if I use any crossbow
other than his,
or if I give heed to any
of Reason's speeches
with which she provides explanations or exhortations,
or if I put riches
in my purse to keep them safe,
or if I plan to safeguard
what I have gained—and not from him—
then I should not count on him.
But he cuts me off
and says that in his company
I'll never play a part,
not for any *lira* or any *soldo*[27]
that I may ever give him.
Love desires these gifts:
body and wealth and soul;
and he forms a single soul with the one
who gives him these things confidently
(and whoever says otherwise lies),
and Love desires that he alone, as a precious object,
be put by this one in his treasury.
And whoever is captured by Love,
Love wants him to be taught
every beautiful custom
that enhances his beauty.
If one pays him appropriately,
so is he properly paid in return.
He wants one to be without pride,
because he has pledged
not to love you very long,
if you don't keep away from pride:
for he sins greatly
who commits the sin of pride.

27. A *soldo* is 1/240 of a *lira*.

Cortese e franco e pro'
Convien che sie, e pro'
Salute e doni e rendi:
Se·ttu a·cciò ti rendi,
D'Amor sarai in grazia,
E sì ti farà grazia.
E se se' forte e visto,
A caval sie avisto
Di punger gentemente,
Sì che la gente mente
Ti pongan per diletto.
Non ti truovi di letto
Matino a qualche canto.
Se ttu sai alcun canto,
Non ti pesi il cantare
Quanto pesa un cantare,
Sì che n'oda la nota
Quella che 'l tu' cor nota.
Se ssai giucar di lancia,
Prendila e sì·lla lancia,
E corri e sali e salta,
Che troppo gente asalta:
Far cosa che·llor seg[g]ia
Gli mette in alta seg[g]ia.
Belle robe a podere,
Secondo il tu' podere,
Vesti, fresche e novelle,
Sì che n'oda novelle
L'amor, cu' tu à' caro
Più che 'l Soldano il Caro.
E s'elle son di lana,
Sì non ti paia l'ana
A devisar li 'ntagli,
Se ttu à' chi gli 'ntagli.
Nove scarpette e calze
Convien che tuttor calze;

You must be courteous
and loyal and valiant,
and you must give and return his greeting graciously.
If you do all of these things,
you'll be in Love's favor,
and he will compensate you well.
And if you're strong and skillful
be advised when on horseback
to use your spurs elegantly,
so that the people
may look at you with delight.
In the morning you must not find yourself
asleep on some street corner.
If you know some songs,
let the singing of them not weigh on you
as much as a *cantare*,[28]
so that your loved one
may hear its melody.
If you know how to handle a lance,
take it and throw it,
then run and jump and dance:
all these things make people glad:
by doing what they like to see,
you make them feel special.
Wear the most lovely clothing you can
within your means,
fresh and new garments,
so that your loved one may hear about it,
the one you hold more precious
than the Sultan holds Cairo.
And if they're made of wool,
it should not be difficult
to design the decorations,
if you have someone to cut them out.
You must always wear
brand new shoes and pants.

28. I.e., a *quintale*, which is 100 kilograms, or 220 pounds.

Della persona conto
Ti tieni; e nul mal conto
Di tua boc[c]a non l'oda,
Ma ciascun pregia e loda.
Servi donne ed onora,
Ché via troppo d'onor'à
Chi vi mette sua 'ntenta.
S'alcuno il diavol tenta
Di lor parlare a taccia,
Sì li dì che·ssi taccia.
Sie largo; e d'altra parte
Non far del tu' cuor parte;
Tutto 'n quel luogo il metti
Là dove tu l'ametti:
Ch'egli è d'Amor partito
Chi 'l su' cuor à partito,
Ch' e' non tien leal fino
Chi va come l'alfino,
Ma sol con que' s'acorda
Che 'l su' camin vâ corda.
Mi' detto ancor non fino,
Ché d'un amico fino
Chieder convien ti membri,
Che metta cuor e membri
Per te, se·tti bisogna,
E 'n ogne tua bisogna
Ti sia fedele e giusto.
Ma, fé che dô a san Giusto,
Seminati son chiari
I buon'amici chiari.
Ma, se 'l truovi perfetto,
Più ricco che 'l Perfetto
Sarai di sua compagna;
E s'à bella compagna,
La tua fia più sicura,

Keep your appearance elegant,
and let no evil things
be heard from your mouth,
but esteem and give praise to everyone.
Serve and honor women,
for whoever sets his mind to do it
will receive much honor.
And if the devil tempts someone
to speak badly about women,
tell him to be quiet.
Be generous, but, on the other hand,
don't divide your heart;
put it all in that place,
where you have placed it:
for whoever has divided his heart
is separated from Love,
for he does not consider that one to be completely loyal
who moves like a bishop in chess,[29]
but he gets along only with the one
who goes straight along his path.
I am not yet finished with my *detto*,
for you must remember
to look for a perfect friend
who will put heart and body
to your service, if you need it,
and who will be faithful and just toward you
in your every need.
But, by the faith I owe to San Giusto,
true friends are
truly hard to find.
However, if you find a perfect friend,
with his friendship you will be
better off than the Prefect.[30]
And if he has a beautiful female companion,
may yours be more trustworthy,

29. That is, diagonally, obliquely and not straight.
30. The Prefect of Rome.

Ché Veno non si cura
Che non faccia far tratto,
Di che l'amor è tratto.
Di lor più il fatto isveglia,
Né ma' per suon di sveglia
Né per servir ch'e' faccia
No'l guarda dritto in faccia. . .

because Venus gives no guarantees
that she will not have another arrow released,
with which love is engendered.[31]
With them[32] she arouses carnal passion,[33]
more than through the chimes of dawn
or through the service that he might give.
She does not look him directly in the face. . . .

31. The interpretation of these verses is uncertain. Contini (823) translates: "e se ha una bella compagna, la tua sarà più sicura, perché Venere non manca di far tirare un colpo (di freccia), di quelli che fanno nascere amore(?)" ["and if he has a beautiful companion, yours will be more secure, because Venus will not fail to have an arrow shot, of the sort that cause love to be born"]. Marchiori (442) interprets as follows: "Qui vuole dire che se uno ha un'amante, può stare sicuro perché *Venere* non si curerà di farla innamorare di un altro uomo, per cui il suo amore possa venire distrutto" ["Here he means that if one has a lover, he can be sure that Venus will not be concerned to have her fall in love with another man, for which reason his love may be destroyed"]. Part of the discrepancy in interpretation stems from the ambiguity of the past participle *tratto*, as meaning either "attratto" or "tolto," "distrutto." We interpret *fia* in v. 473 as a subjunctive which establishes the proper context for the following verses, in which Venus is said to give no assurances (*Veno non sicura*) that she will not refrain from causing the love-inducing arrows to be shot (*che non faccia far tratto, / di che l'amor è tratto*).

32. I.e., love's arrows.

33. Because of the defective condition of the manuscript, we are unable to arrive at a satisfactory interpretation of the concluding verses of the *Detto* (vv. 477–480).

Bibliography

Primary Works

Alan of Lille. *De planctu Naturae*. Ed. Nikolaus M. Häring. *Studi medievali*, 3rd ser., 19.2 (1978), 797–879.

———. *Plaint of Nature*. Trans. and commentary by James J. Sheridan. Toronto: Pontifical Institute of Mediaeval Studies, 1980.

Alighieri, Dante. *The Divine Comedy of Dante Alighieri*. Trans. Allen Mandelbaum. 3 vols. New York: Bantam Books, 1982, 1984, 1986.

———. *Il Fiore e il Detto d'Amore*. Ed. Ernesto Giacomo Parodi. Florence: Bemporad, 1922.

———. *Il Fiore e il Detto d'Amore attribuibili a Dante Alighieri*. Ed. Gianfranco Contini. Milan: Mondadori, 1984.

———. *Il Fiore e il Detto d'Amore attribuibili a Dante Alighieri*. Ed. Gianfranco Contini. Milan and Naples: Ricciardi, 1995.

———. *Il Fiore e il Detto d'Amore attribuiti a Dante Alighieri. Testo del secolo XIII*. Ed. with an introduction by Guido Mazzoni. Florence: Alinari, 1923.

———. *Il Fiore e il Detto d'Amore*. Ed. Claudio Marchiori. Genoa: Tilgher, 1983.

———. *Il Fiore—Detto d'Amore*. Ed. Luca Carlo Rossi. Milan: Mondadori, 1996.

———. *Il Fiore, poème italien du XIIIe siècle, en CCXXXII sonnets, imité du "Roman de la Rose" par Durante*. Ed. Ferdinand Castets. Paris: Maisonneuve, 1881.

———. *Rime*. Ed. Gianfranco Contini. Turin: Einaudi, 1965.

———. *Vita nuova*. Ed. Domenico De Robertis. Milan and Naples: Ricciardi, 1984.

Angiolieri, Cecco. *Le Rime*. Ed. Antonio Lanza. Rome: Archivio Guido Izzi, 1990.

The Bestiary: A Book of Beasts. Trans. T. H. White. New York: G. P. Putnam's Sons, 1960.

Cantare dei cantari. Ed. Pio Rajna. *Zeitschrift für romanische Philologie* 2 (1878), 220–254.

Capellanus, Andreas. *De amore libri tres*. Ed. E. Trojel. Copenhagen: Gadiana, 1892.

Castellani, Arrigo. *I più antichi testi italiani*. 2nd ed. Bologna: Pàtron, 1976.

Dei Faitinelli, Pietro. *Rime di ser Pietro de' Faitinelli*. Ed. L. Del Prete. Bologna, 1874.

Early Italian Texts. Ed. Carlo Dionisotti and Cecil Grayson. 2nd ed. Oxford: Basil Blackwell, 1965.

Guillaume de Lorris and Jean de Meun. *The Romance of the Rose*. Trans. Charles Dahlberg. Princeton: Princeton University Press, 1995.

———. *Le Roman de la Rose*. Ed. Félix Lecoy. 3 vols. Paris: Champion, 1965–1970.

Jacobus De Voragine. *The Golden Legend: Readings on the Saints*. Trans. William Granger Ryan. 2 vols. Princeton: Princeton University Press, 1993.

Ovid. *The Art of Love and Other Poems*. Trans. J. H. Mozley. 2nd ed. Cambridge, Mass.: Harvard University Press; London: Heinemann, 1985.

———. *Metamorphoses*. Trans. Frank Justus Miller (revised by G. P. Goold). 2 vols. Cambridge, Mass.: Harvard University Press, 1984.

Papia. *Papia vocabulista*. Turin: Bottega D'Erasmo, 1966. Reprinted from the Venetian edition of 1496.

Poeti del Duecento. Ed. Gianfranco Contini. 2 vols. Milan and Naples: Ricciardi, 1960.

Le rime della scuola siciliana. Ed. Bruno Panvini. Florence: Olschki, 1962.

Secondary Sources

Arden, Heather. *The "Roman de la rose": An Annotated Bibliography*. New York: Garland, 1993.

Armour, Peter. "Lettura dei sonetti LXI–XC." In *Letture classensi* 22: *Lettura del "Fiore."* Ed. Zygmunt G. Barański, Patrick Boyde, and Lino Pertile. Ravenna: Longo, 1993. 53–74.

———. "The *Roman de la Rose* and the *Fiore*: Aspects of a Literary Transplantation." *Journal of the Institute of Romance Studies* 2 (1993), 63–81.

Baldelli, Ignazio. "La letteratura volgare in Toscana dalle origini ai primi decenni del secolo XIII." In *Letteratura italiana: Storia e geografia, l'età medievale*. Turin: Einaudi, 1987. 65–77.

Barański, Zygmunt G. "The Ethics of Literature: The *Fiore* and Medieval Traditions of Rewriting." In *The Fiore in Context: Dante, France, Tuscany*. Ed. Zygmunt G. Barański and Patrick Boyde. Notre Dame: University of Notre Dame Press, 1997. 207–232.

———. "Il *Fiore* e la tradizione delle *translationes*." *Rassegna europea di letteratura italiana* 5/6 (1995), 31–41.

———. "Lettura dei sonetti I–XXX." In *Letture classensi* 22: *Lettura del "Fiore."* 13–35.

Barber, Joseph A. "Prospettive per un'analisi statistica del *Fiore*." *Revue des études italiennes* 31 (1985), 5–24.

———. "A Statistical Analysis of the *Fiore*." *Lectura Dantis* 6 (1990), 100–122.

Barnes, John C. "Lettura dei sonetti CXXI–CL." In *Letture classensi* 22: *Lettura del "Fiore."* 91–108.

Barolini, Teodolinda. *Dante's Poets: Textuality and Truth in the "Comedy."* Princeton: Princeton University Press, 1984.

Bernardo, Aldo S. "Sex and Salvation in the Middle Ages: From the *Romance of the Rose* to the *Divine Comedy*." *Italica* 67 (1990), 305–318.

Borgognoni, Adolfo. "Il *Fiore*." *La rassegna settimanale di politica, scienza, lettere ed arti* 8, no. 198 (16 ottobre 1881), 247–249.

Boyde, Patrick. "Lettura dei sonetti CCXI–CCXXXII." In *Letture classensi* 22: *Lettura del "Fiore."* 155–178.

———. "*Summus Minimusve Poeta*? Arguments for and against Attributing the *Fiore* to Dante." In *The Fiore in Context*. 13–45.

Brieger, Peter, Millard Meiss, and Charles S. Singleton. *Illuminated Manuscripts of the Divine Comedy*. 2 vols. Princeton: Princeton University Press, 1969.

Brownlee, Kevin. "Jason's Voyage and the Poetics of Rewriting: The *Fiore* and the *Roman de la Rose*." In *The Fiore in Context*. 167–184.

———. "The Practice of Cultural Authority: Italian Responses to French Cultural Dominance in *Il Tesoretto*, *Il Fiore*, and the *Commedia*." *Forum for Modern Language Studies* 33 (1997), 258–269.

Buzzetti Gallarati, Silvia. "La memoria di Rustico nel *Fiore*." In *Studi di filologia medievale offerti a D'Arco Silvio Avalle*. Milan and Naples: Ricciardi, 1996. 65–98.

Cassata, Letterio. "Sul testo del *Fiore*." *Studi danteschi* 58 (1986), 187–237.

Castellani, Arrigo. "Le *cruces* del *Fiore*." *Studi linguistici italiani* 15 (1989), 100–105.

Cherchi, Paolo A. "Tradition and *Topoi* in Medieval Literature." *Critical Inquiry* 3 (1976), 281–294.

Contini, Gianfranco. "Il Fiore." In *Enciclopedia dantesca*. 6 vols. Rome: Istituto della Enciclopedia Italiana, 1984. 2:895–901.

———. "Un nodo della cultura medievale: la serie *Roman de la Rose - Fiore - Divina Commedia*." *Lettere italiane* 25 (1973), 162–189.

———. "La questione del *Fiore*." *Cultura e scuola* 13 / 14 (1965), 768–773.

Copeland, Rita. *Rhetoric, Hermeneutics, and Translation in the Middle Ages: Academic Traditions and Vernacular Texts*. Cambridge: Cambridge University Press, 1991.

Cursietti, Marco. "Ancora per il *Fiore*: indizi cavalcantiani." *La Parola del testo* 1 (1997), 197–218.

Davie, Mark. "Lettura dei sonetti CLI–CLXXX." In *Letture classensi* 22: *Lettura del "Fiore."* 109–130.

De Bartholomaeis, Vincenzo. "Ciò che veramente sia l'antichissima 'cantilena' *Boves se pareba*." *Giornale storico della letteratura italiana* 90 (1927), 197–204.

De Robertis Boniforti, Teresa. "Nota sul codice e la sua scrittura." In *The Fiore in Context*. 49–86.

Dionisotti, Carlo. *Geografia e storia della letteratura italiana*. Turin: Einaudi, 1967.

Dragonetti, Roger. "Specchi d'amore: il *Romanzo della Rosa* e il *Fiore*." *Paragone* 374 (1981), 3–22.

Durling, Robert M. "The Audiences of the *De Vulgari Eloquentia* and the *Petrose*." *Dante Studies* 110 (1992), 25–35.

Durling, Robert M., and Ronald Martinez. *Time and the Crystal: Studies in Dante's "Rime Petrose."* Berkeley: University of California Press, 1990.

Economou, George D. *The Goddess Natura in Medieval Literature*. Cambridge, Mass.: Harvard University Press, 1972.

Erasmi, Gabriele. "Towards a New Interpretation of the *Indovinello veronese*." *Canadian Journal of Italian Studies* 1 (1977–1978), 108–114.

Fasani, Remo. "L'attribuzione del *Fiore*." *Studi e problemi di critica testuale* 39 (1989), 5–40.

Ferrante, Joan M., George D. Economou, and Frederick Goldin, eds. *In Pursuit of Perfection: Courtly Love in Medieval Literature*. Port Washington, N.Y.: Kennikat Press, 1975.

Fleming, John V. "Jean de Meun and the Ancient Poets." In *Rethinking the "Romance of the Rose": Text, Image, Reception*. Ed. Kevin Brownlee and Sylvia Huot. Philadelphia: University of Pennsylvania Press, 1992. 81–100.

———. *Reason and the Lover*. Princeton: Princeton University Press, 1984.

———. *The "Roman de la Rose": A Study in Allegory and Iconography*. Princeton: Princeton University Press, 1969.

Folena, Gianfranco. "Cultura e poesia dei Siciliani." In *Storia della letteratura italiana*, vol. 1: *Le origini e il Duecento*. Ed. Emilio Cecchi and Natalino Sapegno. Milan: Garzanti, 1965. 273–347.

———. *Volgarizzare e tradurre*. Turin: Einaudi, 1991.

Fratta, Aniello. "La lingua del *Fiore* (e del *Detto d'Amore*) e le opere di Francesco da Barberino." *Misure Critiche* 14 (1984), 45–62.

Guerra d'Antoni, Francesca. "A New Perspective on the Veronese Riddle." *Romance Philology* 36 (1982), 185–200.

Hainsworth, Peter. "Lettura dei sonetti XCI–CXX." In *Letture classensi* 22: *Lettura del "Fiore."* 75–89.

Harrison, Robert Pogue. "The Bare Essential: The Landscape of *Il Fiore*." In *Rethinking the "Romance of the Rose."* 289–303.

Hult, David F. *Self-fulfilling Prophecies: Readership and Authority in the First "Roman de la Rose."* Cambridge: Cambridge University Press, 1986.

Huot, Sylvia. "The *Fiore* and the Early Reception of the *Roman de la Rose*." In *The Fiore in Context*. 153–165.

———. *The "Romance of the Rose" and Its Medieval Readers: Interpretation, Reception, Manuscript Transmission*. Cambridge: Cambridge University Press, 1993.

Kelly, Douglas. "'Li chastiaus... Qu'Amors prist puis par ses esforz': The Conclusion of Guillaume de Lorris' *Rose*." In *A Medieval French Miscellany*. Ed. Norris J. Lacy. Lawrence: University of Kansas Publications, 1972. 61–78.

———. *Internal Difference and Meanings in the "Roman de la Rose"*. Madison: University of Wisconsin Press, 1995.

———. *Medieval Imagination: Rhetoric and the Poetry of Courtly Love*. Madison: University of Wisconsin Press, 1978.

———. "*Translatio Studii*: Translation, Adaptation, and Allegory in Medieval French Literature." *Philological Quarterly* 57 (1978), 287–310.

Kleinhenz, Christopher. *The Early Italian Sonnet: The First Century (1220–1321)*. Lecce: Milella, 1986.

———. "Dante as Reader and Critic of Courtly Literature." In *Courtly Literature: Culture and Context*. Selected Papers from the 5th Triennial Congress of the International Courtly Literature Society, Dalfsen, The Netherlands, 9–16 August, 1986. Ed. Keith Busby and Erik Kooper. Amsterdam: Benjamins, 1990. 379–393.

Leonardi, Lino. "'Langue' poetica e stile dantesco nel *Fiore*: per una verifica degli 'argomenti interni'." In *Studi di filologia medievale offerti a D'Arco Silvio Avalle*. Milan and Naples: Ricciardi, 1996. 237–291.

Lewis, C. S. *The Allegory of Love*. Oxford: Clarendon Press, 1936.

Lindberg, David C. *The Beginnings of Western Science: The European Scientific Tradition in Philosophical, Religious, and Institutional Context, 600 B.C. to A.D. 1450*. Chicago: University of Chicago Press, 1992.

Maffia Scariati, Irene. "Spigolature sulle *Letture Classensi* del 'Fiore': il 'salvaggio loco' e il nome di Durante." *Rassegna europea di letteratura italiana* 4 (1994), 35–52.

Marti, Mario. *Cultura e stile nei poeti giocosi del tempo di Dante*. Milan: Rizzoli, 1956.

Mazzoni, Guido. "Se possa *Il Fiore* essere di Dante Alighieri." In *Raccolta di studii critici dedicata ad Alessandro D'Ancona festeggiandosi il XL anniversario del suo insegnamento*. Florence: G. Barbèra, 1901. 657–692.

Mazzotta, Giuseppe. *Dante's Vision and the Circle of Knowledge*. Princeton: Princeton University Press, 1993.

———. "The Light of Venus and the Poetry of Dante: *Vita Nuova* and *Inferno* XXVII." In *Dante*. Ed. Harold Bloom. New York, New Haven, and Philadelphia: Chelsea House Publishers, 1986. 189–204.

Menichetti, Aldo. "Implicazioni retoriche nell'invenzione del sonetto." *Strumenti critici* 9 (1979), 1–30.

Moroldo, Arnaldo. "Emprunts et réseaux lexicaux dans le *Fiore*." *Revue des langues romanes* 92 (1988), 127–151.

Morpurgo, Salomone. "Detto d'Amore, antiche rime imitate dal *Roman de la Rose*." *Il Propugnatore*, n.s. 1 (1888), 16–61.

Nims, Margaret F. "*Translatio*: 'Difficult Statement' in Medieval Poetic Theory." *University of Toronto Quarterly* 43 (1974), 215–230.

Nitzsche, Jane Chance. *The Genius Figure in Antiquity and the Middle Ages*. New York: Columbia University Press, 1975.

O'Donoghue, Bernard. *The Courtly Love Tradition*. Manchester: Manchester University Press, 1982.

Parodi, Ernesto Giacomo. Preface to *Il Fiore e il Detto D'Amore*. Florence: Bemporad, 1922. v–xx.

Patch, Howard R. *The Goddess Fortuna in Mediaeval Literature*. Cambridge, Mass.: Harvard University Press, 1927.

Pertile, Lino. "Lettura dei sonetti CLXXXI–CCX." In *Letture classensi* 22: *Lettura del "Fiore."* 131–153.

Quaglio, Antonio Enzo. *La poesia realistica e la prosa del Duecento*. Bari: Laterza, 1971.

———. "I poeti della 'Magna Curia' siciliana." In Emilio Pasquini and Antonio Enzo Quaglio. *Le origini e la scuola siciliana*. Bari: Laterza, 1971. 171–240.

Rajna, Pio. "Un indovinello volgare scritto alla fine del secolo VIII o al principio del IX." *Speculum* 3 (1928), 291–313.

———. "La questione del *Fiore*." *Il Marzocco* 26, no. 3 (16 gennaio 1921).

Santagata, Marco. *Dal sonetto al Canzoniere*. Padua: Liviana, 1979.

Sebastio, Leonardo. *Il Poeta e la storia*. Florence: Olschki, 1994.

———. *Strutture narrative e dinamiche culturali in Dante e nel "Fiore."* Florence: Olschki, 1990.

Segre, Cesare. *Lingua, stile e società: Studi sulla storia della prosa italiana*. Milan: Feltrinelli, 1976 (1963).

Suitner, Franco. "Dante e la poesia satirica del suo tempo." *Letture classensi* 12 (1983), 61–79.

Took, John. "Dante and the *Roman de la Rose*." *Italian Studies* 37 (1982), 1–25.

———. "Lettura dei sonetti XXXI–LX." In *Letture classensi* 22: *Lettura del "Fiore."* 37–51.

———. "Towards an Interpretation of the *Fiore*." *Speculum* 54 (1979), 500–527.

Vallone, Aldo. "Il *Fiore* come opera di Dante." *Studi danteschi* 56 (1984), 141–167.

Vance, Eugene. *Mervelous Signals: Poetics and Sign Theory in the Middle Ages*. Lincoln: University of Nebraska Press, 1986.

Vanossi, Luigi. *Dante e il "Roman de la Rose": saggio sul "Fiore."* Florence: Olschki, 1979.

———. "Detto d'Amore." In *Enciclopedia dantesca*. 2:393–395.

———. *La teologia poetica del Detto d'Amore dantesco*. Florence: Olschki, 1974.

Vasoli, Cesare. "*Ars grammatica* e *translatio* teologica in alcuni testi di Alano di Lilla." In *Arts libéraux et philosophie au moyen âge: Actes du quatrième congrès international de philosophie médiévale*. Montréal and Paris: Institut d'Études Médiévales and J. Vrin, 1969. 805–813.

———. *La filosofia medioevale*. Milan: Feltrinelli, 1961.

———. "Studi recenti su Alano di Lilla (1950–1960)." *Bullettino dell'Istituto storico italiano per il medio evo e archivio muratoriano* 72 (1960), 35–89.

Wack, Mary F. *Lovesickness in the Middle Ages: The "Viaticum" and Its Commentaries*. Philadelphia: University of Pennsylvania Press, 1990.

Wetherbee, Winthrop. "The Function of Poetry in the *De planctu naturae* of Alain De Lille." *Traditio* 25 (1969), 87–127.

———. *Platonism and Poetry in the Twelfth Century*. Princeton: Princeton University Press, 1972.

Wunderli, Peter. "*Mortuus redivivus*: Die *Fiore*-Frage." *Deutsches Dante-Jahrbuch* 61 (1986), 35–50.

Zingarelli, Nicola. "La falsa attribuzione del *Fiore* a Dante Alighieri." *Rassegna critica della letteratura italiana* 27 (1922), 236–254.

The Rubrics of the Fiore

Sonnet	Rubric
1	[...]
2	L'Amante e Amore
3	L'Amante e Amore
4	L'Amante e Amore
5	L'Amante e Amore
6	L'Amante e lo Schifo
7	L'Amante
8	L'Amante
9	L'Amante e Ragione
10	L'Amante
11	L'Amante e Amico
12	L'Amante
13	Franchezza
14	Pietà
15	Lo Schifo
16	L'Amante e lo Schifo
17	Venùs
18	Venùs e Bellacoglienza
19	L'Amante
20	L'Amante e Bellacoglienza
21	L'Amante
22	Castità
23	Gelosia
24	Vergogna
25	Vergogna e Paura
26	Lo Schifo
27	Gelosia
28	L'Amante
29	L'Amante
30	L'Amante

Sonnet	Rubric
31	L'Amante
32	L'Amante
33	L'Amante
34	L'Amante
35	L'Amante e Ragione
36	L'Amante
37	Ragione
38	L'A[mante]
39	Ragione
40	L'Amante
41	Ragione
42	L'Amante
43	Ragione
44	Ragione
45	Ragione
46	L'Amante
47	L'Amante e Amico
48	L'Amante
49	L'Amante e Amico
50	Amico
51	Amico
52	Amico
53	Amico
54	Amico
55	Amico
56	Amico
57	Amico
58	Amico
59	Amico
60	Amico
61	Amico
62	Amico
63	Amico
64	Amico
65	Amico
66	Amico
67	Amico
68	L'Amante e Amico

Sonnet	Rubric
69	Amico
70	L'Amante e Amico
71	Amico
72	Amico
73	L'Amante
74	L'Amante
75	L'Amante e Ric[c]hez[z]a
76	L'Amante e Ric[c]hez[z]a
77	L'Amante e Dio d'Amore
78	L'Amante
79	La baronia d'Amore
80	Costretta-Astinenza
81	Dio d'Amor e Falsembiante
82	Dio d'Amore
83	Il consiglio della baronia
84	L'ordinanze delle battaglie de la baronia
85	Lo Dio d'Amore
86	La risposta de la baronia
87	Amore
88	Falsembiante
89	Falsembiante
90	Falsembiante
91	Falsembiante
92	Fa[l]sembiante
93	Falso-Sembiante
94	Dio d'Amore e Falsembiante
95	Falsembiante
96	Falsembiante
97	Falsembiante
98	Falsembiante
99	Falsembiante
100	Falsembiante
101	Falsembiante
102	Falsembiante
103	Falsembiante
104	Amore e Falsembiante
105	Falsembiante
106	Amore e Falsembiante

Sonnet	Rubric
107	Falsembiante
108	Falsembiante
109	Falsembiante
110	Falsembiante
111	Falsembiante
112	Falsembiante
113	Falsembiante
114	Falsembiante
115	Dio d'Amore e Falsembiante
116	Falsembiante
117	Amore e Falsembiante
118	Falsembiante
119	Falsembiante
120	Falsembiante
121	Falsembiante
122	Falsembiante
123	Falsembiante
124	Falsembiante
125	Falsembiante
126	Falsembiante
127	Lo Dio d'Amor e Falsembiante
128	L'armata de' baroni
129	Com'Astinenza andò a Mala-Boc[c]a
130	Come Falsembiante andò a Mala-Boc[c]a
131	Mala-Boc[c]a, Falsembiante e Costretta-Astinenza
132	Mala-Boc[c]a, Falsembiante e Costretta-Astinenza
133	Astinenza
134	Mala-Boc[c]a
135	Falsembiante
136	La ripentenza Mala-Boc[c]a
137	Cortesia e Larghezza e la Vec[c]hia
138	Falsembiante
139	La Vec[c]hia e Falsembiante
140	La Vec[c]hia e Falsembiante
141	La Vec[c]hia e Bellacoglienza
142	La Vec[c]hia
143	Bellacoglienza e la Vec[c]hia
144	Bellacoglienza e la Vec[c]hia

Sonnet	Rubric
145	La Vec[c]hia
146	La Vec[c]hia
147	La Vec[c]hia
148	La Vec[c]hia
149	La Vec[c]hia
150	La Vec[c]hia
151	La Vec[c]hia
152	La Vec[c]hia
153	La Vec[c]hia
154	La Vec[c]hia
155	La Vec[c]hia
156	La Vec[c]hia
157	La Vec[c]hia
158	La Vec[c]hia
159	La Vec[c]hia
160	La Vec[c]hia
161	La Vec[c]hia
162	La Vec[c]hia
163	La Vec[c]hia
164	La Vec[c]hia
165	La Vec[c]hia
166	La Vec[c]hia
167	La Vec[c]hia
168	La Vec[c]hia
169	La Vec[c]hia
170	La Vec[c]hia
171	La Vec[c]hia
172	La Vec[c]hia
173	La Vec[c]hia
174	La Vec[c]hia
175	La Vec[c]hia
176	La Vec[c]hia
177	La Vec[c]hia
178	La Vec[c]hia
179	La Vec[c]hia
180	La Vec[c]hia
181	La Vec[c]hia
182	La Vec[c]hia

Sonnet	Rubric
183	La Vec[c]hia
184	La Vec[c]hia
185	La Vec[c]hia
186	La Vec[c]hia
187	La Vec[c]hia
188	La Vec[c]hia
189	La Vec[c]hia
190	La Vec[c]hia
191	La Vec[c]hia
192	La Vec[c]hia
193	La Vec[c]hia
194	La Vec[c]hia
195	Bellacoglienza
196	Bellacoglienza
197	La Vec[c]hia e Bellacoglienza
198	L'Amante e la Vec[c]hia
199	La Vec[c]hia
200	L'Amante
201	L'Amante e Bellacoglienza
202	L'Amante e Bellacoglienza
203	L'Amante e lo Schifo
204	Vergogna e Paura
205	L'Amante
206	L'Amante
207	La battaglia
208	Lo Schifo e Franchez[z]a
209–232	The last section of the manuscript lacks descriptive rubrics

Index of Characters and Places Mentioned in the Poems 

This index contains proper names and toponyms as they appear in the Italian texts. References to the *Fiore* are by sonnet number, and to the *Detto* by line number.

General Index